C000300494

TRUMP: THE HIDDEN HALO

TRUMP
THE HIDDEN
HALO

SIMON DOLAN

Biteback Publishing

First published in Great Britain in 2021 by
Biteback Publishing Ltd, London
Copyright © Simon Dolan 2021

Simon Dolan has asserted his right under the Copyright, Designs and Patents Act 1988 to be
identified as the author of this work.

ISBN 978-1-78590-675-6

10 9 8 7 6 5 4 3 2 1

A CIP catalogue record for this book is available from the British Library.

Set in Minion Pro and Gotham

Printed and bound in Great Britain by
CPI Group (UK) Ltd, Croydon CR0 4YY

MIX
Paper from
responsible sources
FSC
www.fsc.org
FSC® C020471

To the American Republic and the people who defend it.

CONTENTS

FOREWORD
BY NIGEL FARAGE

What will Donald Trump's legacy be? After four tumultuous years, most contemporary commentators will want to focus on the storming of the Capitol on 6 January 2021. When the mob walked up the steps of the Capitol, the President's opponents had the moment they had been waiting for, and they will never let it go. Yet that awful episode did not define Trump's presidency and should not overshadow all he achieved. From the announcement of Trump's candidacy in 2015 to the end of his administration, the Establishment never gave the man who became 45th President of the United States a chance. Early ridicule turned into obsessive condemnation: the phenomenon of 'Trump Derangement Syndrome', which dictated that nothing he ever did was right.

I joined the Trump train in 2016, shortly after the Brexit vote. What I saw was a big personality, full of charisma and – rather to my surprise – charm. I saw a man prepared to take on corrupt elites: a process he knew would be difficult and ugly but was ready to embrace.

At that point, few in Washington took Trump seriously. When, in November 2016, he beat Hillary Clinton, they were in shock – and they stayed that way throughout his tenure. The joke candidate was heading for the White House, and they couldn't believe it.

Trump had come right out of left field. Though he attended an elite college – the University of Pennsylvania – he is not classic Ivy

League. Indeed, he did not excel at school, eventually graduating from college without honours. Disconcertingly for the Washington elite, he had never been involved in mainstream politics. In fact, until the age of seventy, he had not held a single elected office at any point in his life. Before entering the world of showbiz, he'd had a gun-slinging career as a New York real estate guy, where, on occasion, he had to run the gauntlet of the mob. It was rough and tough, and he had to duck and dive to thrive. He developed important life skills, but not of the kind that were appreciated by the liberal elite. There had never been a modern American President with such an unpresidential background, and that is partly why he was so loathed by the media: he was simply not one of them. He was completely different to anything they had encountered in national politics, and they could not accept his rise.

It was not just his background but his language and vocabulary that offended them. The way he spoke alienated the affluent, educated New York, Washington and Los Angeles types. He didn't sound like a politician, and they interpreted his limited use of vocabulary and habit of repeating himself as a sign of stupidity. It was a lazy and offensive assumption. Having spent a significant amount of time with him over the years – sat with him over dinner; talked to him over the phone; appeared at his rallies – I have no doubt that he is incredibly sharp. I was struck by the ease with which he understood the impetus for Brexit: while many European leaders struggled to grasp why millions of British people might want to leave the EU, Trump instinctively understood the desire for freedom from overbearing, distant, bureaucratic institutions. Such was his hatred of globalist corporate structures that sometimes I thought he was more Eurosceptic than I am.

Trump was a leader guided by principles: first and foremost, the fundamental right of sovereign nations to put the interests of their people first, while working with other nations to stamp out war and injustice and promote global prosperity. I remember watching his

2018 speech to the United Nations. At the time I was still a Member of the European Parliament and was listening to him from Brussels. He spoke simply and plainly about the existence of the nation state and why it was the only model that allowed democracy to flourish. That speech defined him. When historians ask, 'What was Trumpism?', the answers are in that speech. He was driven by a firm belief that globalist bureaucracies are expensive and unresponsive and that their power needs to be controlled.

One of his greatest attributes was his natural affinity with voters with whom – ostensibly at least – he had nothing in common. This was not fake: he really did care about the challenges faced by ordinary hard-working Americans, particularly those living in old industrial areas, as they tried to build better lives. I remember sitting with him in Trump Tower, with its lavish gold-inlaid front door, surrounded by Roman-Emperor-scale wealth. There he was, in his magnificently opulent surroundings, talking passionately about the struggling workers of America's Midwest. For all his wealth, he was a blue-collar billionaire, instinctively in tune with the ordinary 'American Joe'. It led to the most appalling snobbery against him. In tones of derision, the commentariat would call him a truck driver, as if driving a lorry should be a source of shame.

During his presidential campaign in 2016, Trump made a series of promises to the American people that he intended to keep. In the White House, he was as good as his word. I remember going into the West Wing in February 2017, when he had been in office for just over a year, and seeing a big whiteboard listing all his election promises. Next to each pledge was a tick or a timetable, setting out what had been delivered and what remained to be done. I told him that I thought he was helping to restore faith in the democratic process. 'I've kept more promises than I've made!' was his proud response.

During the 2020 presidential election campaign I was surprised and honoured when he invited me to join him on stage at a rally in

Arizona. Addressing thousands of his supporters, I called him the bravest man I know, for his sheer resilience and will against a vicious media and the Washington DC swamp. Against overwhelming opposition and the determination of powerful vested interests to portray everything he did in the worst possible light, he never wavered from his principles: to do everything he could to stand up for forgotten and marginalised American voters and make his country great again.

Naturally, I was castigated for my tribute to Trump that day. But as I read *Trump: The Hidden Halo*, I realised that my words in Arizona were correct. As this powerful and important book sets out, his achievements during his four years in office were remarkable. *The Hidden Halo* charts the battles he faced and shows how, in most cases, he overcame extraordinary obstacles to deliver for the American people. It gives him the fair hearing he was consistently denied and the credit he deserves.

Nigel Farage
February 2021

INTRODUCTION

How will Donald Trump be remembered? Thanks to his response to the outcome of the 2020 election and the awful scenes in Washington when his supporters stormed the Capitol, there has not exactly been a clamour to make a positive case. Frustratingly for those who believed he was doing great things for his country, his strategic errors in the final weeks of his presidency played directly into the hands of everyone who had always despised both him and his supporters.

Yet, as the 74 million Americans who wanted to give him a second term know, the 45th President of the United States was so much more than the circumstances surrounding his departure. To many he remains a hero. This book explores why.

I'd never been interested in politics in general – still less what goes on in Washington – until Trump entered the White House. I'd always taken the view that politicians on both sides of the Atlantic, and almost everywhere else for that matter, are either corrupt or incompetent, or indeed both. Surveying the quality of Members of Parliament in the UK, especially during the years of chaos when the government struggled to implement the result of the Brexit vote, just made me depressed. These elected individuals rule us, I thought resentfully, but most of them seem so useless, I doubt they could get any other job.

All my life, I've disliked being told what to do, which is probably why I have always run my own businesses rather than work for anyone else. The fact that these clowns had so much power and authority annoyed me. However, there didn't seem much I could do about it, so, like millions of other people, I switched off.

Then, in 2015, reality TV star and New York real estate mogul Donald Trump decided to run for office. This piqued my interest. Of course, he had no chance of winning: even his own party was against him. The 'Never Trumpers' in the Republican movement dismissed him as an embarrassment and a joke. Initially, the media was amused but wrote his candidacy off as nothing more than a publicity stunt. It wasn't until later, when it became apparent that his campaign was gathering ground, that they started to panic.

As for me? I started to think: what if? What if a businessman actually got to run a country, rather than one of the dull, standard-issue, 'normal' politicians?

In my mind, this was only ever a thought experiment. The badass in me liked the idea of this swaggering figure wrongfooting all the naysayers, winning by a landslide, then going into the White House and smashing everything up. I didn't crave wanton destruction, or the arbitrary jettisoning of carefully crafted policies that had been proven to work; I just liked the idea of a charismatic outsider doing things differently, challenging the status quo.

Imagining this scenario became a kind of guilty pleasure. Like almost everyone else, I assumed Democrat candidate Hillary Clinton would win by a landslide. After all, when Trump entered the race, the front page of his hometown newspaper, the *New York Daily News*, declared that a 'clown' was 'running for Prez'. They chose the worst picture of him they could find and mocked it up with a stupid painted smile and a big red nose. They used variations of this image time and again, under front-page headlines labelling him 'Dopey', 'Brain Dead' and – when they thought he was about to lose – a 'Dead Clown Walking'.[1] Broadsheet newspapers may have used fancier language, but they were no less brutal in their character assassinations. Cover to cover, they routinely depicted the prospect of a Trump presidency as both improbable and a disaster.

It was not just the media but almost everyone else with a platform or voice. Hollywood hated him. Rappers who once idolised him as a boss man, the personification of brash self-made success and an icon of shameless bad taste and bling, suddenly decided he was a dangerous racist. In April 2016, hip hop artists YG and Nipsey Hussle released a song called 'FDT' (F*** Donald Trump), featuring disobliging soundbites from a bunch of black students who had been ejected from a Trump rally in Georgia. It took the pair less than an hour to record, yet the *Los Angeles Times* declared it 'the most prophetic, wrathful and unifying protest song of 2016'.[2] The *bien pensants* in the City of Angels, and everywhere else, had decided Trump was the devil – and should be sent back from whence he came.

Surveying the relentlessly hostile commentary, I felt sure that, come autumn 2016, he would be heading back to his old life as a reality TV star.

Yet something strange was happening. That summer, following his official nomination as Republican candidate, Trump's campaign, which I'd read was chaotic and run by complete novices who had no idea what they were doing, began to gather momentum. At Trump rallies, the crowds seemed to love him. There was an energy and excitement around him. He spoke for voters who felt forgotten. This was broadening out into a powerful anti-Establishment movement.

As his campaign picked up pace, he took aim at the cosy elites and the 'Washington swamp'[3] – and they fought back. I watched, fascinated, as they threw everything at him. They spent tens of thousands of hours and millions of dollars trying to dig up dirt. Of course, anyone who runs for such high office can expect every aspect of their life and background to be raked over, and rightly so. But the treatment of Donald J. Trump was off the charts. Celebrity A-listers were threatening to leave the country if he got in. It was months until the election, but hysterical left-wingers were already trying to figure out how to impeach him. All this struck me as very odd. If he was such a joke, why were they so scared? Did they think he could actually win?

I've always loved an underdog. Now I was really engaged. And then it happened. I was in a hotel in London on 9 November 2016. I turned on the TV in my room and saw news anchors in tears, people rioting, celebrities in a panic.

What natural disaster had occurred? Had Obama died? What could have caused this? It turned out that nobody had been hurt. What had happened was that Trump had done the unthinkable: he had won. The butt of a million jokes was now the President-elect of the United States.

My wish had been granted. A businessman was now running a country. Not any country but the most powerful on earth. That morning, I felt a sense of excitement, anticipation and mischief. One in the eye for the Establishment.

While I was excited about what lay ahead, I knew that mighty forces were stacked against him. They would stop at nothing to get him out. This time, there would be none of the usual warm words from the losers about giving the victor the benefit of the doubt. There would be no temporary suspension of hostilities while the country came together to celebrate the dawn of a new political era in a spirit of unity and hope. As an outsider, all I could detect among the political classes and commentariat in America was fear, horror and disbelief.

As for ordinary American voters? Millions were euphoric. They felt as I did: that this much-reviled and derided figure might actually do some good.

In the years that followed, I watched in disbelief as the worst possible complexion was put on Trump's every utterance and move. As far as the liberal elite and their media mouthpieces were concerned, he could simply do no right. To me, the way he was publicly judged made no sense. In 2009, Barack Obama, whose foreign policy attracts little praise from historians, was awarded the Nobel Peace Prize. Obama had been in office for just nine months when he received the prize, acquiring it for 'extraordinary efforts to strengthen international diplomacy and cooperation between people'. Apparently even he was surprised. 'To be honest, I still don't know what my Nobel Peace Prize was for,' he has said.[4] Former secretary of the Nobel Peace Prize committee Gier Lundestad has since hinted that the decision was a mistake.

To me, this says it all. At the same stage in his presidency, Trump was embroiled in a witch-hunt over allegations of conspiracy with Russia, whipped up by vested interests determined to discredit him. According to the conspiracy theory, this President was not just stupid, ridiculous and racist – he was a traitor. Unlike Obama, who waged military campaigns in Somalia, Yemen, Libya and Syria and failed to extract the US military from either Iraq or Afghanistan, Trump started no new wars during his tenure in the White House – at least not of the conventional military kind. To me, a cool assessment of the facts suggests that he achieved more in foreign policy terms than any of his recent predecessors. Yet, to date, he has received no international recognition for his efforts whatsoever.

Even among Republicans, there has been a wilful blindness to anything positive he achieved. At times, the hypocrisy has been extraordinary. Of course, Trump didn't help himself: quite the reverse. It is evident from multiple authoritative insider accounts of his administration – and indeed his own Twitter account – that the way he treated some of those who worked for him, those people having given up highly rewarding careers in finance and other fields to support him and his administration, left a little to be desired. He ruffled the feathers of decorated military men, captains of industry and all sorts of other distinguished experts and professionals. The way he spoke about other world leaders could come as a shock. When he behaved like this, the word most often used, even by those who sought to see the best in him, was 'unstatesman-like' – and perhaps they were right.

This book is not going to pretend that none of that happened, or that his verbal tirades were not sometimes ugly. I have not set out to reveal that Donald Trump secretly loves small babies and kittens, nor that he makes midnight visits to hospitals to comfort cancer patients. I doubt he has ever volunteered in a soup kitchen, doled out bags of pasta at a food bank or paused to listen to the life story of a homeless man on the street. That is just not him.

What I am interested in is not his character but what he actually achieved. His army of detractors spent four years playing the man not the ball. Now he is off the pitch, it seems worth studying his best moves. This book seeks to separate his policies from his divisive personality. A long line of smart, successful and very well-informed people have articulated the case for the prosecution of Donald Trump, including those who have a great deal of expertise in the aspects of his administration they have examined. Precious few have made the case for the defence. This book sets out to redress the balance.

This man said he was not 'President of the World' but President of the United States, and he would put 'America First'.[5] I want to make the case that, in many ways, Donald J. Trump did just that. In November 2020, 74 million American voters thought he deserved a second term – so it seems they agree.

Some will ask what qualifies me to attempt such an assessment. The answer is nothing more than the impartiality of an outsider who has no vested interest whatsoever in putting an unduly positive gloss on these events. I do not claim to be an international trade or foreign policy specialist, nor even an economist. Then again, neither are the vast majority of Americans who determine the outcome of presidential elections. And perhaps the fact that we are not experts gives us some advantage. 'Experts' have become an increasingly important part of our lives, but how often do they actually turn out to be correct? If 'expert' economists actually understood as much about the real world as they think they do, then they would be billionaire traders. 'Expert' foreign policy advisers have presided over an awful lot of wars. The same can be said for the war on drugs, the war on poverty and so on. Experts abound, but they often achieve little to nothing. Finally, of course, we have Covid. How many expert opinions on the pandemic have been proven wrong?

Sometimes what is needed is less 'expert' opinion, and more basic common sense. But then I would say that – I am not an expert.

Among all those who bitterly resented the decision of some 63 million American voters to put Trump in the White House in the first place, there is an overwhelming sense of relief that he is gone. The brash showman with the vulgar taste for big suits, sunbeds and colossal chandeliers has been stripped of power. The 'basket of deplorables' who supported him have been put back in their place. As Joe Biden begins his presidency after the most toxic election in modern American history, those who always wanted Trump out of the White House will hope that his departure will usher in a new and much less divisive era. They would like to imagine that the 45th President was some kind of aberration, and that all those Americans who felt he understood their worries and somehow shared their hopes and dreams will simply retreat to the shadows, ashamed that they ever fell for his mesmerising sales pitch.

I am not so sure. Trump's supporters have had a taste of a very different kind of leadership, and, for all his faults, they loved it. It seems probable that their continuing belief that the election was rigged and sense that their hero was hounded out of office will only exacerbate the grievances that propelled him to power in the first place.

As for all those who are celebrating the end of his administration and think Biden is the answer to America's problems, perhaps the passage of time will inject some much needed perspective. With the benefit of hindsight, might they come to realise that the man they painted as the devil actually had a hidden halo?

Simon Dolan
February 2021

PART ONE

FIGHTING THE GOOD FIGHT

1

ALIENS - TRUMP AND IMMIGRATION

The big, beautiful wall. What a striking image. Whether you like the idea or not, it's easy to visualise. For me, a wall serves to keep intruders out. It's a physical barrier to stop people going where they are not entitled to go. To Trump's detractors it was a symbol of cruelty and racism.

All countries have borders. Indeed, a country ceases to be a country if it does not have borders. Like many Presidents before him, Trump simply wanted a border that actually worked. Border patrol wanted one that worked. Legal immigrants wanted one that worked. Most American voters wanted one that worked. Some likened it to the Berlin Wall. Of course, that particular wall was designed to keep people in not out. Do you have a wall or a fence around your house? Does that make you racist or simply sensible?

In spring 1989, New York lived up to its regrettable reputation as one of the most dangerous cities in the world when two women were raped and almost killed in unconnected attacks that took place within three weeks of each other. The first victim, aged twenty-eight, was jogging through Central Park after dark when she was violated, beaten to within an inch of her life and left for dead in a shallow ravine. After she was discovered, she spent twelve days in a coma before regaining consciousness. The second victim, aged thirty-eight, was robbed by three teenagers who then coerced her onto a rooftop in Brooklyn. There, she was brutally assaulted before being thrown down a 50ft air shaft. Like the woman who was attacked in Central Park, her survival was considered miraculous.

Any rape is indescribably appalling, but the first of these two cases received significantly more public attention than the second. The US commentariat generally attributed this discrepancy to the fact that the Central Park jogger was a white middle-class American, whereas the woman assaulted in Brooklyn was a Jamaican immigrant. Among a number of high-profile figures drawn into this row was Donald Trump. His personal reaction to these two shocking events is early evidence that he is not, as his critics constantly claim, fundamentally and intrinsically 'anti-immigrant' – still less anti-immigration *per se*.

When the Central Park attack was reported, Trump spent thousands of dollars taking out full-page advertisements in four New York newspapers in which he called for the return of the death penalty for the perpetrators of such felonies. (As it happens, the five individuals who served prison sentences for this crime were exonerated in 2002 after another man confessed.) Following the second – under-reported – attack in Brooklyn, Trump, Mayor Ed Koch and Cardinal John O'Connor, the Archbishop of New York, were all publicly accused of failing to show as much compassion to the victim as they had shown to the Central Park jogger. The charge was led by the Reverend Herbert Daughtry, a civil rights activist. There may be all sorts of reasons why Trump did not take a public stand against this crime sooner, but a seething hatred of the victim on the grounds of race and immigration status was not among them. He was deeply affronted by the accusation, and immediately arranged to visit the Jamaican woman at the Kings County Hospital in Brooklyn, where she would spend a total of four months recovering from her injuries. Afterwards, he pledged to pay her medical bills. Making good on his promise, in November 1989 he sent the Rev. Daughtry a cheque for $25,000 for this purpose.

Stemming the tide of illegal or low-skilled immigration to

America was a centrepiece of the Trump campaign in 2016, but the impetus was economic, not, as his opponents like to suggest, either xenophobic or racist.

After all, Trump's first wife, Ivana Zelníčková, to whom he was married for fifteen years and with whom he has three children, was born and raised in Czechoslovakia and only became an American citizen in 1988, more than a decade after their wedding. His current wife, Melania Knavs, the mother of Trump's youngest child, Barron, was born and raised in the Socialist Republic of Slovenia and became a US citizen in 2006, the year after their marriage. She is only the second First Lady to be born outside America, the other, Louisa Adams, having lived in the White House from 1825 to 1829. Trump therefore knows about immigration at first hand just as well as anybody. Not only that, but his father, Fred, grew up in a German-speaking household having been born in New York in October 1905, three months after Trump's grandparents moved back to America from Germany. His mother, Mary, emigrated to America from Scotland aged eighteen in 1930. That Trump is in fact a product of immigration himself is all too easily forgotten by his critics.

Trump's focus on immigration, pushed during his first presidential campaign and the early days of his administration by his fiercely nationalistic chief strategist Steve Bannon, was all about protecting the livelihoods – and security – of American citizens. It was a response to the practical concerns of voters who know there are two types of immigration: legal and illegal. There are also two types of immigrant: law-abiding and criminal. It was illegal and criminal immigrants to which Trump devoted most of his energy between 2016 and 2020.

• • •

When President Bill Clinton delivered his State of the Union address in 1995, he received a standing ovation from Congress for his forceful comments on illegal immigration. Nobody seemed to mind that he referred to individuals who should not be in the country as 'aliens'. Indeed, he used the phrases 'illegal aliens' or 'criminal aliens' four times in the space of a few seconds – language and emphasis that would trigger a chorus of righteous indignation were it to come from Trump.[1] Clinton said:

All Americans, not only in the states most heavily affected but in every place in this country, are rightly disturbed by the large numbers of illegal aliens entering our country. The jobs they hold might otherwise be held by citizens or legal immigrants. The public service they use impose burdens on our taxpayers. That's why our administration has moved aggressively to secure our borders more by hiring a record number of new border guards, by deporting twice as many criminal aliens as ever before, by cracking down on illegal hiring, by barring welfare benefits to illegal aliens. In the budget I will present to you, we will try to do more to speed the deportation of illegal aliens who are arrested for crimes, to better identify illegal aliens in the workplace as recommended by the commission headed by former Congresswoman Barbara Jordan. We are a nation of immigrants. But we are also a nation of laws. It is wrong and ultimately self-defeating for a nation of immigrants to permit the kind of abuse of our immigration laws we have seen in recent years, and we must do more to stop it.

Within a week, a *Washington Post*–ABC News survey gave Clinton a 54 per cent approval rating, up ten points in a month and the highest rating he had enjoyed in ten months, supporting the view that the public liked what they heard.

Across the Western world, politicians of all parties worry about immigration because of the potential impact on a country's public services, housing stock, wages, employment and national security. The same politicians also know that acknowledging these concerns is crucial to connecting with taxpayers. So it is no surprise that Clinton, a Democrat, made these commitments the year before he sought re-election – and he won.

Has Trump gone much further? Not really. Of all his promises before the 2016 election, his vow to build a wall between America and Mexico attracted most attention. Covering 1,954 miles and with about 350 million crossings each year (up to 500,000 of which are said to be illegal immigrants), this border is the most frequently used in the world; yet it has long been seen by conservative Americans as the principal entry point for gangs, drugs and victims of human trafficking. Trump's very tangible pledge to erect a huge physical barrier between the United States and its southern neighbour – and to make the Mexicans pay for it – was designed to convince voters that on this issue he would be tougher than any of his predecessors. It was a piece of political messaging genius: even the simplest of voters could understand and remember the pledge. In reality, the only real difference between what he was promising, and the border reinforcement works initiated by his predecessors was that he called it a 'wall' and not a 'perimeter' or a 'fence'.

Barack Obama may not have made a similarly tub-thumping immigration speech during his tenure in the White House, but he did deliver a televised address to the nation in November 2014 in which he echoed Clinton's point about the US–Mexico border, proclaiming that he had been even more robust. Obama declared that since taking office in 2008, he had deployed more agents and more technology to secure the border than at any time in America's history. 'Over the past six years, illegal border crossings have been cut by more than half,' he boasted.[2] He was right. Construction of a federally funded border fence began in 1993, during President George H. W. Bush's administration, when fourteen miles were built near San Diego. Bill Clinton continued with the project during his first term. Then, in 2006, the Secure Fence Act was passed during President George W. Bush's second administration, ultimately allowing for about 700 miles of additional double-layered fencing, which was completed by 2015, the year before Obama left office. Significantly, the 2006 legislation enabling the erection of this border was passed with support from three notable Democrat senators: Barack Obama, Hillary Clinton and Joe Biden.[3] None of them has ever been accused of racism for backing it.

Indeed, by the time Trump was elected, some 700 miles of border fencing was already in place. Naturally, most voters didn't know much about the existing infrastructure, and most of those attracted to Trump's policy just liked the sound of it. Ironically, 'the wall' was not even Trump's own idea. It was cooked up as a so-called 'mnemonic device' – a technique used to aid memory – by political consultants Roger Stone and Sam Nunberg, to remind Trump to talk about illegal immigration on the campaign trail. No doubt they were spurred on by polls such as one conducted in 2015 for *Washington Post*–ABC News, which found that 65 per cent of Americans supported building a 700-mile fence along the border with Mexico and adding 20,000 border patrol agents. The same survey found that 52 per cent still wanted a wall even when told it would cost $46 billion. In other words, Trump is not a knuckle-dragging racist, as is so frequently characterised, but was instead responding – via his advisers – to public opinion.

According to Joshua Green, a CNN political analyst, the wall was Stone's brainchild. In his 2017 bestseller *Devil's Bargain: Steve Bannon, Donald Trump and a Nationalist Uprising*, Green revealed:

Inside Trump's circle, the power of illegal immigration to manipulate popular sentiment was readily apparent, and his advisers brainstormed methods for keeping their boss on message. They had learned that Trump was not interested in policy detail: he preferred information and concepts to be presented in a simple, bite-sized way that voters would find easy to understand. They needed a trick, a mnemonic device. In the summer of 2014, they found one that clicked.

Nunberg, who worked with Stone, confirmed: 'Roger Stone and I came up with the idea of "The Wall", and we talked to Steve [Bannon] about it. It was to make sure [Trump] talked about immigration.'[4]

The scale of public enthusiasm for the wall was not that surprising. America may have been built on immigration, but even in this land of opportunity, many voters are at best conflicted about the notion of welcoming in penniless foreigners seeking the so-called American dream.

The Immigration Act of 1924, introduced after the population reached almost 112 million, limited the number of immigrants from southern and eastern Europe in favour of those from Britain and Canada, and banned all immigration from Asia, but subsequent liberalisation made America one of the most immigrant-friendly countries in the world. Over the past forty years, the official population has rocketed to an estimated 330 million. All the while illegal immigration has also thrived, most of it coming via Mexico. This legal and illegal population boom has occurred in tandem with the deindustrialisation of swathes of the country. According to the US Bureau of Labor Statistics, one third of manufacturing jobs disappeared between 2001 and 2009. The impact of this in general terms has been that more people – both Americans and immigrants of all kinds – went in search of fewer jobs at the lower end of the pay scale at the same time, leading to a justifiable sense of apprehension among resident blue-collar workers.

The scale of the challenge was exposed in a 2017 report released by the Federation for American Immigration Reform, a non-partisan not-for-profit group that campaigns to reduce immigration. It claimed that taxpayers 'shell out approximately $134.9 billion [annually] to cover the costs incurred by the presence of more than 12.5 million illegal aliens, and about 4.2 million citizen children of illegal aliens.'[5] (It did acknowledge that illegal immigrants probably pay about $19 billion in tax – and of course calculating such costs is notoriously difficult.) The following year, a study carried out by Yale

University suggested that the actual illegal immigrant population of America may be as high as 22.1 million.[6] The very nature of illegal immigration means it is impossible for anybody to know the real numbers involved at any given time. All that is clear is that illegal immigration in America has become a significant and very costly issue – a reality that Bill and Hillary Clinton, Barack Obama and Joe Biden have all been prepared to acknowledge. Yet since Trump began talking about immigration, a gulf has opened up between the two main parties over how to approach the issue. For reasons which will become clear, it is hard to conclude that this is attributable to anything other than individuals playing politics: what Bill Clinton was able to get away with saying, Trump was not.

• • •

By the time Trump launched his presidential bid on 16 June 2015 at Trump Tower in New York, he said he had spoken to guards on the US–Mexico border. His conversations with these officials led him to conclude that 'the US has become a dumping ground for everybody else's problems'.

'When Mexico sends its people, they're not sending their best … They're sending people that have lots of problems,' he went on. 'They're bringing drugs. They're bringing crime. They're rapists. And some, I assume, are good people.'[7] Then he unveiled the policy that would become the focal point of his campaign: his promise to 'build a great wall, and nobody builds walls better than me, believe me, and I'll build them very inexpensively, I will build a great, great wall on our southern border. And I will have Mexico pay for that wall.'[8]

The commentariat was shocked. This, they predicted, would be the end of Trump's nascent campaign. How could a serious politician get away with such inflammatory language? *Washington Post* writer Jonathan Capehart declared that the speech had sounded 'the death knell' for the Republican Party. 'I'm going to go out on a limb and predict that Trump will not be the next president of the United States or even the GOP nominee,' he wrote the following day, predicting that the candidate's 'harsh rhetoric' and 'xenophobic zingers' he would hurl on the debate stage would hobble his efforts to secure the keys to the White House.[9]

In the weeks that followed, Trump's Republican rivals for the presidential candidacy piled in. Marco Rubio, the Florida senator and son of Cuban immigrants, called the comments 'not just offensive and inaccurate, but also divisive.'[10] Jeb Bush, the former Florida governor whose wife is Mexican and who supported legalising the status of undocumented immigrants, said: 'His remarks ... do not represent the values of the Republican Party, and they do not represent my values.'[11] With Trump leading Rubio in the polls by this stage, and almost neck-and-neck with Bush, it is hardly surprising that they lashed out. Of the other Republican presidential hopefuls in the nomination race during the summer of 2015, the sole fellow candidate to back Trump's remarks was Ted Cruz, the Texas senator who, interestingly, was born to a Cuban father. He said Trump 'speaks the truth'.

Perhaps most crucially for a businessman – especially one who was also a complete outsider to win the White House in 2016 – Trump's hard-line stance had immediate commercial repercussions. Carlos Slim, once the richest man in the world, announced he was ending a joint venture that he and Trump had pursued in Ora TV. Univision, the largest Spanish-language network in the US, and NBC, the US media giant, said it was dropping its broadcasts of the Miss USA and Miss Universe pageants, which Trump co-owned. The department store Macy's axed his line of suits and ties. And Nascar, the motor racing body, said it would no longer use one of his hotels for its end-of-season awards. Speaking to *Fox News* on 4 July, Trump said he was surprised by the strength of the backlash. 'I knew it was going to be bad because all my life I have been told: if you are successful you don't run for office,' he said. 'I didn't know it was going to be this severe.'[12] He defended his ideas, however, and said he had become a 'whipping post' for talking about immigration and crime. Even when the going got this rough, though, he stuck to his course, suggesting he did believe he could fix the immigration problem. It remains a moot point if others in the race would have made such financial sacrifices for the potential of the White House.

When Hillary Clinton's Democrat Party published its manifesto in July 2016, it accused Trump of 'demonising' Mexicans and claimed, 'He wants to build walls and keep people – including Americans – from entering the country based on their race, religion, ethnicity, and national origin.'[13] The Democrats produced no hard evidence to back up this assertion. The fact that Mrs Clinton had voted for George W. Bush's border fence a decade earlier seemed to have slipped the party's mind. Crucially, the Democrats' proposals also included an effective amnesty for the 'more than 11 million people living in the shadows, without proper documentation', who, the party said, 'should be incorporated completely into our society through legal processes that give meaning to our national motto: *E Pluribus Unum*' ('out of many, one'). Anecdotal evidence suggests that immigrants in Western democracies are overwhelmingly more likely to vote for parties regarded as being on the left rather than on the right. Given the biggest landslide in American presidential history was only 17 million votes, it was even suggested that this amnesty was a cynical way of guaranteeing them power.[14]

In any case, four months later this platform was rejected at the polls when Trump defeated Clinton in an Electoral College victory, carrying thirty states and securing 304 electoral votes to Clinton's 227. Furthermore, the House of Representatives and the Senate remained in Republican control, theoretically giving it the power of the White House as well as both chambers of Congress for the first time since 2007. Trump now had a mandate to deliver on 'the wall'. With such numerical advantages, what could possibly go wrong when he tried to deliver the immigration policy that helped to get him to the White House?

•   •   •

Trump's own definition of his US–Mexico border wall changed over time. On 20 May 2015, for instance, he gave an interview to the Christian Broadcasting Network in which he referred to it twice as a 'fence' rather than a wall. There was also significant debate before he was elected about how long it should be – or could be, given that natural terrain such as rivers and mountains along the 1,954-mile route eliminated the need for a wall covering that distance. The other crucial question was who would pay. Despite Trump's claims, the Mexican government had made clear that it would not.

Almost as soon as he was sworn into office as the 45th President of the United States in January 2017, Trump issued a series of executive orders. They included Executive Order 13767, signed on 25 January 2017, which instructed the government to begin constructing a border wall using existing federal funding. A notice on the White House website left little doubt over where the President stood on this issue. It read:

> The United States must adopt an immigration system that serves the national interest. To restore the rule of law and secure our border, President Trump is committed to constructing a border wall and ensuring the swift removal of unlawful entrants. To protect American workers, the President supports ending chain migration, eliminating the Visa Lottery, and moving the country to a merit-based entry system. These reforms will advance the safety and prosperity of all Americans while helping new citizens assimilate and flourish.[15]

Despite Trump's determination, his efforts hit their own wall pretty quickly, partly thanks to Democrat stubbornness. Given that Trump had won the election on a platform of immigration control, that party's opposition to his proposals made a nonsense of its name.

On 11 July 2017, House of Representatives Speaker Nancy Pelosi, a Democrat, issued a statement on the Republican Appropriations Bill to fund President Trump's border wall, in which she referred to the wall as 'immoral, ineffective and expensive'. A stand-off ensued, which would ultimately require Trump to find innovative ways to obtain the necessary funds to get the programme on track. In the process he would be hit by a barrage of lawsuits from states, environmental groups and border communities. The primary legal challenge surrounded the diversion of billions of dollars of military funding towards construction of the wall.

The Trump administration's 'family separation policy' fanned the flames. In April 2018, the then Attorney-General Jeff Sessions announced that all adults arrested while crossing the Mexican border into America illegally would face criminal prosecution on federal charges. While they were in custody, any minor travelling with them would be placed under the supervision of the US Department of Health and Human Services. 'If you don't like that, then don't smuggle children over our border,' Sessions said.[16] It may have been harsh – but nobody could claim they had not been warned. In the preceding decade, tens of thousands of child immigrants had arrived in America, with many ending up in care homes. Trump's policy was tough, but to many American voters, it seemed a reasonable way to tackle an escalating problem that they did not consider their responsibility.

Between 19 April and 31 May 2018, according to a Department of Homeland Security spokesman, nearly 2,000 children were separated from their parents and guardians and placed into holding facilities. The scope for emotive opposition was considerable – and officials carrying out federal government's orders sometimes played into critics' hands. Hostility to the policy intensified when an eight-minute audio recording surfaced in June 2018, apparently of young immigrant children on the Texas border howling after being separated from their parents while a US border patrol agent made mocking remarks. A group of seventy-five former US attorneys wrote an open letter to Sessions calling for a rethink. Three airlines, American Airlines, United Airlines and Frontier Airlines, issued a statement asking the government not to use their planes to transport migrant children who were separated from their parents. Even Melania Trump published her thoughts on the issue, saying she 'hates to see children separated from their families and hopes both sides of the aisle can finally come together to achieve successful immigration reform'. On 20 June 2018, Trump was forced to perform a U-turn, signing an executive order ending family separations at the border.

Multiple Western countries have faced – and continue to face – dilemmas over how to deal with illegal immigrant children, whether or not they are accompanied by adults. There are few easy answers: governments cannot afford to send out the message that anyone with youngsters will be given a free pass. The opposition to Trump's policy was at least partly politically motivated by looming Congressional elections in November 2018. For example, the cover of *Time* magazine, published on 2 July 2018, showed a crying two-year-old Honduran girl, Yanela Sanchez, mocked-up next to a stern-looking Trump. Ten days later, *Time* was forced to issue a correction explaining that the girl had been crying while her mother was *questioned* but the two were never, in fact, *separated*. Meanwhile prominent Trump opponents, including Jon Favreau, President Obama's speechwriter between 2009 and 2013, shared pictures of young immigrants in cages on social media. The ruse backfired spectacularly when it transpired that the images had been taken at an Arizona family detention centre in 2014 – when Barack Obama was in the White House. Evidently, in 2014 Obama's administration had come up against exactly the same problem as Trump faced in 2018, as almost 70,000 child migrants flooded into America. The Obama administration's response was, on occasion, to incarcerate these children – and the media did not make any fuss.

While it may be true that there was a key difference between the way this was handled under Obama and Trump – namely that the Obama administration did not separate families as a blanket policy, as Trump's has done – it is intriguing to note that Democrat Texas congressman Henry Cuellar told CNN in June 2018 that he had released some of the offending photos because 'it was kept very quiet under the Obama administration'. The left-wing American Civil Liberties Union (ACLU) also alleged that month that immigrant children had been physically and sexually abused while in custody. The ACLU claimed to have 30,000 pages of documents detailing the 'monstrous' behaviour of Obama's border patrol force. It is a classic example of the hypocrisy Trump endured throughout his administration.

In October 2018, a growing number of illegal border crossers threatened to trigger what Kevin McAleenan, US commissioner of Customs and Border Protection, described as a 'border security and humanitarian crisis', as officials dealt with nearly 1,900 people per day, either presenting themselves at ports of entry without the required documents or attempting to cross the border illegally.[17]

Yet still Congress had failed to agree to funding 'the wall'. So, Trump deployed 5,200 troops to the border in an attempt to contain the crisis. Matters reached a head on 21 December 2018, when the government began a partial shutdown after Republican senators failed to secure enough votes to approve the $5 billion Trump wanted for construction costs, thanks to opposition from Democrats. Bar the length of time it took to get things going again, there was nothing particularly unusual about this deadlock: the governments of Bill Clinton and Barack Obama had also shut down, putting hundreds of people who work for the executive office of the President on furlough. At thirty-five days, Trump's hiatus was the longest in American history and showed the level of dysfunction over immigration in Washington.

In February 2019, with matters still unresolved, Trump declared a state of national emergency over the border crisis. As the Democrats, now in control of Congress, continued to block his funding request, it was the only way he could unlock billions of dollars to construct additional barriers on the southern border. According to the White House, up to $8.1 billion would become available in this way, from the Treasury Forfeiture Fund, the Department of Defense and a congressional spending package. Although the emergency declaration received criticism from congressional Democrats, it was not without precedent, with several of Trump's predecessors having declared more than fifty such 'emergencies' between them since 1976. In November 2019, Customs and Border Protection chief Carla Provost declared that 78 miles of construction of the border wall system had been completed with 158 miles under construction and 273 miles in a 'pre-construction' phase. Progress continued to be made on the 30ft-high wall. Given the scale of opposition Trump faced both in Congress and among special interest groups who busied themselves filing lawsuits which certain 'activist' judges in America's lower courts were happy to uphold, his determination was impressive.

On 23 June 2020, Trump visited the south-western border in San Luis, Arizona, to sign a plaque commemorating the building of the 200th-mile of new border wall. By the following month his government had obtained a total of $15 billion for the project, only 30 per cent of which was agreed by Congress. The rest came from repurposed funds from Defense Department accounts. By early October 2020, a total of 350 miles of fencing had been completed, using 524,000 tons of steel and 752,000 cubic yards of concrete, according to the US Customs and Border Protection Agency. The administration hoped to complete 450 miles of border wall by the end of 2020.

Trump's critics have found many ways to lambast the wall, pointing out that Mexico has never directly paid for the project despite his initial insistence that it would foot the bill. Yet Trump can talk legitimately about the 15,000 troops that Mexico deployed at the border between 2016 and 2020 to help to stop illegal crossings. Moreover, while he had to refine his original ambition of constructing a barrier along the entire border (which he could never have done anyway because some of the land is impassable), he overcame hurdle after hurdle to complete more than 350 miles of wall.

In fact, much of this border replaced and updated existing fencing that was badly in need of repair, yet its existence acts as proof of Trump's unwavering resolution to fulfil a campaign promise. The entire project has been estimated to cost $20 million per mile, according to a report by US Customs and Border Protection produced in January 2020 – substantially more than the 700 miles of 18ft-high fencing built by President George W. Bush, which cost an estimated $4 million per mile. But Trump's structure is all singing and dancing, featuring floodlights, surveillance cameras and an access road.

As for how effective Trump's border controls were, according to the United States Border Patrol there were 851,508 apprehensions of illegal immigrants in the financial year to September 2019, a 115 per cent increase from the previous year and the highest total since 2006. As impressive as this was, it is ironic to reflect on the fact that this figure fell far below the 1,643,679 apprehensions recorded in 2000 – the peak year – when Bill Clinton, a Democrat, was in power.

Either way, Trump certainly changed the debate about American immigration. In July 2020, the Migration Policy Institute, a non-partisan organisation, produced a lengthy piece of research entitled 'Dismantling and Reconstructing the US Immigration System: A Catalog of Changes under the Trump Presidency'. It calculated that his administration had made 'more than 400 policy changes on immigration'. The report concluded that Trump's administration had had a 'dramatic' effect on immigration and made the first serious reforms in this area since 1996. This includes new rules making migrants ineligible for asylum if they failed to apply for it elsewhere en route to America; establishing asylum co-operation agreements with Central American countries allowing the United States to send asylum seekers abroad; and a new policy of making asylum seekers wait in Mexico for their adjudications, as opposed to being free to live in America. Reversing these policy changes will be a huge political challenge for any successor, so Trump's decisions are likely to continue to have a bearing on America's immigration system for years to come.

POSTSCRIPT

In August 2018, a 95-year-old former Nazi collaborator, Jakiw Palij, who served as a guard at the Trawniki concentration camp in Nazi-occupied Poland during the Second World War, was deported from America. He had arrived in the United States in 1949 and had been a citizen since 1957 but in the 1990s it came to light that he had lied to immigration officials about his role in the war, falsely claiming to have been a farmer and factory worker. When federal authorities learned the truth about his dark past, his citizenship was revoked, and his deportation was ordered by a judge in 2004. It took fourteen years to remove him. Part of the problem was that the United States cannot criminally prosecute Second World War crimes that were carried out abroad. Additionally, perhaps unsurprisingly, no other nation was willing to allow Palij entry. Germany, Poland, Ukraine and other nations refused to take him, and so he continued living in limbo with his wife in New York, the last Nazi war crimes suspect in America. Given that thousands of Jews were slaughtered at the Trawniki camp, his presence was a running sore among New York's Jewish community. It was Trump who made it his business to have this Nazi collaborator taken off US soil. In September 2017, all twenty-nine members of New York's congressional delegation signed a letter urging the State Department to follow through on his deportation. After weeks of diplomatic negotiations, Palij was sent to Germany, where he died a few months later. At the time of his death, Richard Grenell, the US ambassador to Germany, praised President Trump's leadership in helping to resolve the protracted legal dispute, saying: 'I am so thankful to Donald Trump for making the case a priority. Removing the former Nazi prison guard from the US was something multiple Presidents just talked about – but President Trump made it happen.'

Not only did Trump succeed where his predecessors failed in the case of Jakiw Palij, but no meaningful objections were raised to this particular hardline action against an immigrant. Whether this proves that everybody – Democrat and Republican – can agree that some immigrants are less welcome than others in America is an open question. What is more certain is that, seemingly, no other President showed as much will as Donald Trump in addressing this undoubtedly complicated case. Furthermore, it is a near certainty that none of Trump's predecessors was as willing as he was to get their hands dirty. As America's population continues to edge towards 350 million, perhaps future generations will be rather more appreciative of his efforts.

2

HEADS YOU WIN, TAILS I LOSE - RACE AND RIOTING

Antifa. Black Lives Matter. These so-called 'movements' seem very similar and seem to me to be populated by a curious number of white, over-privileged twenty-somethings who feel the need to destroy something. Trump was an obvious target for these rabble-rousers. Here was a rich white man who wouldn't dance to their tune. When George Floyd died at the hands of the police, he was martyred by these groups, who seemed to hold Trump personally responsible for what happened. The implication was always that Trump was a racist, and somehow condoned appalling behaviour towards people of colour by the police.

Floyd's death was unforgivable, but he was no saint: he had a deeply murky past and had spent five years behind bars for aggravated robbery with a deadly weapon. Then again, facts did not matter to millions of protesters, politicians and sportsmen and women all over the world. They just wanted to paint Trump as a racist – as they had all along. They felt no need to provide any evidence, still less any proof.

Martin O'Malley was a charismatic former Maryland governor when, in 2015, he threw his hat into the ring as a candidate for the Democratic presidential nomination. A youthful-looking fifty-two, he based his campaign around appealing to a new generation of voters who felt disconnected from modern politics. As he was little known outside Washington and New York, he had a lot to prove when he appeared at the annual Netroots Nation conference in Phoenix, Arizona, in July that year. The gathering, which usually attracts about 3,000 delegates, styles itself as a forum for 'progressives'. Since 2007, it has hosted every significant Democrat politician of the day, including the Clintons, Al Gore and Barack Obama. But 2015 was different. More than 60 per cent of the panellists were non-white, the most diverse line-up in its history. To O'Malley, it seemed a brilliant opportunity to kick-start his campaign. He could not have been more wrong. The arena swiftly turned so hostile and raucous that he was effectively forced offstage.

The trouble began about fifteen minutes into O'Malley's Q&A session. Seated onstage in the Phoenix Convention Center's main hall and looking relaxed in a grey suit with no tie, he vowed to end wealth inequality. Suddenly, loud chanting began. O'Malley – probably nervously – began tapping his hands in time to rhythmic slogans about racial justice. Then Tia Oso, of the Black Alliance for Just Immigration, who represented the demonstrators, climbed onto the stage. She picked up a microphone and delivered a lengthy monologue about race and immigration. It included a reminder that the Black Lives Matter movement had just marked its second anniversary. Next, demonstrators yelled the names of black women who have died in police custody. O'Malley stood and listened, at one point turning to Oso to say, 'My people came here as immigrants from Ireland.'¹ Shouts of 'Black lives matter! Black lives matter!' ensued, together with more chanting, including the vulgar slogan: 'If I die in police custody burn everything down! That's the only way motherfuckers like you listen!' Soon, Patrisse Cullors, a co-founder of Black Lives Matter, was invited onstage to ask a question. 'It's not like we like shutting shit down, but we have to,' she said. 'We are tired of being interrupted ... We are in a state of emergency. If you don't know that emergency, you are not human ... I want to hear concrete actions and I want to hear an action plan.' Doing his best to maintain his equilibrium, O'Malley sought to soothe the agitators with platitudes about the importance of every life. 'Let me say a couple of things. All of us as Americans have a responsibility to recognise the pain and the grief throughout our country from all of the lives that have been lost to violence, whether that's violence at the hands of police or civilians.'[2]

It is hard to see how these sentiments could possibly cause offence – yet his words prompted furious heckles from the crowd. 'Don't generalise this shit!' was one of the politer responses.

Holding his nerve, O'Malley took questions from the floor, revealing that he was in favour of setting civilian review boards to investigate contentious police matters. 'Every life matters and that is why this issue is important. Black lives matter, white lives matter, all lives matter,' he emphasised. Again, there was a furious response. By now his time was up: the next guest, Bernie Sanders, his rival for the Democratic nomination, was waiting in the wings. O'Malley left the stage humiliated. Through no apparent fault of his own, his appearance at the conference had been a disaster.

Later he took to Twitter to clarify his position, explaining, 'Everyone deserves a voice. #blacklivesmatter. I WILL promote a racial justice agenda as president.' He would subsequently go even further, apologising for his choice of words on a programme called *This Week in Blackness.* 'That was a mistake on my part, and I meant no disrespect,' he said. 'I did not mean to be insensitive in any way or communicate that I did not understand the tremendous passion, commitment and feeling and depth of feeling that all of us should be attaching to this issue.'[3]

The following month, just weeks after formally announcing his candidacy, Donald Trump discussed the Netroots Nation incident and its aftermath on Fox News. He made two points that say much about his political instincts. First, with trademark candour, he declared that by apologising O'Malley had behaved 'like a little baby … like a disgusting little weak pathetic baby'. Then he went for the hecklers themselves, asking, 'How can you apologise when you say black lives matter, which is true; white lives matter, which is true; all lives [matter], which is true? And then they get angry because you said white and all; we don't want you to mention that. What's [O'Malley] need to apologise for?'[4]

It left little doubt over the way he would approach such matters if he were elected President. The language he used might not have been elegant, but clearly he would not buckle at the first sign of difficulty, and he would be unafraid to question why so many individuals involved in racial justice movements seek equality for one group while apparently denying the importance of equality for all regardless of colour. He was instinctively suspicious of the true motivates of groups like Black Lives Matter, feeling that this organisation, and others like it, were intent on further confusing the already complicated question of race in America. He sensed right: Black Lives Matter was at that time developing a far-left anti-capitalist ideology that is closest to Marxism or even anarchism. Its ultimate goals fly in the face of everything for which Trump stands. Indeed, long before other political figures realised that the organisation's agenda reached far beyond the necessary and laudable campaign for racial equality, he was critical of Black Lives Matter, labelling the term itself 'very divisive'.[5] He neither dismissed nor downplayed the importance of the campaign group's fight for racial justice, stating in a prescient interview with the Associated Press his belief that relations between the police and the black community were 'far worse' than people realised. Presenting himself as the 'law and order candidate', he also noted the concerns of some black people in America when it came to police conduct, suggesting a lack of training might be to blame for recent police shootings.

The default for Trump's critics is to suggest that he is somehow either responsible for racism per se – a patently ridiculous charge – or guilty of fuelling it. The O'Malley episode serves as a reminder that the Black Lives Matter movement was active in America long before Trump became President. It was launched in 2013 when

Barack Obama was in the White House, proving that those behind it felt the need to establish this movement even when an African American was running the country.

• • •

Some five years after the O'Malley/Black Lives Matter debacle, Trump was tested on race relations in a way that no President had been since the late 1960s. On the evening of 25 May 2020, a 46-year-old black man named George Floyd died after being apprehended by police outside a shop in Minneapolis, Minnesota, for allegedly using counterfeit money to buy cigarettes. Footage of his arrest taken by a bystander showed a white police officer, Derek Chauvin, pinning him to the ground by kneeling on his neck. The officer immobilised him in that position for between eight and nine minutes while Mr Floyd repeatedly screamed, 'I can't breathe.' The official post-mortem found that the 46-year-old suffered a cardiac arrest while being restrained and classified his death as a homicide. Chauvin was subsequently charged with murder and at the time of writing he is awaiting trial.

This tragedy prompted the most sustained period of civil unrest in American history. In the days following Floyd's death, the father of five was martyred in media coverage that largely glossed over his criminal past. Much was made of the fact that he was known as a 'gentle giant' who had made a concerted effort to turn his life around after a troubled past. A video emerged of him appealing to young people to make good choices and avoid gun violence. Amid the rightful outrage over the grotesque way in which he was crushed to death by the authorities, there was little mention of his numerous previous convictions, nor of the fact that he had served four years behind bars for aggravated robbery. His extensive criminal record in no way justified his treatment – but it *was* important context. The extent to which it was effectively erased by vested interests intent on portraying him not simply as an innocent victim of a sick system (which he *was*) but as a hero (quite some stretch) and the furious condemnation of any mention of his questionable past, illustrates the extent to which the complex debate over racial equality has become distorted. For politicians, the only safe response is to virtue-signal, which is not Trump's style.

Within twenty-four hours of Floyd's murder, civil liberties groups were staging demonstrations in his name in every state. Anti-fascism campaigners Antifa joined protests which continued into September. Louisville in Kentucky and Portland in Oregon each passed the bleak milestone of more than 100 consecutive days of unrest. Many rallies were peaceful, but others were violent riots accompanied by looting, arson and vandalism. Statues were torn down, including one of America's first President, George Washington, which was spray-painted with the words 'genocidal colonialist'. The police were consistently targeted, and by 8 June, the *New York Post* reported that some 700 officers had been injured.

Four days after Floyd's death, secret service agents reportedly rushed the President to a White House bunker designed to be used in a terror attack after a baying mob – some hurling rocks and trying to upend police barricades – gathered outside. According to one estimate, vandalism in just twenty states between 26 May and 8 June would cost the American insurance industry between $1 billion and $2 billion, the highest such bill following riots in US history. Tensions were inflamed when contentious police shootings of other black people came to light, including the case of 29-year-old Jacob Blake, who was shot in the back as he entered a car in which his three children were seated. It prompted weeks of riots in the city of Kenosha, Wisconsin.

With depressing predictability, Trump's critics sought to portray these cataclysmic events as the defining point of his presidency, rounding on him for failing to honour Floyd's death or confront the deep-seated societal questions it raised. This was demonstrably untrue. In fact, his reaction to Floyd's death was swift and decisive and left no doubt as to his sympathies for the victim's family, or his grasp of the huge political implications of the incident. On 26 May, the four police officers involved in his arrest were fired. These sackings took place at lightning speed. Yet protests began straight away as the video of the father of five's final minutes circulated on social media, with hundreds taking to the streets of Minneapolis, vandalising police cars and spraying graffiti over a police station.

On 27 May, two nights after Floyd's death, criminal activity spread to other cities including Memphis and Los Angeles. Demonstrators in Minneapolis set fire to a police station. That night Trump took to Twitter to announce the steps he had taken in response to the tragedy.

'At my request, the FBI and the Department of Justice are already well into an investigation as to the very sad and tragic death in Minnesota of George Floyd...' he declared, adding in a second message that he had asked that the inquiry be quick. Lest there was any doubt over his sympathy for the victim, he declared: 'My heart goes out to George's family and friends. Justice will be served!' Against this backdrop, it is patently unfair to claim – as many did – that his response was somehow hostile or uncaring.

Amid continuing unrest, on 28 May, the President criticised authorities in Minneapolis for allowing the violence to escalate. 'These THUGS are dishonouring the memory of George Floyd, and I won't let that happen. Just spoke to Governor Tim Walz and told him that the Military is with him all the way. Any difficulty and we will assume control but, when the looting starts, the shooting starts. Thank you!' he declared, on Twitter.

What did Trump mean? Was he really threatening to mow protestors down with machine guns, Tiananmen Square style, as his detractors immediately suggested? Or was this a straightforward warning about the way violence can escalate and an appeal to remember where it all began: with the death of a father? 'It means when there's looting, people get shot and they die. And if you look at what happened last night and the night before you see that it's very common. And that's the way that was meant,' was the President's explanation.

That there should be any ambiguity was unfortunate. A spin doctor would have deleted the reference to shooting, but Trump never ran his tweets past his advisers. He thought of himself as his own spokesman.

Under pressure from liberal users, Twitter saw fit to post a 'public interest notice' on the message, claiming the President's words broke rules relating to the 'glorification of violence'. A week earlier, a tweet by Iran's Supreme Leader Ayatollah Ali Khamenei, calling for '#jihad against Israel', passed uncensored. The White House could have been forgiven its indignation over such double standards.

By 31 May, violence had spread even further across the country, affecting more than seventy-five cities and leading to at least 4,400 arrests. Curfews were imposed to try to halt the unrest. On 1 June, Trump threatened to send in the military. He said if cities and states failed to control the protests and 'defend their residents' he would deploy the army and 'quickly solve the problem for them'. Speaking from the White House Rose Garden, he declared that 'all Americans were rightly sickened and revolted by the brutal death of George Floyd' but that his memory must not be 'drowned out by an angry mob'.

'I'm dispatching thousands and thousands of heavily armed soldiers, military personnel and law enforcement officers to stop the rioting, looting, vandalism, assaults and the wanton destruction of property,' he added, calling for the National Guard – the reserve military force that can intervene in domestic emergencies – to be deployed in greater numbers. At that point, about 16,000 troops had been activated. To some, it was heavy-handed – there was controversy over the use of tear gas to clear protestors out of Lafayette Square, apparently to clear a path for the President as he approached the White House – but, then again, on the campaign trail, Trump had repeatedly promised to stand for law and order. Now, he was doing just that. On the left, there was a dogged reluctance to acknowledge the wanton destruction taking place. Referencing the US constitution, which guarantees protestors' freedom to assemble, Democrat presidential hopeful Joe Biden said, 'We're not going to allow any President to quiet our voice.'[6] When Trump tried to act in favour of law-abiding citizens, his opponents apparently decided that he was behaving more outrageously than the looters themselves.

• • •

While federal and state authorities were battling to contain both the riots and the coronavirus pandemic, more than 1,000 health and medical professionals were busying themselves undermining those efforts by signing a letter backing the protests. Published on 4 June, the letter declared that the protests were 'vital to the national public health and to the threatened health specifically of black people in the United States'.[7] The letter spoke of the 'pervasive lethal force of white supremacy'. Many of the signatories were based at the University of Washington's Division of Allergy and Infectious Diseases.

America was in the grip of a double crisis, as cities were ransacked by criminals and Covid-19 was killing tens of thousands of citizens. Yet 'experts' on the liberal left remained determined to undermine the President. They must have known that the mass gatherings they were supporting, purportedly in the name of equality, risked spreading the virus, with potentially fatal consequences – but evidently they considered this a fair price to pay to promote their cause.

On 5 June, Trump gave another press conference in the White House Rose Garden, this time to discuss the latest employment figures. During this appearance he said:

Equal justice under the law must mean that every American receives equal treatment in every encounter with law enforcement regardless of race, colour, gender or creed. They have to receive fair treatment from law enforcement. They have to receive it. We all saw what happened last week. We can't let that happen. Hopefully George is looking down and saying this is a great thing that's happening for our country. A great day for him. It's a great day for everybody. This is a great, great day in terms of equality.[8]

Yet again, some were quick to take offence, accusing him of using employment figures to make political capital out of Floyd's death. His message could, of course, be interpreted in a more straightforward way. Is it beyond the realms of possibility that he was simply saying a strong economy is vital to improving race relations? It is known that George Floyd had tried to turn his life around through employment after being released from prison, after all.

What this long and sorry saga shows is that however Trump responded to the death of George Floyd, and the rocket booster it put under the campaign group Black Lives Matter, he could not win. From the outset, he encountered resistance from three distinct areas: the looters, civil liberties groups and certain liberal commentators and politicians. Whatever he said or did during this fraught period, at least one of these opponents always made it their business to find fault. They actively relished stirring up trouble. What his own supporters saw was a President who showed considerable strength and determination in the face of both a medical and a culture war.

• • •

What exactly does the Black Lives Matter movement stand for? Its precise agenda is difficult to identify because it does not have an official manifesto. The organisation's stated aims vary from one country to another and depend on who is talking. In the UK, for example, according to a statement on a fundraising page, it would like nothing less than to 'dismantle imperialism, capitalism [and] white supremacy' as well as the 'patriarchy and the state structures that disproportionately harm black people'.[9] In America, its chief target is the police. When, in the wake of Floyd's death, New York-based campaigners began demanding the 'defunding' of law enforcement agencies, the city's Democrat mayor Bill de Blasio was swift to act. Instead of standing firm against protestors who surrounded New York's City Hall and courthouse vandalising buildings, he caved in. As a result, the City Council stripped $1 billion from the New York Police Department budget. In one stroke, more than 1,000 junior officers who were due to graduate from the police academy the following month were axed, and a plain-clothes anti-crime unit was also disbanded. Inevitably, violent crime rose. Not unreasonably, Trump presented this as a warning to other states labouring under the misapprehension that reducing resources for law enforcement is likely to make anywhere safer. 'They want to pass federal legislation gutting and hamstringing every police department in America,' he said.

> They want to end cash bail; close prisons; defund police depart-ments – or at least largely defund. You see that with New York. A billion dollars they took out of their police department, and crime has gone through the roof. And appoint far-left prosecutors who side with the criminals and target law-abiding citizens. If the left gains power, no city, town, or suburb in our country will be safe.[10]

De Blasio's response? That Trump was 'making things up' to distract from his own cuts to benefits.[11] De Blasio had not prioritised public safety – while Trump put this basic duty of a political leader well ahead of pandering to the mob.

The city of Seattle learned a hard lesson too. In summer 2020, its political leaders also backed 'defunding' the police after pressure from Black Lives Matter. They claimed reducing police numbers would unlock money which could be reallocated within the com-munity. When the first round of cuts was announced a few weeks later, the city's (black) police chief Carmen Best resigned, saying she would no longer be able to do her job properly. Local authorities also allowed Black Lives Matter protesters to turn part of Seattle into a 'police-free' zone for a month. In a hopelessly naïve show of solidarity, the mayor of Seattle, Jenny Durkan, even spoke of having a 'summer of love'. What actually followed was weeks of violence and destruction in which shops were wrecked and police were injured.

Using Federal Bureau of Investigation (FBI) crime data from the first half of 2019 (the most recent official data source on US cities with populations over 100,000), the President claimed the top-ten American cities for overall violent crime were all run by Democrats, including New York, Los Angeles and Chicago – though his critics were swift to point out that 64 of the 100 biggest cities in the US are controlled by Democrats.

● ● ●

Could America do better when it comes to race relations? Of course it could. Statistics produced by the BBC at this time showed that, in 2019, there were 1,004 fatal shootings by police in America. Of those killed, 36.8 per cent were white; 23.4 per cent were black; 15.7 per cent were Hispanic; the remainder were recorded as being of 'unknown' or 'other' ethnicity. As America's population is 60.4 per cent white, 13.4 per cent black and 18.3 per cent Hispanic, these figures are depressing. Undeniably, a greater proportion of black people than white people are killed by police. The same research claimed that approximately one third of America's prison population is black, and that black people are statistically more likely to be arrested for drug abuse than white people even though they use drugs at roughly the same level – further evidence that the battle for racial equality in America has a long way to go. At no point has Trump denied any of this.

What did prominent Democrats do during this period? As the

riots raged, many remained curiously quiet. On 18 August, however, Michelle Obama used her speech at the Democratic Party convention to denounce Trump and imply that he is racist. 'As George Floyd, Breonna Taylor, and a never-ending list of innocent people of color continue to be murdered, stating the simple fact that a Black life matters is still met with derision from the nation's highest office,' she said.[12] Referring to the unrest, she was critical of the idea that 'pepper spray and rubber bullets are used on peaceful protesters for a photo-op', another gross over-simplification of events and a point-blank failure to mention the violence that had affected areas like Portland, Seattle and Chicago. 'Peaceful protesters' do not throw Molotov cocktails, nor do they loot shops and burn down buildings. They do not assault police officers or their fellow citizens.

Nobody can be sure how Hillary Clinton would have handled these events, but her track record does not inspire confidence. In February 2016, a Black Lives Matters protestor called Ashley Williams bought a $500 ticket to a private fundraiser Mrs Clinton was hosting in South Carolina. Once inside, Williams confronted the then presidential hopeful about a speech she had made in 1996 during Bill Clinton's re-election campaign in which she defended his 1994 crime Bill, a piece of legislation which some believe has increased the number of black and Hispanic Americans being imprisoned. The Bill was designed to crack down on gang members. At the time, the then First Lady described gang members as 'super-predators'. 'We must bring [them] to heel.' Critics have since decried this terminology as racist. Interrupting Clinton, Williams claimed she 'owed an apology to black people'. Clinton later released a statement which was in effect just that.

In the run-up to the 2016 presidential election, the former First Lady went to great lengths to give speaking slots at the Democratic convention to individuals associated with Black Lives Matter. There were no such invitations to the widows and widowers of police officers killed in the line of duty.

• • •

Before 28 June 2020, Mark and Patricia McCloskey were two un-known, if very successful, personal injury lawyers. Within two months of that date, this white, middle-class married couple from St Louis, Missouri, had gained an unwanted notoriety in America that led to an invitation to speak at the Republican convention – an honour they were willing to accept. The McCloskeys were at home relaxing on that Sunday evening in June when hundreds of Black Lives Matter protestors turned into their private gated road, Port-land Place, en route to demonstrate outside Mayor Lyda Krewson's house. Believing that the protestors – some of whom were white – had trespassed onto the front lawn of their imposing and expensive mansion, they ran outside barefoot, each holding a gun, to signal that they intended to guard their property. No shots were fired. They insisted they were motivated by fear, not by race. They were subsequently charged with weapons felony offences. Headline after headline stated that this couple had 'brandished guns at Black Lives Matters protestors', or words to that effect, portraying them as the aggressors – despite evidence that protestors had screamed abuse at them. An audio recording revealed that one member of the crowd shouted, 'We gonna kill you, bitch.'

Echoing the view of many ordinary Americans who are passion-ate about their constitutional right to bear arms, Trump labelled the decision to charge the couple a 'disgrace'. He invited them to make a joint speech at the Republican convention. 'No matter where you live, your family will not be safe in the radical Democrats' Ameri-ca,' Mrs McCloskey said during the speech. 'What you saw happen to us could just as easily happen to any of you who are watching from quiet neighbourhoods around our country.' In a bitter irony, it turned out the McCloskeys were supporters of Black Lives Matter.[13]

The line-up of speakers at the Republican convention showed just how inaccurate it is to suggest that Trump has no support among people of colour. Among those who took to the podium were former football star Herschel Walker, Senator Tim Scott, Kentucky Attorney-General Daniel Cameron, housing secretary Ben Carson and White House staffer Ja'Ron Smith – all black. Another speaker was Clarence Henderson, a 1960s civil rights protestor. 'Donald Trump truly cares about black lives,' he said. 'His policies show his heart.' Trump also pardoned Jon Ponder, a black former bank robber who was convicted three times and who now runs a programme helping to rehabilitate other criminals into society. Would these individuals have appeared if they believed claims of Trump's supposed racism? Would a racist invite them to speak at a party convention?

When, on 26 June, Trump signed an executive order directing federal law enforcement agencies to prosecute anybody who damaged federal monuments, an offence which could lead to a spell of up to ten years in prison, it had an immediate effect. The President was demonstrably doing what he said he would do when elected: cracking down on crime. When he visited the torn-up city of Kenosha on 1 September to witness for himself the destruction of days of rioting and looting there, he did so also to praise the police, who had been under siege. John Antaramian, Mayor of Kenosha – Jacob Blake's hometown – was among those who urged him not to make the trip on the grounds that it was 'ill advised'. The President went anyway. He knew the importance of being seen there, both to encourage the law-abiding majority, and to discourage anybody who thought that breaking the law was a reasonable way of making a point – or making a living.

For many American voters, these were the actions of a leader, a President, a statesman. Wind the clock back to July 2015, when Martin O'Malley fled the stage at the Netroots Nation conference because of the offence he had allegedly caused, and imagine how a figure with a thinner skin and less resolve than Donald Trump would have handled the race riots of 2020.

Had O'Malley won the Democratic nomination and gone on

to become President, and had these violent demonstrations taken place on his watch, the protests could have played out very differently. O'Malley had allowed himself to be pushed around by the mob and bullied into making weak apologies. By contrast, Trump never flinched, meeting the challenge of civil unrest head on.

3

BARBARIAN AT THE GATE – FREE SPEECH AND POLITICAL CORRECTNESS

For the past few years, politicians and big corporates have expended huge energy trying not to offend anyone. The slightest transgression leads to calls for boycotts, resignations and hastily written apologies. Any good businessperson knows that if you try to please everyone, you end up pleasing no one. President Trump understood this. As a result, he upset every conceivable pressure group. The irony is that his share of the Hispanic and black vote increased to record levels over his term.

Nimesh Patel was greeted with rapturous applause as he walked on to stage to perform a comedy act. The set-up was a little basic for an Emmy award nominee – just a black-floored auditorium with a single chair and a mic – but he had not expected anything fancy on a college campus. In any case, he had felt honoured to be invited. A successful stand-up who'd written for the American late-night TV show *Saturday Night Live*, he was performing at New York's prestigious Columbia University. His hosts were a student political organisation called the Asian American Alliance. The audience would be young, enthusiastic and progressive. Patel was sure it would be fun.

Roughly half an hour into the show, all seemed to be going well as he set up the audience for his next joke. It was a skit about a time when he lived in the culturally diverse Hell's Kitchen neighbourhood in New York, and befriended a gay black man named 'Pursey' ('because he always had a bag on him'). Looking at his new friend, Patel explained, he realised that homosexuality could not be a choice. 'No one looks in the mirror and thinks: "This black thing is too easy, let me just add another thing to it,"' he quipped, waiting for a roar of laughter at the punchline. Instead, there was awkward silence.

Patel was confused but he took the belly flop in his stride. He knew from experience that this happens to comedians sometimes: you just have to press on. Moments later, however, three young Asian women appeared on stage. Patel would have to leave, they said. His offensive remarks about race and sexuality were simply not acceptable here. Just like that, the gig was over. Ever the professional, he tried to smooth over the embarrassment with another joke, but his mic had been cut off. Without further ceremony, he was ushered off stage. Patel was the victim of a culture of extreme political correctness that has swept college campuses and other educational institutions in America, the UK and beyond. It dictates what is and is not amusing or entertaining; what can and cannot be said; even what can be thought.

In a sinister attempt to repress certain viewpoints, typically but not exclusively those on the political right, individuals who express opinions that are deemed inappropriate or offensive risk being 'cancelled', often before they have even had a chance to speak. For the crime of questioning or deviating from groupthink, they stand to lose their reputations and their livelihoods. In many cases, distinguished academics, politicians and other invited speakers have been summarily axed minutes before a scheduled appearance, sometimes after noisy demonstrations and even riots in auditoriums. Others have lost their jobs.

The chilling effect of this blunt method of dealing with alternative viewpoints on sensitive issues has been to stifle free speech: that is, the right to express any opinion, however objectionable or politically incorrect, without censorship or disproportionate consequence. Even the greatest champions of this important liberty generally accept some limits – covered by libel laws and measures designed to prevent incitement to terrorism. The political and cultural battleground is over where the boundaries lie.

In one of the most important achievements of his presidency, Trump would take a stand against so-called cancel culture, energetically championing the fundamental right to free speech enshrined in the First Amendment. In his four years in the White House, he led by example, saying exactly what he thought about sensitive issues without fear of consequence. His refusal to adhere to a woke agenda set him apart from other political leaders and was at the heart of the hatred he engendered, but it was what much of America wanted and it guaranteed a robust and healthy debate on important but divisive issues.

All over the world, voters are fed up with being told what they cannot say or think and that their honestly held views on delicate issues like immigration and same-sex marriage have no place in civilised society. If they support tighter border control, they are racist; if they question aspects of other cultures or religions, they are xenophobes. Older generations are particularly bewildered by the ever-expanding array of labels and pronouns used to describe genders and sexual orientations. They are quietly horrified by what can happen to individuals in the public eye who speak candidly on sensitive subjects and inadvertently get their choice of words 'wrong'. As the *Harry Potter* author J. K. Rowling learned to her cost when she waded into the toxic transgender debate, it can result in weeks of public shaming. For politicians in particular, unfashionable views on gender, race and religion can be career-ending, so they self-censor and become very bland. Trump was the antithesis of all that.

In a way, his arrival in the White House was like one of the great shifts in taste for art. The 1960s saw Pop Art explode onto the streets and walls of North America. A symptom of exhaustion with the 'elitist' aesthetics of so-called abstract expressionism, this artistic style was full of confusing jumbles, seemingly random splatters and supposedly meaningful random shapes. It was a decisive move away from abstract works that were difficult to interpret. Pop Art wanted to live in the real world and all its ugliness. It exaggerated colours, silhouetted paintings with harsh lines and put a light-hearted kitsch spin on the subjects it depicted. The most famous examples of the movement are Andy Warhol's works, including his iconic Marilyn Monroe portrait, printed multiple times in different stark colours. This wasn't a rejection of reality; it *was* reality, showing how something or someone can look through lots of different lenses.

Over the past twenty years or so, politicians in the US and the UK have developed their own form of abstract expressionism. The way they speak is designed to soothe voters and avoid controversy at all costs. The language they like to use is so smooth and robotic that it is often almost meaningless. Political spin doctors train their principals to give non-answers to questions on controversial issues that require nuance. The aim of this political speak is to offend no one.

Trump took a fat paintbrush and splashed all over this drippy canvas. His personal style was messy and frequently outraged those of a delicate disposition, but it was never half-hearted. The more his liberal critics wailed, the more colourful he became.

American voters are not the only ones who are tired of blank-canvas politicians. Ukraine elected Volodymyr Zelensky – a former stand-up comedian. France elected Emmanuel Macron – a relative political unknown running a relatively new party – as President, on the back of some powerful rallying cries to people who feel forgotten. This is not a left-wing or a right-wing trend; it is just widespread fatigue with the professionalisation of politics and the culture of spin.

Trump is the ultimate 'anti-politician' and very consciously styled himself as such. His pitch to voters was that he was an outsider, who would 'drain the swamp' of Washington.[1] Given the choice, he probably wouldn't even have lived in the White House – he and his wife Melania were quite comfortable in Manhattan.

In his physical appearance alone, he was very obviously different to the 'standard issue' US Senator or Congressman. Had his image been contracted out to a Washington PR consultant, his trademark blond combover would never have passed quality control, but he saw no need to adopt a more fashionable style. He didn't enjoy criticism any more than the next person, but he was not going to give sneering commentators the pleasure of changing who he was.

Fox News presenter Steve Hilton, former director of strategy to Conservative Prime Minister David Cameron, believes Trump's unique 'look' contributed to the irrational revulsion he triggered among certain groups of people – 'Trump derangement syndrome', as it became known. Hilton argues:

> It's really superficial. These people just think he's vulgar. Their dislike for him is not based on policy or philosophy – it's the fact he looks the way he does; the fact that he goes on a tanning bed. It's snobbery, of a very particular kind. It's even the food he eats – the fact he likes McDonald's. They don't exactly say it, but what they're thinking is, 'Oh my god, this guy is so vulgar! How did this barbarian get here?' They find him embarrassing, and that is the real reason they hate him so much.[2]

If commentators didn't like Trump's looks, they were even more appalled by the way he spoke. In his use of language, he set himself dramatically apart from the professional political classes. It was joyfully, proudly, outrageously base. He refused to run his tweets by Ivy League-educated advisers; ranted in capital letters; made spelling mistakes; and used a ridiculous number of exclamation marks. Sometimes he got his grammar wrong.

He was not above insulting foreign leaders during difficult negotiations, though when the immediate crisis was over, he was always
ready to become best friends. He publicly criticised his own aides
if they disappointed him, obstructed him or let him down. On subjects ranging from the character of illegal immigrants from Mexico
to the poor, he said and tweeted so many things that were politically incorrect that almost every time he opened his mouth, some
organisation or another was outraged. Nobody had ever heard a
President of the United States speak that way before. Some felt he
was demeaning his high office.

However, his colourful, freewheeling linguistic style was as attractive to millions of voters alienated and disengaged by the beige
political speak of other leaders as it was unsettling to others. In four
years, he almost never dodged questions with sleek non-answers: he
replied from the heart and many people loved it. A 2016 poll by Pew
Research revealed that well over half of Americans felt 'too many
people are easily offended these days over the language that others
use'.[3] Who better than an outsider like Trump to administer a shock
to the system?

'You say a word somewhat differently, and all of a sudden you're
criticized – sometimes viciously,' Trump told an audience of college
students in October 2016. 'We will end the political correctness and
foster free and respectful dialogue.'[4] Trump's language and the theatrical way in which he delivered his speeches, frequently deviating
wildly from the script, were what made his rallies electric. Very few
political speeches are a pleasure to listen to. They typically follow
a tried and tested format and are packed with instantly forgettable
empty rhetoric. Audiences simply zone out. Trump's performan-
ces were different, not least because nobody ever knew quite what
he would say next: certainly not his closest advisers; probably not
even the President himself. For his staff and advisers, it could be a
nerve-wracking experience, but audiences were entranced. Either he
was commanding their attention through the sheer outlandishness

of what he was saying, or he was making them feel as if he were having a private conversation with them in a bar.

Written down verbatim, these speeches could look illiterate. He would ramble, allow sentences to tail off and repeat himself. To those listening, they felt honest and authentic. He never condescended and had no trouble convincing crowds of blue-collar workers that, for all his money and success, he somehow understood their lives.

RealClearPolitics' polling average data shows that Trump's popularity remained relatively untouched no matter what he said, including his claims that Muslims in New Jersey celebrated 9/11 during an Alabama rally; calling some Mexicans rapists; and saying that Fox News journalist Megyn Kelly had 'blood coming out her eyes' and her 'wherever'.[5]

His suggestion, in 2015, that Senator John McCain, the Republican Party's 2008 presidential nominee, was not a war hero because he was captured in Vietnam, upset many veterans, but his supporters shrugged it off or even found his candour funny and refreshing. RealClearPolitics' data shows that his ratings actually rose following this comment.

What pushed the future President to make such a remark? It was the fact that McCain had insulted Trump supporters, claiming he 'fired up the crazies' in the Republican Party. Trump lashed out in defence of the millions of American voters this insulted. As Hillary Clinton would learn to her cost when she denounced his fans as a 'basket of deplorables', claiming 'half' of them were 'racist, sexist, homophobic, xenophobic, Islamophobic – you name it', there is no reward for dismissing chunks of the electorate because their views are 'unrefined'.

• • •

No topics were too toxic, no subjects off limits for Trump, including one of the most politically sensitive issues of all: transgender rights.

In the natural world, various beautiful creatures are neither male nor female but have the ability to choose their own gender. Clown-fish, like the one millions of children fell in love with in the movie *Finding Nemo*, are all born male but can switch sex to become the dominant female in a group. Bright yellow banana slugs have male and female reproductive organs and can use them at the same time. Scientists have also observed frogs changing sex. The most interesting gender benders of all are eels, which do not become male or female until the end of their lives. In all, thousands of species have hermaphrodite features, including humans, as many as 1.7 per cent of whom may be born with some intersex traits – roughly comparable to the number of people born with red hair.[6] For many others, the gender they were assigned at birth is not the gender with which they identify.

Interpretations of gender have myriad implications for the way societies are structured and how they operate – an issue that is relatively new in political terms. Fortunately, times have moved on since society stigmatised and ostracised individuals whose gender identity is different to the gender they were assigned at birth. Now the transgender lobby is a powerful force in both US and UK politics. Rightly, these groups enjoy legal protection from discrimination, particularly in the workplace. There are many sensitivities over just how far this should go, however, particularly in unique work settings like the military.

For most politicians, this is a subject to be avoided. It is not a voter priority, and only a tiny number of people are personally affected, though their voices are disproportionately loud. For those in the public eye who are not *au fait* with the complex and ever-changing prescribed terminology, the risk of causing offence is just too great.

The strange new world of emerging gender pronouns indicating identities that don't fall within the gender binary can feel daunting for politicians – and who can blame them? Students on American campuses use an array of confusing pronouns like 'ze', 'e', 'ey', 'hir', 'xe', 'hen', 've', 'ne', 'per' and 'thon' to name just a few.[7] The sheer fear among politicians of 'misgendering' someone is a huge deterrent to any kind of open debate.

Not to Donald Trump, however. Early in his presidency he declared that transgender individuals should not be allowed to serve in the military, knowing perfectly well that it would cause a storm. At the same time, he knew that many millions of American voters can think of better uses for their taxes than paying for soldiers and sailors to have sex changes. While the politically correct brigade bleated, the silent majority cheered him on.

Trump confronted this issue during his first summer in the White House, making his initial attempt to ban trans people from the military in July and August 2017. Obama had done the opposite, wanting those already in the armed forces to be open about their gender identities. He had set a date to allow the recruitment of openly transgender individuals. These individuals would receive transition-related medical care while enlisted, and this would be paid for from the public purse.

Trump looked at how much all this was going to cost, and how much medical treatment associated with gender transitioning was already costing taxpayers, and was determined to throw it out. He was also exercised by ongoing medical costs for personnel who had already transitioned. A 2016 study by the Rand Corp., commissioned by the Defense Department, estimated that gender-transition-related treatment cost the military between $2.4 million and $8.4 million each year. The report also estimated that among active service members, somewhere between twenty-five and 130 gender-transition-related surgeries were taking place per year.[8] Trump claimed the rationale for the ban was purely economic, though it was not unreasonable of his critics to suspect his feelings on the matter were a little more complicated, not least because the Rand Corp's own press release noted that the impact on costs and readiness would be very small.

In any case, his proposed regulation made clear that the military would not cover the medical costs of trans people, though the armed forces would still 'protect the health' of those who had already begun transitioning. Trump expected a fight, and he got one. His own generals were dismayed, having worked hard to champion inclusivity in the military. Legal challenges by advocacy groups repeatedly delayed implementation. Trump doubled down, and two and a half years later, the ban finally came into force.

At the time of writing, at least five lawsuits against the measures are working their way through the courts, and President Joe Biden has said he will revert to the Obama policy. Critics have pointed out that the US military spends some $84.24 million on erectile dysfunction prescriptions, $41.6 million of which goes on Viagra alone.[9] Relative to the US military's colossal overall budget, the cost of gender realignment surgery and other associated expenses was negligible. To Trump, that was not the point. He objected to the principle of US taxpayers paying for what he viewed as a discretionary, complicating distraction, to an organisation that was meant to be focused on preventing, or if necessary fighting, wars.

Whatever transgender activists and politically correct politicians say, the truth is that many voters agreed. Americans are divided when it comes to transgender people in the military; a 2019 Gallup poll showed that while 71 per cent of Americans support allowing openly trans men and women to serve, 'Republicans (43 per cent) are far less likely than Democrats (88 per cent) and independents (78 per cent)' to do so. There is also a large disparity between men and women's views on the issue.

Many also remain deeply uncomfortable with individuals choosing their own gender, then expecting the same access to single-sex facilities or services as everyone else. According to an *Economist/YouGov* poll, one in five adults believe that 'employers should be able to fire transgender workers who wear work clothes that match their gender identity'.[10] Polls suggest public opinion in America remains deeply divided on the use of public restrooms by transgender people.

Many questions remain about how societies built on centuries of layered gendered tasks and roles will adjust as pressure grows for new approaches. Trump has shown that it is reasonable and legitimate to interrogate all this. As he himself said in August 2017: 'It's been a very difficult situation, and I think I'm doing a lot of people a favor by coming out and just saying it.'[11]

• • •

Trump is not a man to do things by halves, and Independence Day 2020 was no different. Arriving in South Dakota's beautiful afternoon sunshine on Air Force One on 4 July, accompanied by Melania, he headed for Mount Rushmore, where he was widely expected to deliver a speech on the coronavirus crisis. The President had other ideas, however. After a military flypast at dusk, and the first fireworks display to have taken place on the site for eleven years, he launched into a 6,000-word address that mentioned the virus only once. What he really wanted to talk about was the ongoing culture war. By this point, the riots had been raging for weeks. Serious debates had taken place about whether America's national anthem should be changed; whether the constitution should be rewritten; and whether history lessons in schools should reflect the country's slave-trade past.

Trump and his advisers had chosen the iconic setting for his speech with great care. Rioters had desecrated scores of historic statues and monuments. The four giant sculptures of presidents George Washington, Thomas Jefferson, Theodore Roosevelt and Abraham Lincoln symbolise America's birth, growth, development and preservation respectively, according to Gutzon Borglum, the sculptor who created this astonishing work of art. Speaking of 'the greatest Americans who have ever lived', Trump paid tribute to the legacies of these presidents, pledging: 'This monument will never be desecrated, these heroes will never be defaced, their legacy will never, ever be destroyed, their achievements will never be forgotten, and Mount Rushmore will stand for ever as an eternal tribute to our forefathers and to our freedom.' In the context of the preceding weeks, this was entirely appropriate from a man who hoped to be re-elected four months thence. Reminding the nation of the quotation 'all men are created equal', which appears in the US Declaration of Independence, written by Thomas Jefferson in 1776, Trump went on to address the latest attempted overthrow of American society. 'Our nation is witnessing a merciless campaign to wipe out our history, defame our heroes, erase our values, and indoctrinate our children,' he warned. He singled out the phenomenon of 'cancel culture' – which he defined as 'driving people from their jobs, shaming dissenters, and demanding total submission from anyone who disagrees' – as the definition of totalitarianism. He went on:

> In our schools, our newsrooms, even our corporate boardrooms, there is a new far-left fascism that demands absolute allegiance. If you do not speak its language, perform its rituals, recite its mantras, and follow its commandments, then you will be censored, banished, blacklisted, persecuted, and punished. It's not going to happen to us.[12]

Blaming the riots on years of 'extreme indoctrination and bias in education, journalism, and other cultural institutions', he added: 'The radical view of American history is a web of lies – all perspective is removed, every virtue is obscured, every motive is twisted, every fact is distorted, and every flaw is magnified until the history is purged and the record is disfigured beyond all recognition.'

After explaining the achievements of the four presidents represented at Mount Rushmore, Trump asserted his belief in 'equal opportunity, equal justice, and equal treatment for citizens of every race, background, religion, and creed' and called for 'free and open debate, not speech codes and cancel culture'. He also praised some of the greatest Americans who have lived, including Martin Luther King, the Wright Brothers, Jesse Owens, George Patton, Clara Barton, Harriet Tubman, Ella Fitzgerald, Louis Armstrong, Elvis Presley and Muhammad Ali. 'Only America could have produced them all,' he said, announcing a new National Garden of American Heroes.

Instead of finding inspiration in any of this in the days that followed, Trump's critics found only fault. The *Washington Post* ran opinion pieces headlined: 'Trump doesn't have a clue what America is about' and 'Trump is running an openly racist campaign'. The *New York Times* carried a piece with the headline: 'Trump uses Mount Rushmore Speech to Deliver Divisive Culture War Message'. Left of centre publications preferred to ignore the fact that the President's principal objective was to protect the country he was elected to lead, a priority shared by most American voters.

As for CNN? On 4 July, the network aired a report questioning whether all races enjoyed the annual commemorations of the birth date of the United States. The provocative news segment suggested that Trump had kicked off the holiday weekend by 'standing in front of a monument of two slave owners and on land wrested away from Native Americans for the national park'.[13]

Was this responsible broadcasting by CNN, or did it just stoke division? To Trump's supporters at least, what it looked like was yet another attempt to examine the past through the prism of the present to make life difficult for the President.

• • •

In March 2019, Trump signed an executive order to protect free speech on college campuses. It legislated for the removal of federal research funding from institutions where this fundamental right was not upheld.

It was something he had threatened to do in early 2017, after right-wing provocateur Milo Yiannopoulos was dramatically no-platformed amid chaotic scenes at Berkeley University. 'If U.C. Berkeley does not allow free speech and practices violence on innocent people with a different point of view – NO FEDERAL FUNDS?' Trump had tweeted at the time.[14]

Announcing the measure in 2019, the President condemned 'oppressive speech codes, censorship, political correctness, and every other attempt by the hard left to stop people from challenging ridiculous and dangerous ideas'.[15] Again in 2017, he had signed a similar measure to protect religious organisations. It was designed to ensure they would not be forced to accept policies that flew in the face of their religious beliefs, in particular Obamacare's contraceptive mandate.* It protected organisations like Little Sisters of the Poor (a Catholic institute for women run by those committed to a life of chastity) from being sued if they declined to provide employees with health-insurance plans that paid for contraceptives.

In yet another symbolic defence of freedom of expression, at the G7 summit in 2019, Trump refused to back measures promoting government censorship online and the policing of internet content. European leaders had drafted an accord that forced technology companies into the role of government censors, obliging them to police content and remove anything insensitive. Trump refused to sign, fearing it was the thin end of the wedge.

His detractors will counter that he cannot be held up as a champion of free speech, because he repeatedly refused to engage with sections of the media. His dysfunctional relationship with the press was a continual theme of his presidency and stemmed from bitter experience with certain news outlets that he regarded as institutionally incapable of giving him a fair hearing. His experience on the campaign trail in 2016 had taught him that attempting to woo

---

* This mandated health insurers or employers that provide workers with health insurance to cover some contraceptive costs in their insurance plans.

certain left-leaning media groups was a waste of time. Certain organisations, most notably the channel he labelled 'fake as hell CNN, the worst', and the 'failing *New York Times*', seemed determined to find fault with everything he did. Instead of attempting to win them over or at least neutralise their hostility, he deliberately antagonised them. From the outset, he simply would not 'play the game', consistently declining to attend the annual White House correspondents' dinner in Washington. Anticipating a disrespectful reception, he simply no-platformed himself.

His interactions with the press in general and with individual reporters whose articles he disliked did not make his presidency easier. However, there was nothing essentially undemocratic about his approach. Those concerned by the proximity of political journalists to politicians might argue the opposite: that the clubby cosiness of these reporters and the powerful public figures they need to be able to write or broadcast dispassionately about is deeply unhealthy. Trump had no truck with that.

That he regularly refused to give an audience to those who never had a good word to say about him does not undermine his status as a defender of free speech. After all, those who champion the First Amendment are also entitled to plead the Fifth. Journalists from organisations he accused of peddling fake news were able to continue churning out their disobliging material – a liberty they wholeheartedly embraced.

4

WITH FRIENDS LIKE THESE – TRUMP AND THE UK

Ah, the good old impartial BBC. Growing up, it was pretty much all we had as a news source. Trusted by all, whatever was said by 'Auntie' was, without question, the truth. Was that ever really the case? Probably not, but only in these past few years has the bias become so blatant. I know from personal experience. In 2020 I brought one of the most important cases in English legal history, challenging the government over the Covid lockdown. It did not get a single mention on the BBC. By contrast, the Gina Miller Brexit case was given endless coverage. That's just my story, but the bias was regularly on display when it came to Trump. The ultimate bastion of the liberal elite, the Corporation showed its true colours whenever Trump came to town, giving ample coverage to all the protests. After broadcasting his final speech before he left office, who did the BBC instantly cut to for comment? One Mary Trump. That's the niece who hates him so much she penned a book subtitled 'How My Family Created the World's Most Dangerous Man'. How the Establishment love to ridicule the outsider.

As a billionaire property magnate, Donald Trump was accustomed to a certain standard of accommodation. Others might not share his taste, but he had a signature style, typically featuring lashings of glitz and gold. It was considerably showier than the traditional interior décor at the White House.

Whether he really labelled his new official residence and work-place 'a real dump', as one report claimed, is disputed, but what is not in doubt is that when he swapped his swanky New York pent-house for 1600 Pennsylvania Avenue, he was dismayed by his new surroundings. Decorators were drafted in for a multi-million-dollar refit.

Out went the 'stained' yellow striped wallpaper the Obamas had chosen for the Oval Office, to be replaced with a creamy-grey damask design selected by the President himself. According to an official, the President 'wanted to bring back the lustre and glory' of the White House. To that end, conventional carpets, curtains and soft furnishings were thrown out and replaced with more ostenta-tious pieces – though to the disappointment of snobby critics, he did not turn it into a 'penthouse fantasy land'.[1]

Most of the improvements were simply cosmetic, but there were a number of symbolic changes, in particular, the return of a bust of Winston Churchill to the Oval Office. At the start of the Obama ad-ministration, the sculpture of the British wartime leader had been bundled into the back of a taxi and taken to the British Embassy, in favour of a bust of Martin Luther King. The move had caused something of a diplomatic spat after it was interpreted by some commentators as a sign of Obama's hostility to the British.

Obama's people would subsequently claim that his office was just too cluttered with busts. One aide even suggested they'd thought the bust was Eisenhower. ('They all look the same to us.')[2] However, the damage was done: the episode set the tone for what would prove to be a marked cooling of the so-called 'special relationship' between the US and the UK during his administrations.

In 2009, Justin Webb, the BBC's reporter in Washington DC, told the UK House of Commons Foreign Affairs Select Committee: 'If you look inside the current Administration, there is a level of real frustration and eye-raising at what they perceive as the obsession of the Brits with their relationship with the Americans.' In preparation for the Committee, Webb had asked a colleague in DC to ask an administration official about the 'special relationship'. The reply was: 'Get out of my room. I'm sick of that subject. You're all mad.'[3]

A creeping sense that Obama had little interest or even respect for the long-established 'special relationship', a term that had been coined by Churchill in 1946 and later blossomed under Reagan and Thatcher, was reinforced in 2016 during the Brexit referendum campaign, when, at the request of the then UK Prime Minister David Cameron, who was desperately trying to keep the UK in the EU, he warned British voters that if the United Kingdom left the European Union they would find themselves at the 'back of the queue' for a trade deal.

The Anglophile Trump was eager to make amends. Within hours of his arrival at the White House, Churchill's bust was ceremonially returned to the Oval Office. Britain would be 'first in line' for a trade deal with Trump's America.

Trump loved the UK – but the UK did not love him back. From the moment it looked as if he had a serious chance of becoming President to his departure from office, elements of the British Establishment sought to undermine him, humiliate him and apply the worst possible interpretation to almost everything he did. He was the most Anglophile President in the White House for decades: an ardent admirer of the Queen; eager to strike a US–UK trade deal in the wake of Britain's decision to leave the EU; and genuinely keen to see the UK succeed after breaking free from Brussels. For his enthusiasm and support, he received no obvious gratitude from anyone except another anti-Establishment populist, Brexit Party leader Nigel Farage. Other prominent figures and organisations who might have been expected to set aside their differences – from the Mayor of London to senior diplomats and elements of the civil service – did not even trouble to hide their disdain. It is hard to imagine how this can ever have been in Britain's interests.

Among the powerful institutions that struggled to remain

neutral when it came to anything Trump-related was the UK's publicly funded broadcaster, the BBC. Three weeks before the 2016 US election, the BBC's flagship current affairs programme *Question Time* devoted a few minutes to debating whether Donald Trump was 'unfit to be President'. The first member of the panel to be asked to grapple with this subject was the then editor-at-large of *The Independent*, Amol Rajan. 'The man is a psychopath,' Rajan declared. 'He has narcissistic personality syndrome. He can't relate to people.' Without any particular expertise in the subject, he went on to say: 'Donald Trump is an extreme loner. He doesn't actually have any friends. He's lived a very sad and lonely life and he's got a quite ludicrous bunch of policies which means that he probably won't get elected.' He then asked: 'If Trump is such a psychopath and a lying, racist, sexist bully, why isn't Hillary [Clinton] way ahead? I'm not saying that because I think she's a terrible candidate; I think it speaks of the fact that America is a very divided country.'[4] Rajan rounded off his tirade by advising those listening that in order to understand Trump properly, they should compare him with King Lear. He then quoted Lear's words from Act II Scene IV of Shakespeare's tragedy: 'I will do such things – What they are yet I know not, but they shall be the terrors of the earth.' For his rather ostentatious efforts, Rajan accepted a generous round of applause from the audience. Five weeks later, he accepted an offer from the BBC to be its first ever media editor, a job that came with a publicly funded salary of £150,000 a year.

It is striking that the UK's taxpayer-funded broadcaster should have seen fit to employ – just two weeks after Donald Trump won the US election – a man who had recently denounced him in such personal terms, particularly as Rajan was being hired to report facts, not opinions. (For what it's worth, he has flourished at the BBC and is now paid more than £200,000 a year.) A national broadcaster in any country bears some responsibility for setting the tone when it comes to how public figures are portrayed. Of course, the

Corporation is entitled – indeed has a duty – to air criticism of the President as part of balanced reporting. What has consistently been missing is the alternative, supporting viewpoint held by the tens of millions of Americans who voted for Trump.

Trump is half-British by blood through his mother, Mary, who was born in the Outer Hebrides in 1912 and lived in Scotland until 1930. He has publicly expressed his 'love' of Britain and the British on numerous occasions. He has also invested millions of dollars in Scotland, where he owns two golf courses, and he employs hundreds of people in the UK. Nonetheless, deriding him has been something of a national pastime for years, and the BBC – the supposed jewel in Britain's cultural crown – was among those leading the charge. In October 2012, for example, it screened *You've Been Trumped*, an independently made documentary directed by Anthony Baxter, which charts the construction of Trump's golf course in Aberdeenshire and the subsequent political and legal difficulties that arose. The film contains the allegation that some local residents were bullied. Trump objected to the BBC's decision to air this project and, through his Scottish lawyers, Dundas & Wilson, asked the Corporation to drop it on the grounds that it was defamatory, biased and misleading. He also demanded a right of reply. His pleas were ignored, and the BBC gave *You've Been Trumped* (which had already been shown at festivals around the world) its television premiere. Disagreements and disputes between a subject and a broadcaster are commonplace in journalism and documentary-making, but it is hard to avoid concluding that an anti-Trump attitude at the BBC was pretty fixed from this point.

The BBC charter obliges the Corporation to be even-handed at all times. That seems to have been forgotten during the third weekend in January 2017 when it reported on two events: Trump's inauguration and a series of rallies against him in cities in America and elsewhere.

On 22 January, the BBC website quoted Trump as saying that

'it looked like a million and a half people' watched his swearing-in ceremony in Washington DC on 20 January. It also quoted his then press secretary, Sean Spicer, referring to 'the largest audience to ever see an inauguration' – a statement that might, in fact, have held water if global television audiences were counted. The BBC website published comparison photographs of President Obama's first inauguration in January 2009 and Trump's inauguration to emphasise that, according to these images, more people had attended the former. It then reported: 'Millions of protesters have taken to the streets of cities in the US and around the globe to rally against the new US President Donald Trump ... The aim was principally to highlight women's rights, which activists believe to be under threat from the new administration.'[5] Even if Trump had been guilty of exaggeration when he claimed that 1.5 million people were in Washington DC to observe his inauguration ceremony – a boast that the BBC appeared to have skewered pretty successfully using photographs – no such scepticism was shown when it came to the number of those who had attended the anti-Trump marches. Indeed, the BBC cheerfully quoted 'city officials' who 'estimated [the number of protestors in Washington DC] to be more than 500,000-strong, followed by New York with some 400,000 and hundreds of thousands elsewhere, including Chicago and Los Angeles.'[6] These statistics were simply taken at face value. Could it be that the BBC wanted to suggest that many more people demonstrated against Trump that weekend than turned out in support of him in Washington DC? To bolster the story, the same BBC article quoted the *New York Times* and television channels CNN and ABC, which had also attacked Trump's claims about how many people had witnessed his swearing-in. Furthermore, the report added: 'Pro-Trump Fox News reported [Trump's and Spicer's] claims unchallenged.' Naturally, the report omitted to mention that the *New York Times* and other media outlets upon which it had relied are openly *anti*-Trump. It was a master class in selective reporting.

Attitudes to Trump at the Corporation did not improve as time went by. Various prominent presenters with a duty to remain politically neutral did little to conceal their contempt. In July 2019, Naga Munchetty, a BBC *Breakfast* presenter, railed against Trump over a controversial tweet he had posted about four Democrat congresswomen of foreign heritage. The group were campaigning over what they perceived to be a humanitarian crisis at the Mexican border and agitating for Trump's impeachment. He retorted that they should 'go back and help fix the totally broken and crime-infested places from which they came. Then come back and show us how it is done'.[7]

Trump's comment was unwise, but it was not for BBC presenters to express a view. Nonetheless, Munchetty waded into the furore, suggesting that Trump was 'racist'. She was 'absolutely furious' at Trump's choice of words, she said. The BBC received a number of complaints about this rant. Initially, bosses at the Corporation agreed that she had breached its editorial guidelines. That was not the end of the affair, however. Sixty-one black and ethnic minority broadcasters, including Lenny Henry and Krishnan Guru-Murthy, wrote a letter to *The Guardian* newspaper condemning the BBC for agreeing that Munchetty had broken its rules. They demanded that the BBC reconsider, saying nobody can be 'impartial' about racism. Days later, the then BBC Director-General Lord Hall acquiesced, reversing the ruling and saying that the BBC complaints unit had been wrong to find against Munchetty, who had not apparently broken the Corporation's guidelines. Trump's supporters could be forgiven for feeling that special rules applied in this case.

It is not as though everybody learned from this episode. In March 2020, an article on the BBC website by its New York correspondent Nick Bryant accused Trump of making 'ridiculous boasts' and having a 'narcissistic hunger for adoration' during his response to Covid-19. The piece, headlined 'Coronavirus: What this crisis reveals about US – and its president', included Bryant's analysis of the early stages of the pandemic. Again, only a complaint from a member of the public forced the BBC to remove these words in August 2020 and to acknowledge that its correspondent had shown a bias against Trump via the 'approach and tone' of certain phrases he used.[8] BBC 2 *Newsnight* presenter Emily Maitlis was another Trump sceptic. Back in 2013, long before he was a White House contender, she had interviewed him. In her book about her broadcasting career, *Airhead*, published in 2019, she devoted several pages to this encounter. Promoting the autobiography, she appeared on an ITV talk show during which she told two anecdotes about the President which were clearly designed to portray him in a poor light. Lest anyone was in any doubt about where she stood, in 2020, she retweeted a number of highly critical social media messages about the President, including a post by American comedian Sarah Cooper, which said, 'Still processing the fact that the President has no clue what he's talking about on national television.' Whatever Trump had been saying, clearly it was not going to get a fair hearing from the leading lights at the BBC.

•　-　•

Trump probably expected nothing better from BBC journalists, but the way some senior political figures in Britain behaved must have come as a shock. In January 2016, ten full months before he won the US election, British MPs spent three hours debating whether he should be forbidden from entering the country. It came after almost 600,000 people signed a petition in response to Trump's call for a temporary ban on all Muslims entering America. His controversial proposal had been prompted by a mass shooting of innocent people in California by couple Rizwan Farook and Tashfeen Malik. The crime was inspired by Islamic terrorism. Trump's reaction was criticised by almost every senior politician in the West, including David Cameron, who was UK Prime Minister at the time. The parliamentary petition in the UK called for him to be 'banned from UK entry' on the grounds that he was guilty of 'hate speech'. The petition stated:

> The UK has banned entry to many individuals for hate speech. The same principles should apply to everyone who wishes to enter the UK. If the United Kingdom is to continue applying the 'unacceptable behaviour' criteria to those who wish to enter its borders, it must be fairly applied to the rich as well as poor, and the weak as well as powerful.[9]

Given that there was never any realistic chance of this debate resulting in Trump being banned from entering Britain, this was only ever going to be an opportunity for certain MPs to grandstand and virtue-signal. They did not disappoint. Among contributors was Labour MP Rupa Huq, who declared that Trump was a 'racist, homophobic misogynist'.[10] Conservative MP Marcus Fysh called him 'the orange prince of American self-publicity'.[11] And SNP MP Gavin Newlands said that he was not only 'racist, sexist and bigoted' but also 'an idiot'. Voices of reason were few and far between, though Home Office minister James Brokenshire did manage to point out that although the government had the power to exclude people who would 'do harm', America was the UK's most important ally, and the UK should 'engage' with presidential candidates even when it 'profoundly disagreed' with their views.[12] Conservative MP Sir Edward Leigh said that Britain had invited despots to its shores in the past who had done 'far, far worse than anything Donald Trump can dream of'. He also warned against 'shutting down an honest debate about immigration'.[13] The debate ended without a vote, having achieved nothing tangible other than potentially alienating a potential future President of Britain's closest ally.

Trump was magnanimous in the face of this opposition and continued to show that he was well disposed to Britain. When asked about the petition by ITV News the following month, he called it 'ridiculous' and said, 'I love the people of the UK. My mother, as you know, was born in Scotland. She loved Scotland. She loved the Queen.'[14] Yet spectacles like the Westminster Hall debate, which took place long before the American people had even cast their votes, surely influenced public opinion in Britain.

Of course, MPs and other political figures are entitled to express fiercely critical views about any world leader, but it is conventional to show basic respect towards democratically elected premiers. Not to do so is to insult the millions of ordinary people who voted for the individual concerned. Government ministers have a particular responsibility not to upset diplomatic relations without good reason – especially with the UK's most important ally. Yet, from the outset, some of the most powerful and influential political figures in the UK failed to extend Trump even the most basic of courtesies. In polite company in the UK, it was simply not fashionable to say anything positive about him, and politicians of all parties were shamefully eager to join in the bear-baiting.

When Trump won the presidential election in 2016, nobody in Theresa May's government had anticipated the result and so no relationship between Downing Street and the new President existed. Indeed, before entering Downing Street, two of May's chief advisers, Nick Timothy and Fiona Hill, had openly mocked him online. Hill referred to him as a 'chump' and Timothy said that 'as a Tory' he did not want 'any reaching out' to Trump.[15] Many Conservative Party politicians had also said before the election that they could not support him. Some had even said they would have voted for Hillary Clinton. All this was unusual: in the interests of diplomacy, UK government figures tend to exercise great caution when it comes to voicing opinions on American election candidates.

One senior minister who set aside these conventions was Michael Gove. On the eve of Trump's inauguration in January 2017, he told BBC *Newsnight*: 'I said during the election, had I been an American,

I would have voted for Hillary Clinton. Now, I think Clinton would be a stronger and better American President for the world than Donald Trump.'[16]

Gove was a cheerleader for Brexit. He felt so strongly about the case for the UK leaving the EU that he was ready to turn his back on one of his closest friends and allies, then Prime Minister David Cameron, to back the campaign to leave. He might, therefore, have been expected to have welcomed the election of a pro-Brexit President to the White House. After all, Clinton thought the UK should remain in the EU. It is hard to avoid the conclusion that Gove somehow felt the need to curry favour with the audience by telling them what they wanted to hear. It was certainly peculiar that he and others should have preferred a US President who did not think Britain could do well outside the EU, as opposed to Trump, who clearly believed in the UK's potential.

Despite this hostility, Trump remained enthusiastic about forging a new trading relationship with the UK as quickly as possible. This goodwill continued even as pro-EU MPs at Westminster embarked on a lengthy attempt to use Parliament to overturn the referendum result, lowering the country into a political spasm which did not abate until late 2019. Throughout this fraught period, Trump continued to speak of his hopes of a new post-Brexit US–UK trade deal, yet, by August 2020, when Boris Johnson had been Prime Minister for a year, the third round of negotiations between the United States and the United Kingdom for a trade deal had come and gone with no result. It was a huge missed opportunity.

• • •

Between his election in November 2016 and December 2019, Trump made three official visits to Britain. Two of these visits were overshadowed by the behaviour of the Labour Mayor of London Sadiq Khan. Trump's first visit, which took place in July 2018, was a working trip in which he went to Blenheim Palace, birthplace of Winston Churchill, for an official dinner with Theresa May. He also visited the Royal Military Academy Sandhurst and had tea with the Queen at Windsor Castle.

During the trip, a giant inflatable figure depicting Trump as a bright orange baby wearing a nappy was flown over London. This stunt was authorised by Khan. Trump later admitted that protests against him, and the blimp's presence, had made him feel 'unwelcome' to visit Britain. While some of the public undoubtedly enjoyed the spectacle of the ugly balloon floating over London, others were deeply embarrassed – including those who did not much like Trump but considered it the height of bad manners. Digby Jones, a former director-general of the Confederation of British Industry, told CNBC that he thought it was 'disgusting' that the Trump baby balloon was being allowed.[17]

Khan and Trump had been engaged in a feud dating back to December 2015, when Khan had described Trump's proposed ban on some Muslims entering America as 'outrageous'. At the time, he had told the BBC that he hoped Trump would 'lose badly'. After he was elected Mayor of London in May 2016, Trump suggested Khan would be exempt from his proposed travel ban on Muslims. 'There will always be exceptions,' he told the New York Times, adding that Khan's victory was a 'good thing'. Within a week of those positive comments, however, Khan said Trump's views on Muslims were 'ignorant', resulting in Trump challenging Khan to an IQ test. 'I will remember those statements. They are very nasty statements,' Trump told ITV.

When, a year later, Muslim terrorists killed eight people and injured forty-eight others during an attack on London Bridge and Borough Market, the war of words was reignited after Trump mistakenly suggested that Khan had said there was 'no reason to be alarmed'. In fact, Khan had said the public should not be alarmed by the increased police presence on London's streets. A spokesman for Khan responded by saying he had 'more important things to do than respond to Donald Trump's ill-informed tweet'.

Trump responded with another tweet, saying this was a 'pathetic excuse' that the mainstream media was 'working hard to sell'. Two days later, on 6 June 2017, Khan called on the government to cancel Trump's forthcoming state visit. 'I don't think we should roll out the red carpet to the president of the USA in the circumstances where his policies go against everything we stand for,' he said. It was this repeated squabbling which gave rise to the Trump 'baby blimp' being flown over London in July 2018.

Given the nature of his 'welcome' to London, it is probably unsurprising that during this trip, Trump said Khan had 'done a very bad job on terrorism', adding, 'I think he has done a bad job on crime, if you look, all of the horrible things going on there, with all of the crime that is being brought in.'

To the Mayor of London's credit, his office did allow free speech activists to give him a taste of his own medicine, by flying a Khan blimp over London in September 2018. It was not the end of hostilities, however. During Trump's state visit in June 2019, permission was given for the Trump baby blimp to fly over London for the second time. As if this wasn't bad enough, shortly before Trump arrived, Khan penned an article for the left-wing *Observer* newspaper comparing the language used by the President to rally his supporters to that of 'the fascists of the twentieth century'.[18]

Moments before landing in the UK, Trump retaliated, declaring that Khan had 'done a terrible job as Mayor of London, has been foolishly "nasty" to the visiting President of the United States, by far the most important ally of the United Kingdom. He is a stone cold loser who should focus on crime in London, not me.'[19]

Trump was given a state banquet and also attended a ceremony in Portsmouth to commemorate the seventy-fifth anniversary of D-Day. He did return to UK shores in December 2019, but only for a NATO summit.

All this was deeply unedifying, and it went right to top of the British Establishment. It is customary for visiting foreign leaders on a state visit to the UK to be invited to deliver an address to MPs and peers. In an extraordinary intervention shortly after Trump was elected, however, the Speaker of the House of Commons, John Bercow, announced that, in this case, he was blocking the move. 'An address by a foreign leader to both houses of Parliament is not an automatic right. It is an earned honour,' he said dismissively. He went on to portray Trump as racist, sexist and opposed to the independence of the judiciary.

Before the imposition of the migrant ban I would myself have been strongly opposed to a speech by President Trump in Westminster Hall. After the imposition of the migrant ban by President Trump, I am even more strongly opposed ... I feel very strongly that our opposition to racism and sexism and our support for equality before the law and independent judiciary are hugely important considerations in the House of Commons.[20]

In a dramatic breach of protocol, MPs on all sides of the House greeted Bercow's announcement with loud applause.

Where were these MPs and their lofty principles when China's President Xi Jinping made a four-day state visit to Britain in 2015? The leader of the deeply dubious Communist regime, with its appalling human rights record, was invited to address MPs and peers in Parliament's Royal Gallery and attended a state banquet at Buckingham Palace. There was barely a ripple of public protest, nor any objection in Parliament. Indeed, MPs and peers flocked to hear what he had to say. To put this in perspective, state murder in China is commonplace. Persecution of Muslim Uighurs has led to an estimated 1.5 million being held in Chinese state 're-education' camps. Thousands of Uighur women have been forcibly sterilised. Members of the Falun Gong spiritual movement have been subjected to forced organ harvesting by the authorities. And the Chinese state has presided over a ruthless programme of rape, murder and torture in the disputed territory of Tibet since the mid-twentieth century.

Could it be that the British liberal left is somehow obsessed with Donald Trump and his alleged misdemeanours to such a degree that it has lost sight of what a politically extreme regime actually is? Casting Trump in the role of pantomime villain certainly required less moral courage than tackling the wickedness over which President Xi presides.

• • •

Political neutrality is one of the most important features of the civil service. All mandarins have a duty to impartiality to ensure the smooth running of government, whoever is in power. When it came to Trump, however, many senior figures seemed to struggle with this concept.

A month after Trump's state visit to London, leaked diplomatic cables revealed that the UK's ambassador to Washington, Sir Kim Darroch, a career civil servant, thought Trump was 'inept', 'insecure' and 'incompetent'. Darroch also thought Trump could be indebted to 'dodgy Russians' and suggested that his economic policy could wreak havoc on the world trade system. Once again, a major diplomatic rift with Britain's closest ally was a serious possibility thanks to one man believing that his subjective opinions about Trump – whom he scarcely knew – were of primary importance. In the diplomatic cables, Darroch suggested that Trump's presidency might one day 'crash and burn'.[21] Yet it was his own career which suffered that fate. He was forced to resign almost immediately after Trump made it clear that US officials would no longer deal with him. With friends like these, Trump must have thought, who needs enemies?

Unlike civil servants, celebrities are entitled to say what they like, and when it came to Trump, they didn't hold back. In October 2020, the British actor Dominic West gave an interview to ITV's breakfast programme *Good Morning Britain* in which he declared that on hearing Donald Trump had tested positive for Covid-19, 'I did slightly leap in the air with joy.' He added:

> I just hope it doesn't interfere with him being elected out of office that's all … there's an element of schadenfreude, I suppose. I'm not a fan of his, as you can probably tell, and I just hope Biden stays healthy and gets the presidency as quickly as possible. I think Trump is a catastrophe for America and for the world.[22]

The actor John Cleese was cattier: 'Eager to hear what President Trump's physician will say about his positive testing,' he tweeted sarcastically.

> Apparently, his statement will be dictated to him shortly. A doctor friend of mine tells me that Covid-19 symptoms include delusions of grandeur, compulsive attention-seeking, extreme narcissism, inability to tell fantasy from reality, obsessional thoughts about money, obesity, coarse behaviour, unpredictable outbursts of anger, inflated ego, wandering hands, short attention span, abusive language, compulsive lying, contempt for democracy, and cheating at golf.

Cleese then added: 'Apologies. I misunderstood the doctor friend of mine. The symptoms I described are those of Donald Trump Disease, and are not connected in any way with Covid-19. Such symptoms are increasingly common among white supremacists but are curable by a little education.'[23]

Here were two well-known Britons, both of whom have high profiles in America but are unable to vote on that side of the Atlantic, publicly delighting in the fact that the President of the United States was facing a life-threatening illness. They appeared to see no contradiction between such casual spite and any entitlement to the moral high ground.

A few weeks before these ugly interventions, tributes were paid to US Supreme Court Justice Ruth Bader Ginsburg, who passed away on 18 September 2020. Her death attracted extensive media coverage in the UK. Normally, the British have little interest in American judges. In a reflection of how much attention was paid to Ginsburg's passing, Glasgow City FC announced that its players would wear her name on their shirtsleeves for the rest of the season in her honour. The team's manager Laura Montgomery explained, 'We champion change and equality. RBG certainly gave all of us hope of an empowered future and we want to be able to honour her in this simple way.'24 It is not clear what this American judge ever did for women in Scotland, or what she had to do with the game of football. The gesture seemed to suggest that she was a familiar figure in Scotland, particularly among fans of the sport. This was clearly nonsense.

What had happened was that Ginsburg's death had opened up a major political opportunity for Trump – and those on the left in the UK didn't like it. The liberal trailblazer had been nominated to the Supreme Court by Bill Clinton in 1993. Now Trump had an opportunity to replace her with a nominee of his choosing, giving the nine-member top court an in-built 6–3 conservative majority and potentially leading to policy shifts that could last for a generation on highly divisive issues such as abortion. The notion that Trump might seek to fill the vacancy left by Ginsburg before the presidential election just a few weeks later sent the liberal media in Britain and America into a tailspin. Trump wasted no time. Within twenty-four hours of Ginsburg's death, he announced that Amy Coney Barrett was among those being considered for the post. Barrett is a staunch Catholic mother of seven whose social conservatism is diametrically opposed to the world view of newspapers like the *New York Times* and *The Guardian*. Eight days after Ginsburg's death, Barrett was officially nominated by Trump to succeed Ginsburg. It will be interesting to see whether Scottish women's football teams find a moment to honour Barrett's extraordinary professional achievements.

5

MUCH ADO ABOUT
A NOTHINGBURGER?
– TRUMP AND RUSSIA

Russia. The once mighty Soviet Union was America's No. 1 enemy, and indeed the No. 1 enemy of the West, for fifty years. It collapsed a generation ago, but some people have struggled to move on. The Great Russia Conspiracy was a desperate attempt to get rid of Trump. To the enormous disappointment of those who hoped to impeach him, four years, millions of dollars, countless man-hours and numerous investigations found no smoking gun.

One July morning in 2016, FBI agent Michael Gaeta's daily routine at the US Embassy in Rome was interrupted by a most unusual phone call. Former MI6 agent Christopher Steele – an informant with whom Gaeta had successfully collaborated in the past – insisted he get to London urgently. This is big; you won't be wasting your time, was the gist of it. On 5 July, Gaeta made it to the Big Smoke, heading directly to an office near Victoria Station. On arrival, he was presented with a mysterious document that would come to be known as the 'Steele dossier'.

Quite whether Gaeta's reaction was as flabbergasted as has been widely reported, history doesn't relate. The content of the dossier was certainly intriguing, however – even if a good deal of it sounded far-fetched. Skim-reading it, Gaeta could see it merited serious investigation. He would have to show it to his superiors. 'I couldn't just sweep it under the rug,' he would later tell the House Permanent Select Committee on Intelligence.

The dossier went straight to the top. A few weeks later, the FBI would open a formal investigation into the Trump campaign's possible co-ordination with Russia.* By any standards, this was sensational. The notion that a serving US President or individuals acting on his behalf might secretly have been in cahoots with a regime that was no friend of the West, and indeed that had long represented a threat to the rules-based international order, was extraordinary. To a liberal elite still reeling from Trump's victory, it offered a tantalising explanation for something they still could not understand: how this vulgarian could have tweeted, showboated and blustered his path all the way to the White House. If he'd had a secret leg-up, or more, from the Russians, perhaps it all made more sense?

Fusion GPS, the corporate due-diligence company that commissioned the research, later claimed that the dossier was never meant to see 'the light of day', though there was speculation in some quarters that it was designed to be leaked. Ten days before Trump's inauguration, it found its way into the public domain.

Former journalists Glenn Simpson and Peter Fritsch had set up Fusion GPS – a 'research and strategic intelligence' agency – in 2010. Hungry for political work, the pair set out to investigate Trump when he began to gain media attention in 2015. Seizing the initiative, they emailed an unidentified conservative donor they knew 'who disliked Trump', offering their services.[1] This mystery figure put Fusion in touch with the Washington Free Beacon, a conservative website, which bankrolled their research until Trump's nomination. When cash from Free Beacon dried up, Fusion reached out to Marc Elias of Perkins Coie – the Democratic National Committee's and

---

* The agency was by this stage already investigating evidence of improper links between George Papadopoulos, a foreign policy adviser to the Trump campaign, and Russia. Papadopoulos would later plead guilty to lying to the FBI.

Hillary Clinton's attorney of record. According to reports, Perkins Coie went on to hire Fusion to continue its opposition research on Trump in April 2016. In June that year, Fusion drafted in Steele to research Trump's links to Russia.

The resulting dossier seems to have been doing the rounds for some weeks before it was published in full by BuzzFeed, with a caveat that the content was unverified. According to Simpson and Fritsch, their office in Washington became 'something of a public reading room' for journalists seeking damaging information about Trumpworld.[2] Indeed, the pair appear to have been talking to the *New York Times* about running some of the material as early as July 2016. The trouble for media outlets was that most of the allegations were impossible to substantiate. Some claims were plausible: the suggestion that Russia was responsible for the hack of over 19,000 Democrat National Committee emails; the idea that the Kremlin kept a dossier on Hillary Clinton; and the claim that there had been an attempt to cultivate Trump for years. Trump's historic tweets, periodically expressing open admiration for President Putin and flaunting his own popularity in Russia, appeared to lend weight to the latter suggestion.

Other claims, such as the suggestion that Trump associates and the Kremlin established 'an intelligence exchange' for at least eight years, or that his former attorney Michael Cohen had a secret meeting with the Russian government in Prague in 2016, were more of a stretch and would subsequently be comprehensively debunked.

Finally, there were lurid allegations of sexual shenanigans, the most scandalous of which was a suggestion that the Kremlin promised not to use *kompromat* against Trump, in return for 'high levels of co-operation'. According to the dossier, the information they were willing to suppress related to Trump's participation in a depraved orgy with prostitutes in the Ritz-Carlton Hotel. The erotic high jinks purportedly involved 'golden showers' on a bed that had been previously slept in by Barack and Michelle Obama.

As tittle-tattle it was tantalising, but, journalistically, it was a struggle. Could editors justify publishing such sensational un-founded claims? The fact that the 35-page document was riddled with spelling mistakes did nothing to inspire confidence. No wonder most credible news organisations baulked.

For internet-based publishers, the calculations were different, however. They did not require the same evidential standards as newspapers and television channels before posting material. Buzz-Feed, a left-wing internet entertainment company whose core business is pumping out viral content, was particularly excited by the opportunity for worldwide publicity if it took a risk. On 10 January 2017, bosses decided to publish the draft dossier in full, giving other media outlets the cover they needed to follow suit.

Ironically, one of the biggest critics of the decision to publish the dossier was Steele himself, who in subsequent testimony at the High Court in London labelled BuzzFeed's actions 'one of the most irresponsible journalistic acts' ever.[3] Nonetheless, the dossi-er electrified Washington and delighted Trump's critics, who were less interested in whether any of it could be substantiated than the thrill of an apparent scandal with the President-elect at the centre. Whatever the truth or otherwise of the sexual allegations (Steele himself apparently only believed them to be '50/50 true'), any secret co-ordination between Putin and the Trump campaign could be tantamount to treason. It was exactly what the Democrats had been looking for: potential grounds to impeach. Trump's reaction was to dismiss the entire story as 'fake news'. According to insider accounts, he assumed he could just tough it out. Privately, however, he knew that killing the story would not be straightforward. Chief among his difficulties was the fact that in the run-up to the presidential election, three senior members of his campaign team – his own son Donald Trump Jr, his son-in-law Jared Kushner and lobbyist Paul Manafort – had met a Russian attorney, Natalia Veselnitskaya, and Russian–American lobbyist Rinat Akhmetshin in Trump Tower.

The rendezvous took place just two months before Fusion GPS hired Steele.

Details of this meeting would not emerge until late March 2017, but the knowledge that it had taken place was deeply uncomfortable for Trump's team. Even worse was to come.

• • •

Twenty-four days. It's long enough to learn conversational French, take up a new hobby or drive across the US coast-to-coast many times over. It's also long enough to serve a tenure as US national security adviser. Michael Flynn broke a record on 13 February 2017, for the shortest time served in this position, resigning over links to Russia. For the increasingly hysterical army of Trump haters, this was a sensational scalp.

Flynn's difficulties stemmed from a number of phone calls he had exchanged with the Russian ambassador to Washington, Sergei Kisilyak, during the transition period after Trump won the presidential election. Vice-President Mike Pence and other White House officials had downplayed the significance of these discussions when details emerged, claiming the conversation had been limited to pleasantries about Christmas and arranging a future discussion between Trump and Putin. Unfortunately for the President, it swiftly transpired that the exchange had been far more substantial. Crucially, it covered the possibility of lifting sanctions the Obama administration had been about to impose on Moscow for interference in the presidential election. Flynn was forced to resign, admitting that he had 'inadvertently' misled the Vice-President.

All this was manna from heaven for Trump's critics, adding to a growing impression of multiple contacts between the President's aides and Putin's regime. In preceding months, Trump had already lost two senior aides in controversies over their Russia connections. In August 2016, his campaign manager, Paul Manafort, had quit after coming under intense pressure over past lobbying work for pro-Russian Ukrainian oligarchs. The following month, his foreign policy adviser, Carter Page, would also step down over allegations he had private communications with Russian officials. Both Flynn and Manafort would later 'retroactively' register themselves as foreign agents. None of this could be dismissed as 'fake news'. One such connection was unfortunate; two looked careless; three or more looked deliberate. Even for those who wanted to believe the best of the President, it seemed murky.

In the early weeks of the Trump presidency, there was such a hue and cry over all this that he would privately complain that it was almost impossible to get on with the job. The endless speculation and media salivation was exhausting and humiliating, especially when he was dealing with foreign leaders. Sometimes they would openly question how long he was going to be around. Trump tried to ignore it, but it was clear he would have to confront the claims.

Three days after Flynn's resignation, the President staged a memorable press conference that only fanned the flames. Instead of calmly addressing allegations against him, taking each claim in turn and setting out why it was misleading, exaggerated or false, Trump spent seventy-five minutes ranting at the assembled press and dismissing the entire story as a 'ruse'. He insisted, 'I have nothing to do with Russia. Haven't made a phone call to Russia in years ... I own nothing in Russia. I have no loans in Russia. I don't have any deals in Russia ... Russia is fake news.'[4]

If he hoped his obvious fury would somehow make it all go away, he was mistaken. It would not be long before details of the Trump Tower meeting emerged, accompanied by suggestions that Kushner had had several additional undisclosed contacts with the Russian ambassador. For anyone who had not voted for the new President and was still struggling to accept the notion of a swaggering showman in the White House, this was gold dust. It was tangible evidence of a relationship with Russian state operatives that justified much deeper investigation.

• • •

The Trump National Golf Club in Washington DC oozes exclusivity. The meandering Potomac river weaves around rich green fairways, always vibrant no matter the season. Lovely as it is, in 2011, then FBI director Robert Mueller, a member of the prestigious club, sat down to write a letter resigning his membership. He was just too busy to use it enough to justify the outlay. In his letter he explained simply that his family was 'unable to make full use of the Club'. The annual fees were hefty, so he politely asked for some of his money back. In the same letter he asked the club whether he would also be entitled 'to a refund of a portion of our initial membership fee', originally paid in 1994. The Muellers had contact with officials from the club only once after that, when they received a polite note informing them that they would be 'placed on a waitlist to be refunded on a first resigned/first refunded basis'.[5] The family is said to have made various further attempts to get their money back, including writing to Trump himself, to no avail. That should have been that; save that, six years later, Robert Mueller would go on to lead an FBI investigation into the man he perhaps believed owed him a refund: Donald Trump.

The President would later suggest, somewhat fancifully, that Mueller had it in for him, because he was still bitter about the golf-club money. In reality, after an exhaustive investigation into links between the Trump campaign and Russia, Mueller's conclusion allowed Trump to claim that he had been 'totally exonerated'.

The FBI investigation (dubbed the Mueller Inquiry) began in May 2017 and took nearly two years. It covered Russian efforts to interfere with the presidential election; allegations of conspiracy or co-ordination between the Kremlin and the Trump campaign; and allegations of obstruction of justice, prompted by Trump's sensational decision to fire FBI director James Comey. The intelligence chief was dismissed on 9 May that year after repeatedly refusing to help clear the President's name by making it apparent that he was not under investigation.

In the end, the FBI did not find sufficient evidence that the Trump campaign had co-ordinated or conspired with the Kremlin, nor that the President had committed any crime. It found no evidence that the Russian authorities had been cultivating Trump for five years, nor was there sufficient evidence that Michael Cohen had met with Kremlin officials in Prague in 2016. To the obvious disappointment of Trump's detractors, it seems he had not participated in depraved romps with hookers in the Ritz-Carlton Hotel.

None of this was to say that the Russians did not attempt to cultivate the future President and his entourage. That, after all, is exactly how the Kremlin operates, inveigling its way into opposition parties and political disrupters the world over, with no higher objective than to gather intelligence and fuel instability. Indeed, the Mueller Report concluded that, just as the dossier had suggested, Russia did seek to get Trump into the White House and take out his opponent Hillary Clinton. This should be no surprise. The fact that Trump was not fundamentally hostile to Putin, and indeed appeared receptive to forging a closer relationship with the Russian regime, was convenient, but those familiar with the Russian state's *modus operandi* will know that it was the deep division and uncertainty he would cause both domestically and abroad that most excited the Kremlin.

As the *Wall Street Journal* reported, many of the validated assertions in the dossier had been circulating in the media and among Western intelligence agencies for some while by the time Steele began his research in 2016, including the idea that Russia was trying to harm Hillary Clinton. In other words, Steele's work was a mix of old stories, unsubstantiated rumours and some truth. Russian interference in the campaign had been real, but there was no great conspiracy; Trump was naïve and over-exuberant in his dealings with Putin, but he was not a dumb American puppet being manipulated by the Kremlin. It was not quite a 'nothingburger', but the burger had no meat.[6]

Mueller would continue to draw criticism for failing to take the investigation further (Andrew Weissmann, a senior prosecutor on Mueller's team, took the trouble to write a book to that effect, firmly believing the prosecutorial stance wasn't aggressive enough),[7] but it seems likely that those who were not satisfied by a two-year federal investigation would have been unhappy with anything that did not eventually find Trump guilty of high treason. Those reluctant to let it go were fairly obviously driven by a determination to oust the President, rather than by any real concern for the state of democracy insofar as it arose from Russian meddling.

But if there was no smoking gun, Trump supporters wondered, how had he got into such a mess?

• • •

The 1963 Bond film *From Russia With Love* features one of the most comically theatrical Soviet antagonists in cinema. Mr Bond is on the phone in a hotel room as a seemingly frail hotel maid tries to walk off with his bags. Dismissing the woman's actions as simple confusion, Bond pauses his call to ask her not to touch his stuff. 'Leave that, I'll take it,' he says, before returning to a robust exchange with whoever is on the other end of the line.

When he turns around, the old maid, secretly a villainous secret agent by the name of Rosa Klebb, is pointing a pistol at him. In the dramatic scene, Klebb's comrade, also in the hotel room, turns on her to help the unarmed Bond, but is knocked out by the old woman. The audience sees a poisoned blade shoot out of Klebb's apparently ordinary black shoes as she stampedes towards the celebrated MI6 agent in an attempt to kill him.

This is how many people still imagine the Kremlin operates. After all, it's what the West has been told over and again. Moreover, from time to time, the Russian state is behind genuinely shocking and extraordinary crimes on foreign soil, such as the radiation poisoning of Russian defector and former FSB agent Alexander Litvinenko in London in 2006, and the attempted murder of Russian double-agent Sergei Skripal and his daughter, Yulia, in the English market town of Salisbury in 2018.

Dreadful as they are, these periodic outrages pose far less of a threat to Western democracy than the debilitating hybrid warfare techniques the Russian state deploys to further its aims abroad – as those who worried about the corrosive effects of interference in important Western elections recognised. It was reasonable and right to explore how far these activities might have gone in the US presidential election, and to what effect. It was clear that there had been multiple contacts between Trump's associates and individuals linked to the Russian regime, and that those concerned were not always transparent about what had taken place. All too often aides lied or dissembled or suppressed relevant information. In some cases, there may have been legitimate business and political reasons for such interactions, but the way individuals responded to questions gave rise to more, not less, suspicion.

A fair assessment of the whole sorry saga starts by acknowledging that it was entirely natural for his campaign team to pursue information that might undermine or even derail Hillary Clinton. That is how high-stakes political campaigns work. However honourable the candidates and their teams, most of those engaged in a national campaign would actively investigate potentially compromising tip-offs about their opponents. In many cases, it would be foolish *not* to follow up credible-sounding leads. After all, such information might be in the national interest. What more experienced political campaigners recognise is the importance of doing due diligence before engaging with sources peddling negative material about rival candidates. Even once such checks have been carried out, seasoned strategists know that suppliers of disobliging material should be kept at arm's length, so the candidate and his or her most senior aides have plausible deniability against accusations of dirty tricks.

These precautions are all the more important when a campaign receives an approach from a foreign organisation or agent, particularly representatives of a hostile state. This is very much more dangerous and questionable territory and is generally best avoided or, if it seems of real public interest, approached with the utmost caution.

All this seems obvious, which is what makes the decision by Donald Trump Jr, Jared Kushner and Paul Manafort to meet personally with Russian lobbyists in Trump Tower so surprising. Many of Trump's detractors would eventually come to accept that the reason they allowed themselves to get into this position was not that they intended to establish a treasonous relationship with the Russian regime but rather that they were hopelessly naïve. Even the BBC, never an organisation to seek excuses for the President, has acknowledged his campaign's habit of 'novice mistakes' and taking 'unprecedented risks'. Under pressure to explain how it happened, Kushner hasn't exactly admitted naïveté but has conceded that he is 'free of preconceived notions' – a flowery way of saying much the same.[8]

In their highly entertaining accounts of the first year of Trump's administration, both Michael Wolfe and Bob Woodward describe the abject absence of political experience in the Trump campaign, which contributed to the Russia mess. Put simply, nobody in Washington had thought the *Apprentice* star stood a chance, as a result of which no heavyweight political strategists wanted to be associated with his operation, still less to join what they assumed to be a rapidly sinking ship. The Russian debacle, which would have had considerably fewer legs had it not been for the Trump Tower meeting, was one of many catastrophic consequences.

Such was the media fixation with the nature of Trump's relationship with Putin's regime, and such was the scale of the political opportunity it presented his political opponents, that, by summer 2017, almost anything he did on the world stage was viewed through that prism. When Trump withdrew troops from Syria in 2019, for example, some described it as a 'gift' to Putin, whose military had been behind Assad in the Middle East.[9]

The reality was much more nuanced. The truth was that Trump did have more than a sneaking admiration for Putin's personality and leadership style, and he did want to cultivate better diplomatic relations with Russia. The first of these things may not reflect particularly well on his judgement about what makes a fine leader; the second is an entirely reasonable foreign policy objective. Neither – as the official investigation found – constitutes a crime.

From the outset, the US political and media establishment was desperate to find a basis on which to impeach the President. The Russia conspiracy was perfect: captivating, salacious and, in contrast to many esoteric political scandals, easily understood by most voters, at least in broad-brush terms. If true, it could hardly have been more serious. Trump's personality and unfortunate history of public praise for Putin played into the hands of his critics. His extraordinarily ill-advised firing of FBI director James Comey and other intelligence chiefs only added to the appearance that he had something to hide.

It is no coincidence that all this came at the same time as the agonies of the UK Establishment over Brexit. Between 2016 and 2018, there were endless Russia-related conspiracy theories over the vote to leave the EU, peddled by a left-wing liberal elite who could not understand the antipathy of ordinary people towards an institution that had served the professional classes so well. Putin himself saw this quite clearly. 'They don't want to recognise [Mr Trump's] victory. That's disrespect of voters. The same in Britain: Brexit happened, but no one wants to implement it,' he observed.[10] The theme was clear: Western societies were frustrated that they couldn't blame the changing of the status quo on Russia.

As Trump leaves the stage, there is a postscript. Shortly after losing the 2020 election, he announced that Michael Flynn would receive a full presidential pardon. Trump expressed the hope that this act of munificence would allow his disgraced former national security adviser to enjoy a very happy Christmas. He also knew and relished the fact that it would wind up his political opponents and the left-leaning commentariat. Former Democratic Speaker of the House of Representatives Nancy Pelosi said she was disgusted: 'Trump's pardoning of Flynn, who twice pleaded guilty to lying to the FBI about his dealings with a foreign adversary, is an act of grave corruption and a brazen abuse of power,' she puffed.[11]

But by this time, neither the President nor many others in Washington much cared. Trump was leaving office, and the Great Russia Nothingburger had gone well and truly stale.

• • •

Perhaps the greatest shame of the nothingburger is the lost opportunity. It is worth considering how previous administrations approached Russia and the resulting poor state of the diplomatic relationship Trump inherited.

As Obama's Secretary of State, in 2009 Hillary Clinton had famously presented Russia's then Foreign Minister Sergey Lavrov with a bright red 'reset' button, a light-hearted joke designed to underline her commitment to improving relations between the two nations. Ironically, the Russian word for 'reset' was misspelled, and instead the button said 'overload' – *peregruzka* instead of *perezagruzka* – but the two leaders laughed it off. A month later, at the 2009 G20 summit in London, Obama and Russian President Dimitry Medvedev also agreed to a 'new start'. Unfortunately, it did not materialise. Vice-President Joe Biden had made no secret of his opposition to a third Putin term, allegedly flying to Moscow in 2011 to attempt to convince Medvedev to stand for re-election. Medvedev wasn't convinced and chose to back Putin. Later, the two powers would clash over military intervention in Syria and Bashar al-Assad's use of chemical weapons; Moscow's decision to offer refuge to Edward

Snowden after he fled to Russia seeking political asylum; and Putin's illegal annexation of Crimea. In October 2016, Russia's UN ambassador, Vitaly Churkin, described the relationship between the two global powers as 'the worst since 1973'.[12]

By 2013, Clinton was actively discouraging Obama from engaging with the re-elected Putin, writing in a memo that the Russian leader should not be flattered 'with high-level attention'. Obama should decline any invitation for a summit, she said. In the same note, she declared that 'strength and resolve' were the only language Putin would understand.[13] Had she won in 2016, the relationship would almost certainly have deteriorated further. She had done nothing to conceal her contempt for Putin personally, once going so far as to say that he 'doesn't have a soul'.[14] Nobody can know where this mutual dislike would have led, but it seems unlikely it would have been helpful in relation to issues of mutual interest, particularly over Syria.

Trump was perfectly positioned to change all this. The outcry over links between his associates and individual Russians were based on the false premise that it was fundamentally wrong for anyone associated with the President-elect to attempt to cultivate anyone associated with the Russian regime. The assumption was that all interaction should be treated with suspicion and must have stemmed from bad motives.

In fact, as the Kremlin becomes ever more enmeshed in the politics of the Middle East and more entangled with China, the case for attempting to improve the state of US–Russian relations grows more powerful by the day. Some links between Trump aides and Russians were historic and commercial, and of no great consequence, since the individuals concerned were not working for Trump or were only loosely associated with him at the time. Across the West, plenty of perfectly legitimate businesses have Russian interests. More importantly, there was a genuine and worthy ambition on the part of those involved in Trump's campaign to improve the deeply dysfunctional relationship between the Kremlin and the West. Under an obscure eighteenth-century US law known as the Logan Act, private citizens are not allowed to conduct their own negotiations with foreign powers in disputes with the United States. However, there is a long (and sensible) tradition of members of the incoming administration reaching out to foreign officials to introduce themselves and begin to build connections during transition periods.

Long before he ran for the presidency, Trump had laid the foundations for a more positive and constructive relationship with the Russian regime through a series of positive tweets about President Putin. As far back as 2013, ahead of attending a Miss Universe Pageant in Moscow, he had joked on social media about the possibility of bumping into Putin, and the prospect that the Russian President could become his 'new best friend'. Later, having met Putin on another occasion, he would repeatedly describe him as 'so nice'.[15]

The Kremlin's naked disregard for the rules-based international order – exemplified by the annexation of Crimea in 2014; the Novichock poisoning of the Skripals; the brutal repression of political dissidents; and malign meddling in the domestic affairs of Western democracies – were a deeply uncomfortable backdrop to his more fawning social media messages.

But flattery can be strategic, and Trump's apparent admiration for aspects of Putin's leadership style and open acknowledgement of Putin's personal popularity among Russian voters would have given him a huge advantage in efforts to establish more positive diplomatic relations once he reached the White House.

Unfortunately, all that was derailed by the toxic suggestion of some secret and even treasonous alliance between the pair. As an exasperated Trump himself put it at the beginning of the furore:

> The false, horrible, fake reporting makes it much harder to make a deal with Russia. And probably Putin said, you know, He's sitting behind his desk saying, you know, I see what's going on in the

United States, they follow it closely. It's going to be impossible for President Trump to ever get along with Russia because of all the pressure he's got with this fake story.[16]

It would be hopelessly naïve to imagine that Putin will abandon efforts to shore up his domestic and international position by fuelling division in America simply because Trump no longer occupies the White House. Indeed, the Kremlin will doubtless see many political opportunities in a weak and ageing Biden. The links between the 46th President's son Hunter and a Ukrainian energy giant only increase the opportunities for mischief-making. As Vice-President under Obama, Biden Senior was heavily involved in US foreign policy in Ukraine – while Hunter had a highly lucrative position on the board of Ukraine's largest gas company, Burisma Holdings. It was founded by an ally of Viktor Yanukovych, the former pro-Russia President of Ukraine, who was driven out of power in February 2014 by mass protests. Had one of Trump's sons been paid $83,000 a month to be a 'ceremonial figure' for a foreign-owned energy company, especially one with links to Russia, Democrats would of course have been salivating.

6

TEN MEN - TRUMP'S ATTITUDE TO WOMEN

'Grab 'em by the pussy.' That one line, that one snippet of private conversation, was the only real bit of 'dirt' the huge Clinton and Democrat investigation managed to find on Trump, despite two years and millions of dollars spent digging. Contrast that with Bill Clinton's record. When it came to women, Trump was no angel – nor was he was the dangerous 'predator' his critics suggest.

Few inside Trump's 2016 presidential campaign ever expected him to win, but there was one moment in particular when they were certain it was game over. This was the nadir, what seemed like the point of no return, and even his staunchest allies doubted he could survive it. Back in 2005, in a bus on the way to film an episode of the news entertainment show *Access Hollywood*, Trump and TV host Billy Bush had engaged in a vulgar exchange in which the future President described his attempt to seduce a married woman and boasted about the sexual advantages of his celebrity status.

During the lewd conversation, which was captured on tape, Trump bragged that he had tried unsuccessfully to seduce and then 'fuck' Nancy O'Dell, a married woman, by making a pass at her. He stated that he was at that time 'automatically attracted to beautiful [women] … I just start kissing them. It's like a magnet. Just kiss. I don't even wait.' He also boasted that if you're a 'star', women will let you do 'anything'. Expanding on this point, he said, 'You can do anything. Grab 'em by the pussy.'

On 7 October 2016, four weeks before voters were due to go to the polls, details of the excruciating recording were published by the *Washington Post*, sending shockwaves across America. As far as the media was concerned, at least, it was game-over for Trump.

There is no point trying to defend his words. Trump said them, he did not deny having said them, and the tape recording that proved it was soon being played all over the world. Even though no evidence was produced that Trump *had* ever grabbed a woman's genitals in the way he intimated in 2005, the timing of the leak, two days before the crucial second presidential debate between him and Hillary Clinton, was devastating and obviously designed to cause the maximum amount of damage to his bid for the White House.

Mrs Clinton was swift to react, tweeting that day: 'This is horrific. We cannot allow this man to become president.'[1] Her running mate, Senator Tim Kaine, also weighed in, telling reporters that the audio 'makes me sick to my stomach'.[2] Political commentators then made their way to the moral high ground, most of them concluding that the tape had almost certainly derailed Trump's campaign. This bolstered further the notion being pushed by members of the Washington elite that Trump was a predator, a sexist, a misogynist and someone with a fundamental lack of respect for women.

Hours after the story broke, Trump's campaign team issued a statement of apology but also of justification. In it, Trump said, 'This was locker room banter, a private conversation that took place many years ago. Bill Clinton has said far worse to me on the golf course – not even close. I apologize if anyone was offended.' With his back against the wall, it was undeniably astute of Trump to reference Hillary Clinton's husband. Bill Clinton's tarnished reputation in light of the Monica Lewinsky scandal might have encouraged the public to compare the two and, Trump no doubt hoped, to recognise that while Trump was guilty of loose talk, Clinton, while President, had embarked on an extra-marital affair with an impressionable White House aide twenty-seven years his junior. People might ask themselves: whose behaviour was worse?

In the event, Bill Clinton was the gift that kept on giving, helping to prevent Trump's campaign from sinking and instead inflicting significant damage to his own wife's tilt at the White House. In what must rank as one of the best examples in history of a politician successfully countering a crisis, Trump's team managed to gather together, at extremely short notice, three women – Paula Jones, Juanita Broaddrick and Kathleen Willey – who had accused Bill Clinton of sexual assault or sexual harassment in the past. They were joined at a hastily arranged press conference held immediately before the second presidential debate by a fourth woman, Kathy Shelton, who was allegedly raped aged twelve by 41-year-old Thomas Alfred Taylor. Hillary Clinton had defended Taylor at a criminal trial in 1975, securing a plea deal which meant that he was charged with 'unlawful fondling of a child under the age of fourteen' and was sentenced to just one year in a county jail with four years on probation.[3]

During the press conference, Juanita Broaddrick volunteered: 'I tweeted recently, and Mr Trump retweeted it, that actions speak louder than words. Mr Trump may have said some bad words, but Bill Clinton raped me, and Hillary Clinton threatened me. I don't think there is any comparison.' When a reporter asked the group if Trump's star power entitled him to grope women without their consent, Paula Jones shot back: 'Why don't y'all ask Bill Clinton that? … Go and ask Hillary as well!' And Ms Willey then confirmed that she was a supporter of Trump's campaign and she believed in his slogan 'Make America Great Again'. She said:

I cried when he said that because I think that this is the greatest country in the world. I think that we can do anything. I think we can accomplish anything. I think we can bring peace to this world, and I think Donald Trump can lead us to that point.[4]

It seems that these women recognised the difference between 'banter', as Trump had described it, and something far more sinister. In the event, significantly more white women voted for him than voted for Hillary Clinton – 53 per cent vs 43 per cent – not only a reflection of America's historic reluctance to elect female Presidents, but evidence that they took a considerably more philosophical view of the lewd remarks than did the commentariat.

The press conference against the Clintons added some much-needed perspective to what Trump had said – and not *done*, so far as anybody knew – during his conversation with Billy Bush in 2005. His language that day was careless and disrespectful. It is probable that he was simply showing off to another man for reasons best known to himself. Yet plenty of other respectable men – and doubtless women – have made equally off-colour remarks in the company of friends when the idea that a third party was recording them was furthest from their mind.

Moreover, he has a long track record of hiring and promoting women to powerful positions, both in his companies and at the White House – hardly indicative of a hardened misogynist.

• • •

In 1978, Barbara Res was working as an engineer for the New York building firm HRH Construction, on a project for Donald Trump that involved renovating the old Commodore Hotel into the Grand Hyatt on 42nd Street next to Grand Central Terminal. During a meeting about how long it would take, five male engineers told Trump they were adamant that a ballroom in the new hotel could not be completed by the date he wanted. Res, who was in her late twenties at the time, raised her hand and said, 'I'll be able to do it.' A decade later, Trump gave an interview to *Newsday* in which he recalled with some pride what happened next. 'Everyone said, "You've got to be crazy",' Trump told the magazine. 'I put her in charge of the ballroom, and she not only did it by that date but she did it sooner.'[5]

Res's efforts earned her Trump's immediate attention and admiration. She was soon put in charge of overseeing the construction of Trump Tower when work on the skyscraper began in 1980. Throughout the 1980s, she rose to become one of the highest-ranking executives in the Trump Organization. In the male-dominated world of New York construction, her elevation was highly unusual. In 2018, Res explained,

> I was better than the others, and that's the truth. I went into meetings and told people they were wrong and that we're not paying for this. Trump loved it. When he hired me he called me a 'killer'. And that's what he wanted. He hired me to build Trump Tower. He told me that men were better than women, but a good woman was better than ten good men. He thought this was a compliment.[6]

The pair worked together for years, though they eventually went their separate ways following a disagreement over how to approach a construction project. Later, she turned on the man who gave her what he has called 'the break of a lifetime', penning a poisonous account of her time working for him. She concedes that he was never sexist towards her but makes this out to be an exception. She claims that as well as being a racist, Trump routinely showed 'contempt' for women.[7]

Yet it is not as though Res was the only woman to whom Trump gave considerable responsibility when he was building his business. In 1988, when he acquired the Plaza Hotel in Midtown Manhattan for $390 million, he made his then-wife, Ivana, its president. Before then, she had been the CEO of Trump's Castle Hotel and Casino in Atlantic City, where she was in charge of eight vice-presidents, 150 directors and managers, plus 3,500 employees. The casino's gross gaming revenues for 1987 were understood to be in the region of

$300 million – hardly the sort of responsibility that Trump would have handed to anybody if he did not believe they were equal to the task, whether they were male or female. Famously, Ivana Trump was paid a nominal salary of $1 per year and an unlimited number of dresses. Some women – including Res – believed this proved that Trump did not pay women properly and considered them lesser mortals. Inconveniently for these critics, Ivana Trump herself disagreed, telling one interviewer:

> I think it's really ridiculous to ask my husband for a salary. We are a team. We are working together. We are building our empire together. My husband gives me anything I want. I don't need to have a salary. So it was cute. This is the way it was meant. Other people, they turn it around, twist it around.[8]

In the 1980s, three of Trump's top thirteen executives in the Trump Organization were also women: developer Louise Sunshine, and executive vice-presidents Blanche Sprague and Susan Heilbron. Each was also entrusted with a prominent leadership role, leading Trump to remark: 'I have found in many cases [women] are more effective than a man would be. They're very dedicated to showing me that they can do it.'[9] None of this suggests that Trump was a hopeless male chauvinist. If anything, he was something of a trailblazer.

Nonetheless, on 21 January 2017, a women's march took place in cities around the world. According to its organisers, its purpose was to mark Trump's first full day in power as President of America and protest at his stance on a range of issues, including women's rights and the rights of immigrants and other minorities. They said they wanted to 'send a bold message to our new administration on their first day in office, and to the world that women's rights are human rights'. A co-founder of the event Tamika Mallory explained, 'We want to ensure that this country knows women are not happy. And when we get angry, change happens. We make things happen.'[10]

There is no denying the success of this event in terms of the number of those who took part and the media coverage it gained. Millions of women marched through hundreds of cities around the world on that day, some accompanied by husbands or boyfriends. One march even took place in Antarctica. A significant proportion of women who marched wore so-called 'pussyhats', knitted hats with cat ears on them in reference to the remark about women's genitals that Trump made in the *Access Hollywood* tape. Perhaps predictably, large numbers of actors and musicians of both sexes joined in, keen to associate themselves with this anti-Trump festival, the pop star Madonna among them. In a speech in Washington, the singer said that she had 'thought an awful lot about blowing up the White House'.[11]

Strangely, these marchers and the celebrities who joined them had nothing to say when, in May 2018, hundreds of women in Iran bravely staged protests over being forced to wear the hijab. For this show of defiance, scores were imprisoned by the Iranian state. There were also stories of beatings and even unlawful killing. These women were marching against real oppression – but the anti-Trump marchers did not take to the streets again in solidarity.

If Trump was such a terrible sexist, why were some of the most powerful and long-serving figures during his tenure in the West Wing female? From the outset, he wanted to work with women, and they were happy to accept jobs in his administration. Kellyanne Conway was Trump's campaign manager in 2016, making her the first woman to have run a successful presidential campaign. In January 2017, she was appointed counsellor to the President, making her one of Trump's top advisers. She was promoted to senior counsellor to the President the following year, a position she held until 2020, when she left for personal reasons.

Then there was Hope Hicks, who served as White House director of strategic communications from January to September 2017 and as communications director from September 2017 until March

2018. Although she left the White House at that point, she returned in March 2020 as Trump's senior counsellor.

A third woman who worked with Trump was Omarosa Manigault Newman. Although she declared herself a die-hard Democrat Party supporter and had backed Hillary Clinton's presidential run initially, she knew Trump through his television work. During the Republican national convention in July 2016, when Trump was confirmed as the Republican Party presidential candidate, it was announced that Newman had been named director of African American outreach for his presidential campaign. In January 2017, Newman became the assistant to the president and director of communications for the Office of Public Liaison. She was sacked eleven months later after apparently flouting rules on the use of a government car. There had been no fall-out with Trump himself.

Above all, there was Ivanka. Trump's daughter acted as a sounding board for her father from 2015, and in March 2017 was appointed First Daughter and senior adviser to the President, making her a government employee. (She opted not to be paid a salary.) There was precedent for such an arrangement – in 1969, Richard Nixon had appointed his daughter Julie as First Daughter, and relied on her for advice for the next five years. What is interesting about Ivanka Trump's position in the White House is that it put her ahead of both his grown-up sons, Donald Jr and Eric.

Trump's Cabinet included female secretaries of education, transportation and homeland security, plus a further two women with Cabinet rank. Such numbers of women at the top table put him on a par with Bill Clinton and George W. Bush, if not Barack Obama, who had four women in his Cabinet and four with Cabinet rank. Yet Trump outdid Obama in other areas. For example, on Trump's watch Gina Haspel was made the first ever female chief of the Central Intelligence Agency. Her appointment in 2018 again reflected his faith in women to handle responsibility just as well as any man.

Furthermore, in June 2019, *Forbes* magazine carried out an

audit of how many women were in senior roles within the federal government. In many ways, the magazine pointed out, because its business is conducted across many different agencies, offices and departments, it provided as good an indication of women's progression under Trump as any. It found approximately 300 politically appointed roles and dozens of judges and ambassadors who had been given their jobs since Trump took office, again demonstrating his commitment to equality of the sexes. It noted that 'the Office of the President alone has over 100 women in politically appointed roles, many as chief, secretary, director, deputy director, and counselor to the President'. The article also stated that women lead various commissions, singling out Eileen Lappin Weiser, who was chairman of the commission on presidential scholars, and Liz Sara, chairperson of the National Women's Business Council. It further noted that Trump had by that stage appointed forty-four female judges to various courts, an amount that matched the number of female judges nominated by Barack Obama. 'Women lead in the White House as director of the office of administration, deputy director of the office of administration, and chief financial officer in the office of administration,' it stated, adding that Heather Wilson had served as Secretary of the Air Force for two years and that, at the Department of Defense, 'half a dozen women have Senate-confirmed roles for acquisition, research and engineering, finance, readiness and force management, and intelligence'. It also noted that in every other area of government including the Department of Energy; the Department of Health and Human Services; the Department of the Interior; the Department of Justice; the Department of Labor; the Department of State; the Department of Transportation; the Department of Veterans Affairs; the Office of the Director of National Intelligence; and the Environmental Protection Agency (EPA), women had been promoted to senior jobs.[12]

In his most important final appointment, Trump put Amy Coney Barrett in the Supreme Court. From breaking the mould by hiring

Barbara Res to oversee the building of Trump Tower in 1980, to giving his wife and daughter senior positions in business and politics, to nominating Amy Coney Barrett as only the fifth ever female Supreme Court Justice in 2020, Trump has done as much as any male leader to advance women's careers. He certainly did more for women in public life between 2016 and 2020 than one of his political heroines, Margaret Thatcher, who was notoriously reluctant to appoint women to senior roles in her eleven years in power.

In April 2017, Bill O'Reilly, a star presenter at Fox News, was forced to quit the channel over allegations of inappropriate conduct. Liberal and left-leaning celebrities and commentators quickly found ways to drag the President into it. After Trump described O'Reilly as a 'good person', arguing that the TV star should have contested the claims, singer Cher suggested they were each as bad as the other. 'O'Reilly and Donald Trump have sexually harassed women 4 yrs', she tweeted. Comedian Rosie O'Donnell joined in, calling Trump and O'Reilly 'sexual predators of a feather'. Writer Stephen King tweeted that Trump and O'Reilly were both 'members of the odious boys' club where members feel they can abuse and humiliate women at will'.[13] Not one of this trio produced any evidence to back up these highly charged assertions. They simply tarred Trump with the same brush, no doubt because he had been interviewed by O'Reilly on numerous occasions, giving him a platform to air his political positions.

Cher, O'Donnell, King and other stars would presumably have been perfectly happy to see Hillary Clinton elected as US President in 2016. But how would they have felt about Bill Clinton – accused of multiple serious sexual offences by at least three women – becoming 'First Gentleman'? It is hard to imagine they would have taken to the streets.

In litigious America, where anybody of means has a lawyer on speed dial, it would be truly remarkable if a billionaire with a career spanning almost half a century at the highest level in real estate, showbiz and politics had not attracted any allegations of inappropriate behaviour. Trump made himself all the more vulnerable to such claims by repeatedly appointing women to senior roles and welcoming them into his inner circle: in other words, treating them in exactly the same way he treated men. When he reached the highest office in the land, naturally there was a very receptive media audience as a tiny minority of those with whom he had been associated in the past, whether personally or professionally, decided the time was ripe to complain.

7

DRILL, BABY, DRILL – TRUMP AND THE ENVIRONMENT

No one would accuse Donald Trump of being soft and fluffy: I don't think 'saving the planet' was ever high on his to-do list. His decision to pull out of the Paris Agreement on climate change infuriated environmentalists, who did not accept his rationale. Quite simply, he believed the Climate Change Accord was a bad deal for America. He thought it put an unfair burden on American businesses, workers and taxpayers – while giving China a free pass. He wasn't elected on a platform to reduce carbon emissions: he was elected on a platform to protect and create American jobs. And that is what he set out to do. Clearly fossil fuel forms a large part of the US economy. Trump embraced this and made the most of it. As for becoming energy self-sufficient, one of his other missions? Even lefties can buy into that. If the US does not need foreign oil, it might – just might – reduce the number of wars.

There are no roads leading to the pristine wildlife reserve in north-eastern Alaska, nor any within it, only millions of acres of rugged mountains, frozen tundra, valleys, rivers and lakes. The protected area stretching from the Brooks Range mountains to the Beaufort Sea is a vast wilderness with great herds of caribou and precious flora and fauna that are vanishing elsewhere as their habitats are destroyed: golden eagles and arctic foxes; grizzlies and polar bears; wolves and lynx; as well as some 200 species of birds. Some call this the place where life begins.

All 19.6 million acres of the Arctic National Wildlife Refuge (ANWR) have been a no-go zone for development for decades. The special status of this remarkable ecosystem dates back to 1960, when President Dwight Eisenhower made it a federal protected area. As the scattered settlements of Native Americans can attest, it is an almost uninhabitable place, with temperatures dipping below -30 degrees Celsius in winter, when there are just four hours of light each day. In extraordinarily challenging conditions, these tiny communities live much as they did thousands of years ago.

What the ANWR lacks in infrastructure and amenities, it more than makes up for in natural resources, however. These hidden riches have made it a target for some of the world's worst, most powerful and most polluting energy companies – corporations whose ambitions Trump was ready to back.

The most coveted part of the reserve is a 1.5-million-acre stretch, known to oil barons as '10-02'. It is a coastal plain where the land meets the Arctic Ocean, a place of exquisite beauty and unique environmental importance. Every year, tens of thousands of wild reindeer known as Porcupine caribou come to calve near the sea, following the longest overland migration made by any animal on earth. These are the creatures on which native tribes have depended for some 25,000 years. If they are displaced by humans and machines, nobody knows how, or whether, the herds will adapt. This, and much more, is at stake if the delicate ecosystem is ravaged by drilling.

The trouble is, 10-02 is the access point for anywhere between 4.3 billion and 11.8 billion barrels of oil, and oil company executives are not paid to prioritise the future of wildlife habitats. Moreover, many political leaders in Alaska believe the state and its people will benefit from the expansion of energy exploration and have long lobbied hard in support of plans to exploit the reserve. Even the Native American communities that would be most affected are bitterly divided over the issue. On the northern edge of the refuge is the Iñupiat village of Kaktovik, which, at the latest official count, had a population of just 258. When the oil was first discovered in the 1970s, they quickly signed over their land in exchange for shares in native corporations. By contrast, the Gwich'in settlement of Arctic Village, home to little over 150 people, on the southern boundary of the reserve, vehemently oppose the move, fearing it will destroy their way of life.

As for Trump? He has said he 'really didn't care' about the future of ANWR, until someone told him that other Presidents had tried and failed to open it up to drilling. Then, and only then, did he become interested, vowing on a point of principle to succeed where they had failed.[1]

· · ·

For those who understand its value as a final frontier, the status of the ANWR is totemic. During his 2016 presidential election campaign, Trump horrified environmentalists by making clear that it would no longer be off-limits if he became President. Already, there was serious doubt over whether he believed in climate change.

In 2009, he had been a signatory to an open letter from a group of businessmen calling for urgent action on climate change. Addressed to Obama and the US Congress, the full-page advert in the *New York Times* said America should lead the way in making the changes 'necessary to protect humanity and our planet … If we fail to act now, it is scientifically irrefutable that there will be catastrophic and irreversible consequences for humanity and our planet', it said.[2] It was also signed by Trump's three grown-up children.

Quite why he added his name is unclear: other high-profile backers were liberal business types and celebrities. Perhaps he believed it at the time; perhaps he felt he had to be seen to be making the case. Either way, in the years that followed, his position on man-made climate change was inconsistent with those comments, increasingly leaning towards outright scepticism. He has variously described climate change as 'non-existent', 'mythical' and a 'hoax', and he has claimed that it was 'created by and for the Chinese, in order to make US manufacturing non-competitive'.[3] When he periodically comes under pressure to demonstrate that he is not a climate change denier, he tends to acknowledge that something strange is happening to the weather but express doubts over any link to human activity.

His decision within months of entering the White House to withdraw the US from the Paris Climate Change Accord, a legally binding international treaty designed to limit global warming, confirmed how little importance he attached to the issue relative to his political priorities. Announcing the move, Trump nonetheless claimed that he cared 'deeply' about the environment and that under his leadership, America would continue to be 'the cleanest and most environmentally friendly country on earth'. He declared: 'We're going to have the cleanest air. We're going to have the cleanest water. We will be environmentally friendly.'[4]

This was no more than lip service. The clear focus of his speech was the importance of protecting American jobs and the extent to which America would be at a competitive disadvantage globally if he did not abandon legally binding commitments to reduce carbon emissions and pay into various green funds. Drawing heavily from a study by a controversial New York-based economics consulting firm, the President claimed that complying with the treaty could cost America some 2.7 million jobs by 2025, including 440,000 in the manufacturing sector. By 2040, he claimed, the 'onerous energy restrictions' would cut iron and steel production by 238 per cent; coal by 86 per cent; natural gas by 31 per cent; cement by 23 per cent; and paper by 12 per cent. 'The cost to the economy … would be close to $3 trillion in lost GDP and 6.5 million industrial jobs, while households would have $7,000 less income and, in many cases, much worse than that,' he said.[5]

To American voters who took these shocking figures at face value, the case for jettisoning the agreement must indeed have seemed overwhelming. Few of those listening would have come away in any doubt over his commitment to put US taxpayers first. In comments that played directly to his base, he repeatedly emphasised that his only obligation was 'to the American people' and made clear that he did not regard the treaty as fair.

The way he saw it, the obligations placed a grossly unfair burden on American taxpayers relative to taxpayers in China and India. It was 'simply the latest example of Washington entering into an agreement that disadvantages the United States to the exclusive benefit of other countries, leaving American workers ... and taxpayers to absorb the cost in terms of lost jobs, lower wages, shuttered factories, and vastly diminished economic production,' he declared.[6]

What really riled him was that the terms of the agreement allowed China and India 'to do whatever they want for thirteen years'. They would be, he said, 'allowed to build hundreds of additional coal plants', while America was forced to curtail production. As he saw it, levelling the playing field in global trade was a key part of his job, and this did the very opposite. Rounding off his speech, he declared that the Paris Accord would 'undermine our economy, hamstring our workers, weaken our sovereignty, impose unacceptable legal risks and put us at a permanent disadvantage to the other countries in the world'. It was, he said, time to put 'Youngstown, Ohio, Detroit, Michigan, and Pittsburgh, Pennsylvania – along with many other locations within our great country – before Paris, France' and make America great again.[7]

Democrats and environmentalists were appalled. Barack Obama, Bill Clinton and Al Gore all condemned the move. In an emotional press release, Democratic Congresswoman Eddie Bernice Johnson said, 'Today, I am not proud. I am saddened and embarrassed that this country will not be working in coordination with the international community to address the threat of climate change.'[8] French

President Emmanuel Macron filmed an address in English, saying that Donald Trump was making a 'mistake', bitingly adding that the American, French and other allies should 'make our planet great again'. Even North Korea condemned the decision as the 'height of egotism'.[9]

Yet Trump had a point. The economic burden on the US *was* disproportionate. Under the terms of the accord, America faced higher costs mitigating climate change until 2030 than China and India. Indeed, China's voluntary plan allowed for emissions to rise until then, and the regime continues to open new coal mines. Moreover, while there were serious implications for protecting the environment, the case for weaning America off foreign energy imports was overwhelming.

•   •   •

Morgantown in West Virginia is an idyllic-looking place. Divided by the shimmering Monongahela river ('The Mon'), it is thought to have inspired Joni Mitchell's song, 'Morning Morgantown'. The reality is less romantic. If the Mon is shimmering, it may be because of toxic chemicals swirling beneath the surface. Salts, metals and gas waste high in radium have been polluting the water, a huge source of concern for the town's 30,000 inhabitants. The toxins are naturally occurring in the Marcellus shale formation nearby. But how do they get into the Mon? The culprit is, of course, hydraulic fracturing – referred to as fracking – a process that uses a combination of drilling and a high-pressure water mixture to recover gas and oil from shale rock.

Fracking is controversial. Environmentalists hate it because it requires huge volumes of water, and there is a considerable threat of carcinogenic chemicals seeping into groundwater. On the other hand, this new type of energy gives drilling firms access to oil and gas, which are otherwise difficult to source. It has significantly boosted American domestic oil production and reduced fuel prices. According to Obama, fracking offered the US and Canada gas security for some 100 years and halved the potential emissions needed to generate electricity.

The 2020 US election saw candidates divided on the issue. Biden's position was confusing. He veered between stating that he was against any 'new fracking' and would end subsidies for 'any fossil fuel' to claiming that he had never opposed it. His energy plan did not specifically mention the word fracking, focusing instead on 'banning new oil and gas permitting on public lands and waters'.[10]

By contrast, Trump's position was clear: he repeatedly stressed his support for the industry. Towards the end of October 2020, he signed an executive memorandum to defend the jobs and interests of American workers in energy through support for fracking. 'Under my administration, we are no longer beholden to foreign powers or domestic radicals. We are powering our Nation on our own terms,' he said.[11]

Of particular importance to the fracking debate is the swing state of Pennsylvania where shale gas production has soared over the past decade. 'The Great Commonwealth of Pennsylvania would absolutely die without the jobs and dollars brought in by Fracking. Massive numbers!' Trump tweeted in October 2020.[12]

For Trump, supporting this industry was a no-brainer. Not only did it create jobs, it also played into his 'America First Energy Plan', a mission to make the US energy independent. Until recently, domestic energy output in the States simply could not keep pace with demand. Heavy reliance on energy imports continually distorted foreign policy and left the US exposed to rogue states and terror organisations in the Middle East. It was behind diplomatic rifts, sanctions and even wars. It is a habit that will die hard – even Trump, a campaigner for energy independence, has spoken of wanting to 'secure' Syrian oil – but the President was determined to make progress.[13] Fracking presented a route out of all this. By the time Trump entered the White

House, it was making a dramatic difference. In 2006, the United States imported 60 per cent of its oil. By 2019, largely thanks to this new energy source, the country had become a net exporter of oil for the first time since records began in 1973. As for jobs, according to the Bureau of Labor Statistics, shale operators, pipeline companies and service companies together employed nearly 32,000 people as of June 2020 in Pennsylvania alone.

While fracking booms, the US oil industry remains in its deepest recession since the '80s. During the 2016 presidential election campaign, Trump repeatedly backed more drilling. In an energy-focused speech in North Dakota that July, he laid into President Obama for taking Alaska petroleum 'completely off the table' and accused Democrats of introducing so many environmental regulations that it was almost impossible for the oil industry to make a decent profit. In an indication of where his allegiances lay, he invited billionaire oil baron Harold Hamm to be his warm-up act at the speech. In a 2008 vice-presidential election debate, Republican candidate and Alaska governor Sarah Palin had famously urged crowds to chant 'drill, baby, drill' to express their support for exploiting domestic energy sources. Trump's attitude was much the same. However, he was not the uniquely destructive influence of environmental activists' imagination.

•   •   •

Bristol Bay in Alaska has the largest salmon run in the world. At certain times of year, crystal-clear creeks, branching to and from Lake Iliamna in the Kvichak river watershed, fill with floundering fish as they return to their birthplace after years maturing in the ocean. It is particularly rich in sockeye salmon, known for their distinctive bright red bodies, which can grow up to 3ft in length. Sometimes bear cubs run in and paw at the fish, as if they are grabbing glittering rubies from the water. According to predictions by the Alaska

Department of Fish and Game, over 51 million sockeye salmon will return to Bristol Bay in 2021. As a result, the bay is crucial to commercial fishing – its salmon fishery alone creates $14.7 million of revenue for local government entities. All this is threatened by the proposed construction of a gold mine near the salmon run.

'Pebble Mine' has been in the works since 2010. Its backers want federal permits to mine for gold, copper and molybdenum, endangering 80 miles of streams and 3,500 acres of wetlands. There are particular concerns about copper, which can be harmful to salmon. Pollution from the site at the headwaters of the Nushagak and Kvichak rivers, two 'arteries' of the Bristol Bay ecosystem, could spread out to the entire watershed.

Alaskan public opinion polls consistently show that more people oppose than support the scheme. Multiple jewellers in the US and across the world have gone so far as to pledge not to buy gold from the development if it is ever given the go-ahead. Among the many opponents, one surprising voice stood out: Donald Trump Junior. An avid fisherman, Trump's son agrees that the project would ruin a key salmon fishery. In August 2020, in response to a tweet posted by Nick Ayers, former chief of staff to Vice-President Mike Pence, which urged the Trump administration to block the project, Trump Jr said, 'As a sportsman who has spent plenty of time in the area, I agree 100 per cent. The headwaters of Bristol Bay and the surrounding fisheries are too unique and fragile to take any chances with. #PebbleMine.'[14]

According to an un-named *New York Times* source, Trump Jr repeatedly raised the proposed development with his father. His lobbying appears to have paid off. Eventually, the President blocked an essential permit for the Pebble from the Army Corps of Engineers. As the *Los Angeles Times* recognised, Trump had done something spectacularly 'good' for the environment.

In the same month, Trump also backed the Great American Outdoors Act, which aimed to restore, maintain and protect national parks. The idea was to use funds from offshore oil and gas drilling to maintain public land, national parks and Native American schools. The act permanently directed $900 million a year to a federal programme that acquired and protected public lands. At the signing ceremony, Trump declared it to be the 'most significant investment in our parks since the administration of the legendary conservationist President Theodore Roosevelt'.[15]

It would be foolish to pretend that Trump is any kind of environmentalist or that he has sought to do great things for wildlife and wildlife habitats. His climate change scepticism, his rollback of multiple hard-won environmental protection regulations and the fact that what he could have positioned as difficult decisions taken despite a genuine care for the environment were never presented in those terms, render it extremely difficult to make the case for the defence. His opposition to the gold and copper mine and his support for the public lands act do not offset the negatives, but they do demonstrate that, on occasion, he was ready to take positive environmental steps.

His position on ANWR is particularly difficult to stomach, not least since it seems to have stemmed less from a principled and well-reasoned economic position than from an arrogant and egotistical quest to out-do his predecessors. Crass as his comments were, they serve as a reminder that previous Presidents have been no angels on the environment. Obama himself opened up Arctic drilling in some areas. His decision to approve Dutch Shell's return to oil and gas extraction off Alaska was slammed by many environmentalists at the time and seen as a contradiction to his supposed commitment to environmentalism. Earlier, Obama had signed a proposal to prohibit drilling on 1.4 million acres of the ANWR. It wasn't until December 2016 – his last month in office – that he permanently banned new oil and gas drilling in most US-owned waters in the Arctic and Atlantic Ocean, in a last-minute effort to protect his climate legacy.

It is worth noting that, according to the International Energy Agency, in 2019, the US saw the largest drop in energy-related carbon emissions of any country, a fall of 140 million tons or 2.9 per cent, to 4.8 gigatons. US emissions are now down almost 1 gigaton from their 2000 peak, the largest absolute decline by any country over that period. Comparatively, China remains by far the world's biggest carbon polluter, contributing 28 per cent of global emissions in 2019. Between 2000 and 2018, India's carbon pollution increased by 157 per cent.

America remains the second largest producer of carbon emissions. All over the world, environmentalists have great hopes for Biden. It remains to be seen whether he will deliver much more than hot air.

PART TWO

GOOD WORKS

8

MOON TO MARS – TRUMP'S RECORD ON JOBS

When Trump was suffering from Covid, doctors conducted various tests. Someone put it about that he tweeted, 'They didn't find DNA, they found USA.' This was fake news, but it's hardly surprising it went viral: it's exactly the sort of thing he might have said. Who wouldn't want a leader who loved his country so much? Make no mistake, Trump put America first. He saw jobs going to China and Mexico and vowed to get them back. In office, he did everything he could to achieve just that.

Some 500 miles north of Moscow lies a testing site for weapons designed to give Russia the edge in future wars. Naturally, only a fraction of what goes on in the secretive research laboratories at Plesetsk Cosmodrome ever makes it into the public domain: when a disaster at the site killed forty-eight workers in 1980, it took nine years for the truth to emerge. With characteristic indifference to the truth, Russian state-sponsored newspaper *Pravda* reported the launch of the rocket Vostok-2M as a success at the time. In fact, it had exploded two hours before scheduled blast-off, a mixture of kerosene and tanks of liquid oxygen and nitrogen creating a deadly inferno.

To the consternation of American defence chiefs, recent experiments at the Russian spaceport have proven rather more successful.

Of particular concern during Donald Trump's third year in office was a satellite codenamed Cosmos 2542. At first, US intelligence analysts monitoring space activity did not notice anything unusual about the object, which was launched from Plesetsk on 25 November 2019. Then they saw something extraordinary: Cosmos 2542 was giving birth to a second satellite, codenamed Cosmos 2543. Tracking the two objects, the analysts became increasingly concerned: they appeared to be tailing a US spy satellite. At times, the Russian spacecraft were creeping within 100 miles of the multi-billion-dollar American device – behaviour described by US defence chiefs at the time as 'unusual and disturbing'.[1] Just as Russian military aircraft regularly 'buzz' UK airspace, flying ever closer towards zones they know are off-limits to test UK vigilance and resolve, President Putin's armed forces were seeing what they could get away with hundreds of miles above Earth.

The US government immediately communicated its displeasure to the Russians, and, for a while, Cosmos 2542 and 2543 slipped away. That was not the end of it, however. A few months later, Cosmos 2543 embarked on an even more audacious mission. To the alarm of US defence and intelligence analysts, the spacecraft was observed launching an unknown projectile. It looked very much as if Putin's regime was attempting to develop the capability to attack and disable satellites belonging to other nations.

The implications were huge: a hostile state with this technology could cripple another country within a matter of seconds. For America and her allies, the episode underlined the looming threat to the critical satellite infrastructure that provides everything from GPS systems to the ability to launch nuclear weapons.

It was not even as if the Russians were the most dangerous aggressors: the Chinese had been experimenting with the technology required to destroy foreign satellites for years. An international agreement governing the 'Exploration and Use of Outer Space, including the Moon and Other Celestial Bodies' was designed to prevent future 'star wars', but it had been drawn up in the 1960s. In the twenty-first century, this potential new warfighting domain had become what one US commander described as the 'wild, wild west'.[2]

On 19 February 2019, Donald Trump announced the establishment of the US Space Force: the first new military service in the US for more than seventy years. Created by executive order, it would have an annual budget of more than $15 billion (equivalent to around a third of the entire UK defence budget), its own flag and uniform and a staff of some 16,000 Air Force active duty and civilian personnel.

When it came to defending America, it was 'not enough to merely have an American presence in space. We must have American dominance in space,' Trump said.[3] As the Russians, the Chinese and other hostile states seek military and commercial advantage high above Earth, it may not be long before Trump's critics are forced to acknowledge his foresight in establishing the US Space Force. At the time, he didn't get much credit. Most people still seem to think that war in the sky will only ever happen in the movies. (Men's glossy magazine *GQ* loftily dismissed the new space force as 'ludicrous' – a view that was not shared in defence circles.)[4] It may take an unpleasant shock to persuade voters of the very real threat posed to the international rules-based order by the weaponisation of space, at which point Trump's foresight in establishing a dedicated branch of the military to meet this formidable challenge may be viewed more sympathetically.

In America's Deep South, however, thousands of US voters are already benefiting from the initiative, as the Trump administration's push on both military and commercial space exploration supports jobs. There's an old saying in that part of America that anyone who wants to go to the moon must go via Mississippi. That's because NASA's Stennis Space Center, in the so-called Magnolia State, is America's premier rocket engine test complex. Every rocket that has ever powered an American into space has been tested there.

For local people, extra federal money for space exploration and defence systems means extra employment opportunities. Indeed, shortly after Trump announced the creation of the new national space force, the then Governor of Mississippi, Phil Bryant, unveiled measures designed to put his state in pole position for the extra federal investment, with the creation of Mississippi's own space force and a new space-related economic development arm.

Bryant says the President's military and scientific space initiatives contributed to record employment figures in his state. Until 2016, he says, politicians in Mississippi assumed that unemployment could never fall below 5 per cent. It never had, and it never would. Then Trump came along, and it turned out a chunk of the workforce that everybody had long written off were ready to roll their sleeves up and do a hard day's work. In the run-up to the presidential elections of 2020, Mississippi had the lowest unemployment figures in the state's history.

'It's 4.7 per cent – that is a dramatic reduction to unemployment here,' Bryant says.

In Mississippi, everyone thought 5 per cent was full employment. They thought at least 5 per cent of the potential workforce just won't work. Under Trump, we saw historic revenue numbers coming into the state of Mississippi – more people working; more people investing in homes; more people buying new products. So we were able to put half a billion dollars into reserves – into what we call our Rainy Day Fund, because we had so much money coming into the Treasury. That had never been done before![5]

This was no one-off phenomenon. Under Trump, employment surged in almost all states – and certainly not just as a result of federal-funded programmes like the new space force. It was exactly what the President had promised on the campaign trail. Just as Labour Prime Minister Tony Blair put 'education, education,

education' at the heart of his first administration in the UK, Trump swept to power in 2016 promising 'jobs, jobs, jobs'. Nobody could accuse him of lacking ambition. He would, he told an audience of business leaders at the Waldorf Astoria Hotel in New York in September 2016, create an astonishing 25 million jobs over the next decade. These numbers were widely dismissed as fantasy figures.

'Far-fetched' was the verdict of the *New York Times*, while other commentators labelled the pledges 'wildly unrealistic'.[6] The general view was that, unless he planned a wave of immigration, even if he could create all those new openings, he would not be able to find anyone to do the work. In fact, in the three years prior to the pandemic, an additional 6.4 million jobs were created. Had Trump secured a second term and succeeded in maintaining approximately this rate of growth, the number of jobs created would have exceeded 20 million. It would have been significantly short of the 25 million headline figure he boasted of but would nonetheless have represented a remarkable achievement.

Following his 2020 defeat, nobody will ever know whether he could have pulled it off, though the shattering impact of coronavirus would certainly have made it a very long shot. What can be said for sure is that during his one-term presidency, he delivered the lowest unemployment rate in America in half a century, a record he would have been determined to build on when the pandemic ended.

Among the many economic reforms he spearheaded to boost job creation was a programme of deregulation, designed to cut unnecessary red tape that was throttling the US economy. In the first full year of his administration, the cost of federal regulation alone was estimated at $2 trillion annually – a huge drain on businesses across the United States. Trump's response was to issue an executive order requiring federal departments and agencies to scrap two existing regulations for every new regulation they created. This wasn't easy: indeed, as fast as he tried to scrap rules introduced by previous administrations, left-wing organisations and other vested interests launched legal battles to retain them, resulting in long drawn-out wrangles that often ended up in court. He suffered multiple defeats in cases involving protections for migrants, the environment, the disabled, affordable housing and student loans.

Nonetheless, by February 2019, the pace of regulatory growth in America had slowed by almost a third, and almost seventy significant rules – defined as those with an economic impact of at least $100 million – had been eliminated, with only three new ones issued. Comparing his record to that of his predecessors, US website Investor hailed him as an 'all-time record rule-cutter', crediting him with rolling back more red tape than any modern American President.[7]

Governor Bryant describes how these changes had a very real impact at state level, particularly in relation to infrastructure:

> Previously, if you were going to build, say, a highway, there were about a dozen different federal agencies you had to get permits from, just to build a bridge! So, if you've got a new plant coming in, but you need a railroad and a bridge, or an extension of a highway, in the old days, you'd have to say, 'Thank you for bringing us your plant, but it will be eight years for me to get you a bridge.' Or it would take you three years to get EPA to approve the environmental impact study. In the Obama years, if the EPA showed up, you were in trouble. They'd find some way to shut you down or fine you. They were doing it to create businesses for trial lawyers. The Obama EPA would always say, 'They're violating rules.' It was adversarial. The federal government was a state adversary of corporations and businesses. Trump came in and all of that changes. I can remember having the EPA come to Mississippi and welcoming them, knowing that they were here to work *with* us. We now have co-operative federalism, by which I mean, federal government is co-operating with states; co-operating with reducing burdensome regulation. It has been a totally new and different and wonderful environment.[8]

• • •

The international race for domination in space played perfectly to Trump's narrative of 'making America great again'. This was not just about defence, it was about commercial opportunity and scientific prowess. When it came to space exploration, he wanted to be first, because it reasserted America's place in the world. 'So important for our psyche,' was how he put it.[9] Quite literally, he wanted to plant the American flag on new frontiers. Less than a fortnight after the 2020 presidential election, four astronauts from a spacecraft named *Resilience* boarded the International Space Station, in the first of what NASA hopes will be a series of missions ending US reliance on Russian rockets. '@NASA was a closed up disaster when we took over. Now it is again the "hottest", most advanced, space center in the world, by far!' Trump tweeted, with his usual chutzpah.[10]

If NASA was 'hot', so was the American economy before the pandemic. Such was Trump's economic success that, in 2019, pollsters and political analysts believed the 2020 election was his to lose. On 7 September 2018, a CNBC commentator published an article acknowledging that Trump had 'set economic growth on fire'. The piece described an economic boom that was 'uniquely his' – a 'tremendous achievement'. It continued: 'During his time in office, the economy has achieved feats most experts thought impossible. GDP is growing at a 3 per cent-plus rate. The unemployment rate is near a fifty-year low. Meanwhile, the stock market has jumped 27 per cent amid a surge in corporate profits.'[11] Wages had increased by 2.9 per cent year on year to the highest level since April 2009 – the best gain since the end of the recession linked to the financial crisis in June 2009.

Pre-coronavirus, there were so many positive economic indices that only a *force majeure* could have dramatically weakened Trump's position as he fought for re-election – as indeed it did. Throughout his first three years in office, real wages, adjusted for inflation, grew, with average hourly earnings in April 2019 standing 3.2 per cent higher than the previous year, the ninth month in a row in which growth topped 3 per cent. Crucially, it wasn't just the better-off getting wealthier: wage growth among low-paid workers outstripped that of higher earners by the widest margin in two decades. Pay for those in the bottom quarter rose 4.5 per cent in November 2019, relative to 2.9 per cent for the highest 25 per cent of earners.

Contrary to the perception that left-wingers sought to propagate – that black and ethnic communities were oppressed under Trump – minority workers had particularly benefited from the economic boom. In 2019, for example, the median black female worker benefited from an 11 per cent wage rise. Meanwhile, in the first three years of his presidency, median household incomes rose from $61,000 to an all-time high of $66,000. Just as Trump had promised on the campaign trail, manufacturing jobs in particular rebounded, with 284,000 new positions created in 2018 alone, the most in a year for more than a decade.

How could his critics argue with this stunning record? They standard way was to credit the last guy, which is exactly what they did. An analysis of Trump's economic record by his nemesis CNN grudgingly acknowledged that his job record was 'better' than that of his predecessor but highlighted the challenges Obama faced when he entered the White House in 2008, in the midst of the worst financial crisis since the Great Depression. 'In comparison, Trump took office with a string of seventy-six straight months of job gains. Job creation under the Trump administration is a continuation of an improving job market, not the turnaround that occurred in the early years of the Obama administration,' the channel sniffed.[12]

In a self-congratulatory tweet in February 2020, Obama played the same game, seeking to take credit for the state of the US economy more than three years after he had left office. Commemorating the eleventh anniversary of the Recovery Act, the $831 billion economic rescue package he put in place following the global financial crash, Obama highlighted 'the longest streak of job creation in

American history', the clear implication being that the achievement was mostly down to him.[13] The tweet was guaranteed to provoke his successor. A furious Trump immediately hit back, labelling Obama's social media message a 'con job'.

'He had the WEAKEST recovery since the Great Depression, despite Zero Fed Rate and MASSIVE quantitative easing. NOW, best jobs numbers ever. Had to rebuild our military, which was totally depleted. Fed Rate UP, taxes and regulations WAY DOWN,' Trump raged.[14]

The President's indignation was understandable. Indeed, a point-by-point CNN analysis of Trump's claims, which boasts of putting 'facts first', gives Trump some credit for the rate of growth and accepts that he had less help from the Federal Reserve than his predecessor, because the federal funds rate, a key interest rate, remained near zero during Obama's two terms. Moreover, between 2009 and 2014, the central bank purchased trillions of dollars in bonds (quantitative easing), which juiced the economy throughout that period. By contrast, during Trump's administration, the Fed raised key interest rates seven times, with reductions only beginning in July 2019.

As Fox News presenter Steve Hilton puts it, the 'immediate go-to argument on the left' – that Trump simply inherited a booming economy from Obama – just doesn't wash. 'It's economically illiterate,' Hilton says, arguing that economies work in cycles. 'When you've come out of recession, you get big growth, then it slows down. It's much harder to get growth towards the end of the cycle. It was petering out under Obama. Then Trump came in and gave it the turbo boosters. His critics just won't acknowledge that.'[15]

•   •   •

On the morning of 16 May 1939, a long queue began forming outside a grand municipal building in the city of Rochester in Upstate

New York. The men and women gathering outside the old post office building looked downtrodden. Many had been struggling to feed themselves and their families for months.

The irony was that American farmers were producing more food than they knew what to do with. The Great Depression had impoverished so many people that they could not afford to buy basics like butter, meat, fruit and vegetables. Yet agricultural land was as productive as it had been prior to the crash. Farmers did not have enough customers for all the food they were producing, but people were going hungry. To resolve this desperate mismatch, President Franklin D. Roosevelt's administration came up with a scheme, under which the poor were able to use government-issued stamps to buy surplus farm produce. In an indication of the scale of demand, on the day the historic initiative was launched in Rochester, some 2,000 people waited their turn for the stamps, which they were able to take to one of 1,200 participating grocery stores and exchange for items like eggs, flour, oranges and beans. The scheme was a huge success. In due course, it was rolled out nationally, and it formed the basis of what would become the Food Stamps system in America today.

There's nothing fun about living off food stamps, as Nina McCollum, a struggling freelance writer, can attest. She has told of her despair and humiliation at having to resort to what is now called the Supplemental Nutrition Assistance Program to avoid going hungry.[16] Fortunately, beneficiaries of the scheme are now spared the embarrassment of having to produce vouchers at the supermarket checkout, an experience that McCollum recalls from her childhood as a source of 'crippling shame'. Yet the subsidy system only covers certain items, and many users are still forced to turn to charitable food banks to keep the wolf from the door.

Under Trump, food stamp enrolment fell to its lowest level in eight years, not because the poor did not qualify for assistance but because fewer families actually needed help. According to official data, in 2019 around 4.2 million fewer people were living in poverty in the US compared with the previous year – not quite the 'largest poverty reduction under any President in history' that Trump claimed, but certainly the largest drop in modern times. You have to go back more than half a century to Lyndon B. Johnson in 1966 to find a President who did better, with a drop of 4.7 million. Indeed, according to Department of Agriculture data, by February 2020, some 7.7 million Americans had been lifted off food stamps since the 2016 election.

How did he do it?

The 2017 Tax Cuts and Jobs Act was pivotal. It lowered the punitive business taxes of the Obama administration to levels similar to most European countries. Corporation tax was slashed from 35 per cent to 21 per cent, making America a more attractive destination for inward investment and a better place to do business. As employers sent less money to the Treasury, they could afford to pay workers more. In 2018, workers received some of the highest wage gains in a decade. Average Americans received a tax cut of $1,400, while the average family with two children saw taxes reduced by more than double that figure.

The combination of these and other fiscal measures sent stock market and investor confidence soaring. At the start of 2020, the Dow Jones Industrial Average reached record highs. By February, it had risen 39 per cent since Trump's election. In the first year of his presidency, the index rose by almost a third – the second best record of any President in history.

A 2017 analysis of the state of the economy by investment bank Schroders acknowledged that Trump's policies had 'lifted confidence'. It continued, 'He wants to spend huge amounts of money on infrastructure, has promised to create millions of jobs and bring business back to the US. This should be good for economic growth in the US. It could even kick-start faster growth elsewhere.'[17] The bank's chief economist, Keith Wade, concluded that investors had 'bought fully into Trump's promise to "Make America Great Again"'. In perhaps his most significant observation, Wade predicted that future trade deals would be more favourable to the US.

Making that happen would be one of Trump's biggest and most important battles in the White House.

9

STEEL RESOLVE – TRADE DEALS, TARIFFS AND MANUFACTURING JOBS

Tariffs don't sit well with me, as a libertarian. In an ideal world, there would be free trade, free movement and a perfectly free marketplace. This would undoubtedly lead to lower prices for the consumer in the longer term. The trouble with that is, it only works if everyone plays by the same rules. Sadly, every country, either overtly or covertly, imposes tariffs and restrictions on almost all overseas goods and services, or else provides state aid to give the same effect. Trump knows this, but rather than do the usual diplomatic, political thing of trying to appease other leaders and haggle around the edges, he embraced tariffs openly and honestly and used them for the blunt, effective tools they are. Lo and behold – it worked.

For bosses at the *Pittsburgh Post-Gazette*, the run-up to presidential elections do not generally bring difficult editorial decisions. For almost five decades, the newspaper has simply backed the Democrat candidate as the more likely of the two to make life better for people in the old industrial city. Since 1972, no Republican candidate has ever convinced the publisher and editorial board that he would do a better job for people in this crucial swing state of Pennsylvania. Reflecting the left-wing politics of its readers, the

Pittsburgh Post-Gazette had no reservations about endorsing Barack Obama in both 2008 and 2012.

In 2016, however, the editors wobbled. The truth was, they did not much like either of those running. Trump, they declared, was a 'vulgarian, who never seems to study, to apologize or to learn. He is also a sexist and a cad.' Yet Clinton had been under criminal investigation into her use of a shadow computer server while in government, with impeachment 'a very real possibility from day one'. Worse, they considered her deeply dishonest. 'Nothing about her is genuine,' was their brutal assessment.[1]

For some readers, the editors acknowledged, the choice might seem as if it were between a 'crook and a nut'. Breaking more than forty years of tradition, the publisher decided against any endorsement. Instead, readers were offered a kind of crib sheet showing how Clinton and Trump matched up in specific policy areas. They were encouraged to vote according to what mattered most to them. If the answer to that question was trade and manufacturing, the paper argued that they should back Trump. 'For many Americans, this is the premier issue of the election … If trade and manufacturing are your issues, Donald Trump is your man,' it declared.

The 2016 editorial created quite a stir in a state that is always crucial to the fate of presidential candidates. Many readers cancelled their subscriptions. On the other hand, the *Pittsburgh Post-Gazette*, whose sister paper is *The Blade* in the neighbouring state of Ohio, won new readers in hard-pressed areas just outside the city, where folk were as passionately pro-Trump as their metropolitan neighbours were against.

In any case, the decision was, according to the paper's editor Keith Burris, a matter of journalistic integrity. Some time ago, he and the publisher decided to move the paper away from what he calls 'kneejerk leftism'.[2] That meant giving credit where credit was due – including to Donald Trump.

In 2020, the *Post-Gazette* doubled down, taking the radical step of publishing an editorial that actively endorsed the President, knowing full well it would alienate even more readers. Why? Because they believe that in the four years he was in office, Trump demonstrated that he genuinely cared about people in states like Pennsylvania and Ohio and would fight for their future. The President's commitment and enthusiasm was in sharp contrast to the attitude of so many other political leaders, who treated these parts of America as little more than 'flyover country' – unless, of course, an election loomed.

'It took courage for the publisher to run the 2020 endorsement,' Burris admits.

Our readers are furious with us! They are still furious about four years ago. We've taken a significant commercial hit. Even saying, 'Look, we know he has all these character flaws, but are there other things we should look at, like his actual record' – just saying that in itself is considered blatantly and blindly pro-Trump, and if you are that, people seem to think you are also de facto a racist!

But we have tried to make the paper more aware of all these people who live around the rim of Pittsburgh, and to speak for the whole region not just one part of the city. It is about what Establishment politics has done to these two cities and these two regions.[3]

Pittsburgh is one of the poorest cities in the United States: only Detroit, Cleveland, Miami and Buffalo have lower average household incomes. Like other towns across this huge north-eastern state, for forty years it was hammered by the decline in the US manufacturing industry. Coal and steel plants struggled to survive in an era of cheap metal imports from China. Many were forced to lay off swathes of their workforce or shut altogether. Even before China started undercutting them, the steel industry in Pittsburgh was in trouble, as dwindling local supplies of coke and iron ore deposits sent the price of raw materials soaring. Many steel mills simply became unviable. As for coal production, the economies no longer stacked up. There wasn't a supply issue – coal still ran deep across Pennsylvania, and the industry still employed some 17,000 people in the state. According to some local politicians, left to its own devices, the industry could keep producing anthracite and softer bituminous coal for another thirty years. But coal is heavily polluting, and environmental regulations have decimated profits. Many pits have simply been abandoned. The derelict infrastructure is a hazard, but those responsible for it are out of cash to bury the skeletons of their once thriving businesses.

While coal and steel towns continue to suffer, the city of Pittsburgh is on the up. Successive mayors have been remodelling it as a hub for tech companies and research and development at Carnegie Mellon University. There is a particular focus on the development of robotics. Uber and Google are there. The main employer is no longer ailing US Steel, which continues to rack up huge losses, but the University of Pittsburgh Medical Center, a not-for-profit healthcare enterprise which is headquartered in the city and has a 90,000-strong workforce nationwide. Burris goes so far as to say that Pittsburgh is becoming 'hipster'.

Nonetheless, thousands of blue-collar workers there and across the states of Pennsylvania and Ohio still depend on jobs linked to steel and coal production and see their livelihoods disappearing. To Trump, this part of the United States typified the impact of globalism on the American economy. He put the two states at the heart of his 2016 presidential election campaign, holding a succession of rousing rallies where he set out a vision for repositioning the economy to 'Make America Great Again'. His 'America First' message offered real hope to hard-pressed workers, who loved the tub-thumping rhetoric about 'bringing their jobs home'.

'When I'm President, guess what, steel is coming back to Pittsburgh,' Trump declared at one such event, promising to restore the work that had been 'stolen' from them.[4] American steel would send new skyscrapers 'into the clouds. Way, way, way into the clouds,' he said. This would be 'American hands' rebuilding the nation.

These were pledges he repeated time and again in Pennsylvania, Ohio and the other Rust Belt states of Michigan, Indiana, Illinois and north-eastern Wisconsin. In coal mining areas crowds roared their approval, waving placards declaring 'Trump Digs Coal'. Explaining his vision, he promised to be a champion for jobless Americans. He boomed:

My economic plan rejects the cynicism that says our labour force will keep declining; that our jobs will keep leaving; and that our economy can never grow as it did once before...

All of these things and so much more are possible, but to accomplish them we need to replace the policy of globalism which has moved so many jobs and so much wealth out of our communities and so much wealth out of our country, and replace it with a new policy of Americanism.[5]

The big question was how he intended to deliver. In a PBS debate in June 2016, Obama demanded to know 'what exactly' Trump would do. 'There's no answer to it. He just says, "Well, I'm going to negotiate a better deal." Well, how exactly are you going to negotiate that? What magic wand do you have? And usually the answer is, he doesn't have an answer,' he added dismissively.[6]

In fact, Trump did have an answer: it was just that most economists and Wall Street types did not like it. It involved tearing up international trade agreements and introducing a raft of protectionist measures that had long ago fallen out of fashion as Western nations embraced global free trade. Vested interests and trade experts lined up to decry his plans. He also found himself up against senior figures in the White House, who believed his radical approach would do great economic harm. The more these 'experts' objected, the more many American voters seemed inclined to support the President's approach. After all, it was widespread suspicion of Establishment figures and disillusion with the way things had always been done that had propelled Trump to the White House in the first place. Trump's supporters did not need to understand complex economics or the history of trade and tariffs to see that the status quo was not delivering for them. Little wonder they were ready to embrace a different approach.

Some did everything in their power to block or water down the measures he proposed. He was ready to face them down.

• • •

Almost every day, the sun shines bright on the towering blue-and-white billboard welcoming workers to the Ford factory in San Luis Potosí. The climate is arid subtropical in this part of Mexico, and the motor car giant's familiar elliptical blue logo, with its swirly capital F, is usually a perfect match for the hot azure sky.

The weather is great, but, for the car company, the political climate was not, when Trump came to power. In common with other American car manufacturers with a taste for cheap Mexican labour, as soon as Trump was elected, Ford began feeling the heat. The President's repeated insistence on the 2016 campaign trail that American companies should employ American workers was a clear warning to those tempted to offshore more jobs. Firms that planned to expand overseas production operations risked public humiliation, being named and shamed by a President who painted them as unpatriotic and exploitative. This unappealing prospect encouraged many, including Ford, to think again.

It was Henry Ford who first made cars affordable for ordinary Americans, changing the course of history by developing the assembly-line technique of mass production. Unveiled in 1908, Ford's famous Model T was so cheap that by the 1920s, it was everywhere, revolutionising transport and industry in the US. Ford himself was an internationalist who embraced the opportunity to expand overseas. To some extent, he shared Trump's 'America First' ideology, in that he was adamant that the US should be economically self-sufficient. He still wanted Ford cars to be sold all over the world, though, and by 1929 he had dealerships on six continents and was helping the Russians develop Soviet car plants.

With this proud history, at the tail end of the Obama administration, Ford bosses had no qualms about drawing up plans to open a new plant in San Luis Potosí. The idea was to use low-paid Mexican workers to churn out small vehicles, allowing higher-paid American workers to focus on the production of larger, more expensive cars. There was nothing remotely irregular about this: American car companies have been outsourcing production to Mexico since the North American Free Trade Agreement (NAFTA) was signed in 1994. Financially, it was a no-brainer. After all, Mexican labourers are willing to work for a few dollars an hour without the many benefits US workers enjoy. If more Mexicans had steady jobs, that created wealth. Moreover, in the past decade, Mexican car plants, once less well equipped to produce complex components, had become more sophisticated and efficient, churning out some 11,000 vehicles a day. Most US car companies were taking advantage of this opportunity in some way: a few miles from Ford's 'welcome' billboard, for example, US tyre company Goodyear Tire and Rubber Co. has been building a $550 million tyre facility, and Ford rival General Motors Co. has various production sites in the area. Free traders would see this as a win-win. Mexican wages might have been comparatively modest, but the money went far further than it would in the US. It was not only good for Mexico but it was also good for American shareholders.

Trump's point was that it has not been good for American blue-collar workers. During his 2016 campaign and as President-elect, he repeatedly made clear his disdain for such outsourcing, threatening to punish companies choosing Mexican workers over Americans. Days before entering the White House, he threatened to slap a 35 per cent tax on cars made in Mexico and sold in the US.

'Instead of driving jobs and wealth away, AMERICA will become the world's great magnet for INNOVATION and JOB CREATION,' he tweeted, on 3 January 2017.[7] And at a Made in America product showcase in July that year, he stated: 'We want to build, create and grow more products in our country using American labor, American goods and American grit … No longer are we going to allow other countries to break the rules, steal our jobs, and drain our wealth – and it has been drained.'[8]

Around the same time, he began singling out particular companies for attack. First, he laid into General Motors for making their Chevy Cruze model in Mexico then sending it to car dealers 'tax free across the border'.[9] Then he turned on Japanese car maker Toyota over plans to make their Corolla for the US market in Mexico. 'NO WAY! Build plant in US or pay big border tax,' was his response to those schemes.[10]

Watching nervously from the sidelines, Ford bosses knew they could well be next. The San Luis Petosí project had become too hot to handle. The welcome sign would stay up, as would the skeletal structure of the factory that had already been constructed on an industrial estate – perhaps in the hope of better days to come – but almost everything else about the $1.6 billion project would have to be abandoned. It was a tortuous process that cost the company tens of millions of dollars in compensation claims from disaffected contractors and left many Mexicans and other suppliers grievously out of pocket, but Trump had made it politically untenable to press ahead. Had they done so he could have inflicted huge damage to their brand.

In the end, despite repeated threats, the President never did impose tariffs on imports of foreign-made cars and auto parts. What he did was renegotiate the NAFTA free trade agreement with

Mexico and Canada, which he considered 'perhaps the worst trade deal ever made'.[11] Under the re-drafted agreement, known as United States–Mexico–Canada Agreement (USMCA), at least three quarters of a vehicle's materials had to be made within the trading area, and 40–45 per cent of that quota had to be made by workers paid at least $16 per hour. The wage requirement was specifically designed to target Mexico.

In 2018, he also imposed a slew of tariffs on the import of foreign goods, from steel and aluminium, to washing machines and solar panels. Domestic producers were delighted: on the day of the washing-machine announcement, shares in Whirlpool, which had accused overseas rivals Samsung Electronics and LG of dumping cheap white goods on the American market, rose by 1.8 per cent in after-hours trade. 'President Trump has ensured American workers will compete on a level playing field with their foreign counterparts,' Whirlpool chairman Jeff Fettig said at the time.[12]

Such was Trump's enthusiasm for this blunt method of protecting domestic producers that he began to style himself 'Tariff Man'. He declared:

> When people or countries come in to raid the great wealth of our Nation, I want them to pay for the privilege of doing so. It will always be the best way to max out our economic power. We are right now taking in $billions in Tariffs. MAKE AMERICA RICH AGAIN.[13]

Wall Street executives were appalled. It flew in the face of everything they had been taught about the benefits of unfettered free trade. All it would do was raise consumer prices, they warned. It would hurt the ordinary Americans Trump claimed he wanted to help. To some extent, they were right. American producers hit by tariffs would pass at least some of their extra overheads on to customers. On a point of principle, Trump was robbing Peter to pay Paul – and both Peter and Paul were American. (Down in Mexico, Pedro was also losing out, but the President would have been the first to say he did not care about that.) His tariffs were also hurting the Canadians, neighbours and allies few Americans were keen to alienate. Amid mounting political and diplomatic pressure, in May 2019, the levies were lifted, Trump having concluded that they had served their purpose.

The President had shown that he was willing to do what few of his predecessors had seriously considered and use tariffs to correct market distortions. Arguably, the way he went about it was too blunt: some world trade experts who back the use of levies to correct iniquities in global trade arising from practices such as state subsidies will argue that he should have targeted specific injustices, as opposed to imposing blanket import taxes. But it was a heavy shot across the bows.

He was also ready to use tariffs as a political tool. In a move that sent shockwaves through his own party, just weeks after dropping the levies, he threatened unilaterally to reimpose a 5 per cent tax on all imports from Mexico, a figure he said would rise to 10 per cent on 1 July, and by another 5 per cent each month for three months, 'until such time as illegal migrants coming through Mexico, and into our Country, STOP'.[14] Republicans including Ted Cruz signalled that they would block the measures in Congress, and Trump did not follow through. However, Mexican leaders could not have been left in any doubt that he would make good on his threat if they were seen not to be doing something about it.

NAFTA was not Trump's only trade target. Within days of his inauguration in 2017, he honoured a campaign pledge to withdraw the US from the Trans-Pacific Partnership (TPP), an agreement between twelve countries. Together they represented a third of all global trading. The deal had been hammered out under the Obama administration in an attempt to maintain US dominance of trade in the region. The idea was to draw signatories including Japan,

Australia and Vietnam around an American nucleus before China attempted to do the same. The problem was that while the free trade agreement boosted corporate profits, it didn't translate into more jobs for American workers. Worse, it had become a way for unscrupulous multinationals to sidestep Congress and chip away at workers' rights. Thus, it became as toxic for Democrats as for Republicans. As Obama's Secretary of State, Hillary Clinton had described TPP as the 'gold standard in trade agreements', but when labour unions lined up to attack the agreement, she changed her mind.[15]

During the 2016 presidential election campaign, Trump labelled it a 'disaster done and pushed by special interests' and likened it to a 'rape' of the US.[16] He vowed to cut America loose in favour of bilateral agreements that would bring jobs and industry back on American shores. On 23 January 2017, he signed a presidential memorandum doing just that.

Neither the renegotiation of NAFTA nor the withdrawal from TPP created anything like the angst inside the White House as Trump's threat to rip up the United States–Korea Free Trade Agreement (KORUS). The President had become fixated by Washington's $18 billion annual trade deficit with Seoul. The long-standing agreement was intricately connected to joint security operations in the region, but the President did not seem interested in that.

According to various insider accounts, he repeatedly dismissed the importance of the lengthy US military presence in South Korea, an arrangement that would be plunged into doubt if the two countries fell out over KORUS. In one of the most important benefits of the arrangement, US intelligence assets in the region would provide a thirty-minute warning in the event of a nuclear missile strike – an advantage that could fall to a few minutes if co-operation ceased.

Yet Trump felt the US was being ripped off by the South Koreans on both trade and defence. Despite the continuous threat posed by North Korea, he struggled to see the rationale for the multi-billion-dollar cost of maintaining US forces on the Korean peninsula, prompting Defense Secretary James Mattis to warn him that it was vital to 'prevent World War III'.[17] The exasperated general is said to have privately complained to colleagues that the President's understanding of the security situation in the region was no more sophisticated than that of a 'fifth or sixth grader'.

In his account of the controversy over the future of KORUS, Watergate journalist Bob Woodward claims the President's trusted economic adviser Gary Cohn conspired to save the agreement by removing a cancellation letter from Trump's desk. The document gave South Korea notice of America's intention to withdraw and had been placed there for the President to sign. Woodward quotes Cohn telling a friend, 'I stole it off his desk. I wouldn't let him see it. He's never going to see that document. Got to protect the country'.[18] If this is true – and Cohn has never denied it – it goes to show what the President was up against. Cohn might have been right, but, as an unelected official, it was not for him to take an executive decision.

In the end, Trump let it go. The treaty underwent some minor revisions relating to the regulatory burden on US car exports and tariffs on Korean truck imports, allowing Trump to claim it had been renegotiated, but there seems little evidence that the changes made much difference in either country. Had he followed through on his threats and ripped up KORUS, the national security implications would have been immense. Setting aside how they went about it, those who fought to preserve the agreement probably served their country (and the rest of the world) well. In any case, while Trump reportedly did not much like South Korean leader Moon Jae-in, there were far more dangerous dragons to slay. His most important trade war would be with China, the empire that truly threatened America's place in the world.

10

WINNING – TRUMP
AND CHINA, PART ONE

*China. 1.4 billion potential customers! At the turn of this century, West-
ern governments and corporates were desperate for a slice of the action.
Partnerships were formed with educational establishments, business
forums were set up and politicians rolled out the red carpet for visiting
representatives of the Chinese regime. Huge brands were desperate to gain
a foothold in this lucrative market. They grew drunk on the promise of
free trade and cheap goods. Tiananmen Square was just a memory. They
all thought China had changed. The entire Western world bought into it.
By the time they realised just how malign the regime remained, it was
too late: China owned huge swathes of Western infrastructure and had
embedded nearly 2 million Chinese Communist Party members across
governments, universities and the world's biggest banks and financial institutions. Make no mistake: President Xi Jinping sees the Chinese model
of tech fascism – by which I mean control and repression of populations
aided by technology – being rolled out all over the world, apparently welcomed by many governments. Donald Trump saw this. He was ready to
stand between the West and that dystopia. His stance against Huawei,
after other Western governments caved, was one of his finest hours.*

There was a moment at the height of the coronavirus crisis when
Donald Trump revealed his true feelings about the nation that
poses the single greatest threat to America's place in the world. It

only took one word: 'China'. It was the way the President said it, pausing very briefly for dramatic effect before spitting out the two syllables with naked contempt. Covid-19 had come from China, he declared, so calling it 'the Chinese virus' was 'not racist at all; no, not at all'. He was simply telling it as it was. In a fiery exchange with a reporter, he explained that in blaming China for the pandemic, he just wanted to be 'accurate'.[1]

Had Trump known that the 'Chinese virus' would prove so pivotal to his fate in the 2020 presidential election, he would doubtless have had even more venomous words for a regime whose sinister commercial, foreign policy and military activities he confronted with more focus, energy and effect than any of his predecessors. If he has a hidden halo, it is arguably here, in his approach to China that it shone brightest. Not only did he grasp the full extent of the Chinese economic and geopolitical menace but he also recognised that the policy of appeasement that had been adopted by Barack Obama and supported by vested interests all over the world, would not serve America or her allies well. His instinct, reinforced by his confidant and chief political strategist Steve Bannon, was that America should not behave as if there were nothing to be done about China's quest for global pre-eminence, nor accept the regime's eventual success in this mission as an inevitability. The rise of China was not, Bannon told students at the University of Oxford in England, some kind of 'second law of thermodynamics' that nobody could change. Bannon's view was that all those business types who gathered for the World Economic Forum at Davos every year and talked about 'the Asian century', blithely assuming that with a bit of gentle pressure the Chinese would eventually embrace Western ways, were 'absolutely dead wrong'.[2] Trump agreed. His approach to the 'dragon' would be much more confrontational. As a result, according to world trade expert Shanker Singham, the Trump administration would be 'the first administration to actually cause the Chinese to have any respect for the US'.[3]

• • •

Western visitors to parts of China could be forgiven for imagining that it is light-years away from replacing America as the most powerful nation in the world – especially if they chance upon one of the country's now notorious 'wet markets'. They eat cats and dogs in China, and, as the world now knows, they also eat pangolins, the scaly anteaters scientists believe may have been a staging post in the spread of coronavirus from bats to humans. 'If it has got four legs and it is not a chair, if it has got two wings and it flies but is not an aeroplane, and if it swims and it is not a submarine, the Cantonese will eat it,' the infamously politically incorrect HRH Prince Philip once declared disparagingly about people in southern mainland China, and there is still a grain of truth in that.[4] While attitudes to animal welfare remain medieval, however, other aspects of China have changed beyond recognition as it has urbanised, and the middle classes – as defined by income – have swelled from 39.1 million people (3.1 per cent of the population) in 2000 to 707 million (50.8 per cent of the population) in 2018.

For the time being, America remains the biggest economy in the world by GDP. In 2019, the US economy was valued at $21.43 trillion while the Chinese economy was two thirds that size, at $14.3 trillion. However, nominal GDP fails to account for the relative cost of goods and services, as well as inflation in other countries. GDP in purchasing power parity (PPP) terms is often considered a more accurate measure. According to the IMF, back in the 1990s, the United States' share of the world's GDP in PPP terms was 21.7 per cent while China's share was only 4.03 per cent. By 2017, China had overtaken the US. Come 2020, the gap had widened, with China on 18.56 per cent of the global share and the US on 15.98 per cent. Watching these trends, Trump was appalled, noting the hugely ambitious growth targets the Chinese set themselves. 'If China has a GDP [growth] of 7 per cent it's like a national catastrophe. We're down at 1 per cent.

And that's like, no growth. And we're going lower, in my opinion,' he argued during the presidential debates in 2016.[5]

As far as the Chinese regime was concerned, this was about restoring China's rightful place in the world. For centuries it had been one of the greatest civilisations on earth, leading technological development on everything from shipbuilding to the invention of paper and the discovery of gunpowder. However, the 1800s descended into a 'Century of Humiliation' that left deep scars on the national psyche. During the two Opium Wars, British gunships forced China to open up its ports to trade. In the Boxer Rebellion of 1900, Beijing was stormed by American, British, Russian, Japanese and French forces. Chinese President Xi Jinping has described it as 'a period of ordeal too bitter to recall'. He has said, 'In the 100 years from the Opium War in 1840 to the founding of the People's Republic in 1949, China was ravaged by wars, turmoil and foreign aggression.'[6]

The rise of the revolutionary Mao Zedong transformed China's national identity and set it on a different, though no less damaging, path. Chairman Mao's attempts to restructure the agrarian economy created the worst famine in human history, killing 45 million people, but the tragically misnamed Great Leap Forward did pave the way for a very different era of partial economic liberalisation. Mao's more moderate successor, Deng Xiaoping, abandoned many orthodox communist doctrines and began opening up the economy to free markets and special economic zones. What followed in the 1980s and 1990s was the beginning of rapid export-led growth for China.

In the West, it was naïvely assumed that as China became more prosperous, it would embrace the rules-based international order. Unfortunately, the Communist regime was playing a very different game. What President Xi called the 'China Dream' was not limited to national rejuvenation. The aim was nothing less than to make the so-called Middle Kingdom the world's dominant power.

Obama recognised that the twenty-first century was likely to be contested in Asia but was more inclined to lean into the competition than fight it. His administration drew up plans for a 'Pivot to Asia', a foreign policy initiative designed to prompt a strategic rebalancing of US interests from Europe and the Middle East to Asia, but the plans were troubled from the start and were soon derailed by the impact of the 2008 financial crisis and the ongoing wars in Iraq and Afghanistan. Between 2008 and 2016, he failed to contain or shape China's growing economic influence or prevent the brazen militarisation of the South China Sea. Trump set out to correct that.

For him, being President was all about winning. On the campaign trail, he would declare:

We're going to win. We're going to win so much. We're going to win at trade, we're going to win at the border. We're going to win so much, you're going to be so sick and tired of winning, you're going to come to me and go, 'Please, please, we can't win any more.'[7]

He looked at the world as if it were a balance sheet. If China was winning, the US was losing. It was zero-sum. From the outset, levelling the economic playing field with China was top of his agenda. He was not going to stand idly by while the US fell down the global pecking order. Second place is first loser, after all.

It was not a theme that Trump discovered only as he launched his first presidential campaign. He had been exercised by the rise of China for years. In February 2012, he tweeted, 'Next to Chinese VP Xi Jinping yesterday, @BarackObama said he welcomes China's "peaceful rise". China is laughing because their "rise" is at our expense.'

Trump's first ever meeting with Steve Bannon, in 2010, was dominated by this issue. Recalling their two-hour exchange, Bannon has said:

He turns on about China, and we get into this conversation about China. And we talk about trade. We talk about non-trade barriers, talk about the South China Sea; we talk about currency manipulation. Of a two-hour meeting, the China thing is twenty or thirty minutes long. It's the one thing he knows.[8]

Bannon was impressed by Trump's expertise, noting that not many people in political circles at that time could discuss the issues with such fluency.

I can't, in Washington DC, outside maybe some noodge at a think tank, have the conversation I just had with this guy on China. Nobody will talk about non-trade barriers; nobody will talk about currency manipulation. They couldn't pick the South China Sea. He talks about the South China Sea … It's amazing to me he actually has what I think is one of the biggest threats, if not the biggest threat we've got coming, he understands China better than anybody in this city.

It was a view echoed by economists Stephen Moore and Arthur Laffer. 'Trump wasn't just shooting from the hip. He knew his stuff,' they write in their book *Trumponomics*, after meeting him before he was elected, in March 2016.[9]

By the time Trump reached the White House, he was ready to take measures against the Chinese regime that his predecessor would never have contemplated.

•   •   •

With its palm-fringed beaches, highland tea plantations and elephant reserves, Sri Lanka is among the world's most attractive tourist destinations. From the Buddhist temples and ancient fortified city of Galle to the waterfalls and jungles, there is something for everyone, which is why the island's second largest airport ought to be very busy. Accordingly, Mattala Rajapaksa International Airport is designed to cater for up to 1 million passengers a year. In reality, there are almost none. Even before coronavirus paralysed international travel, the check-in desks lay closed; there were no queues at security; the departure lounges were mostly empty; and only a trickle of people ever came through arrivals. The ghostly terminal receives a dozen passengers each day. For this privilege, Sri Lanka pays China $23.6 million a year – and will do so for almost a decade. This giant white elephant is one of a raft of infrastructure projects across Asia, Africa and Europe, funded and built by the Chinese as part of their Belt and Road Initiative. By pouring capital into road construction, energy plants and transport hubs in grateful developing countries, China is attempting to recreate the old trading route of the Silk Road – traversed by the explorer Marco Polo – linking sixty-five countries across Africa, Asia and Europe. Such is the scale of this global endeavour that investment bank Morgan Stanley estimates it will cost the Chinese state some $1.2–$1.3 trillion by 2027. As far as the regime is concerned, it is money well spent.

In his book *China's Asian Dream*, China analyst and former journalist Tom Miller suggests the objective is to attract lesser powers into China's chilly grip, from where there will be little release. 'China's aim is to use economic incentives to build closer relationships with its neighbours, drawing them ever tighter into its embrace. In return for delivering roads and power lines, it expects its partners to respect its "core interests", including its territorial claim in the South China Sea,' he writes.[10]

Well before it started colonising parts of Asia and Africa, China's role in global trade had grown exponentially as a result of joining the World Trade Organization (WTO) in December 2001. Back in the year 2000, the US exported more than China to 148 of the 192 nations that provided trade figures to the IMF. By 2019, the figures had flipped on their head, with China exporting more than the US in 144 countries. The United States had lost its trade dominance in most of Europe, Africa, Oceania and South America, only remaining the biggest player in France, the UK, Israel, its near abroad in

Latin America, Canada and Mexico, and a handful of other countries. Trump was deeply disturbed by this shift.

In the run-up to the 2016 election, his campaign produced a document entitled 'Reforming the US–China Trade Relationship to Make America Great Again', setting out how he would tackle China's growing trade monopoly. It featured a damning assessment of the way previous US administrations had approached this issue, singling out Bill Clinton for particular criticism. He had, the document declared, 'boldly promised' that welcoming China into the WTO would be 'a good deal for America'. Voters had been told that US products would get better access to Chinese markets and every sector from agriculture to telecommunications to automobiles would benefit. Instead, 'none of what President Clinton promised' came true.[11]

Shanker Singham, who was involved in the fifteen-year negotiation over China's accession to the WTO between 1986 and 2001, agrees that the Chinese pulled the wool over everyone's eyes.

> Everyone at that time was very focused on getting China into the WTO. We very naïvely believed that all we had to do was get them into the WTO, get them to liberalise their markets, lower tariffs and open up, and competition would automatically follow. We thought that about lots of other countries as well, and we were wrong. We thought they would automatically open up, and we thought that economic democracy would ultimately bring political democracy.[12]

What actually happened was that WTO membership allowed China to flood world markets with cheap goods. Other countries simply could not compete with the mass production in state-subsidised factories and grim sweatshops. China was also accused of artificially devaluing its currency. The Chinese yuan had been fixed to the US dollar in 1994 at 8.28 yuan per dollar, which significantly undervalued the yuan. As a result, their goods were more competitive on the international market than they would have been had they been using an unhindered market-based floating exchange rate.

Trump's trade manifesto spelled out the damage done to the US:

> Since China joined the WTO, Americans have witnessed the closure of more than 50,000 factories and the loss of tens of millions of jobs. It was not a good deal for America then and it's a bad deal now. It is a typical example of how politicians in Washington have failed our country.[13]

With loss of trade comes loss of money. By 2006, the United States had a record-breaking current account deficit of $816.6 billion (-5.9 per cent of GDP), more than double the deficit in the trade of goods and services of $401.9 billion (-3.9 per cent of GDP) at the start of the millennium. China has a different story. From a minor trade surplus of $20.4 billion (1.7 per cent of GDP) in 2000, it has since soared to a peak current account surplus of $420.6 billion (9.9 per cent of GDP) in 2007. Sustained current account deficits and surpluses pose a significant risk to the global economy. Indeed, some believe China's rise was one of the catalysts for the 2008 financial crisis, as credit poured into the States, fuelling unsustainable consumption.

Trump saw rebalancing trade as a priority. 'We can't continue to allow China to rape our country, and that's what they're doing,' he declared at a rally in Indiana during the 2016 election campaign.[14] Speaking in the first presidential debate, he said 'nobody' in Obama's administration was addressing this economic threat.[15] He asked his economic advisers to draw up plans for punitive tariffs to level the playing field.

Liberals and free-trade-supporting Republicans scoffed at his protectionist instincts and warned of dire consequences if he started a trade war with the Chinese. 'A President Trump could destroy the world economy,' declared the editorial board of the *Washington Post*.[16] A doom-laden Larry Summers, Obama's director of the National Economic Council and Bill Clinton's Secretary of the Treasury, predicted a 'protracted recession within eighteen months' if Trump became President, labelling economic nationalism 'highly dangerous'.[17]

Biden was similarly scathing, still arguing in 2020 that no other nation in the world could catch up with America. Trump would not be deflected. In office, he did exactly what he said he would. What almost beat him was something odd: the fact that he got on rather well with President Xi.

In April 2017, the Chinese leader made an early visit to Mar-a-Lago. The chemistry between the pair was surprisingly good. Trump would later declare that they had 'developed a friendship'. He enthused, 'I think, long-term, we are going to have a very, very great relationship, and I look very much forward to it.'[18] It was classic Trump: the warm embrace that could quite quickly be followed by a kick in the guts.

Trump fired the first shots of his trade war in January 2018 with the washing machines and solar panel tariff, shortly followed by the levy on steel and aluminium. The dumping of millions of tons of Chinese steel on American and European markets had long been an international bugbear, sending prices into freefall in 2015. 'The fact is we weren't treated and haven't been treated fairly by other countries,' Trump said, in justification for the move.[19] At the tariff signing ceremony, he was joined by workers from the steel community. 'Steel is steel. You don't have steel, you don't have a country,' was how he put it.[20] Spontaneously, he invited workers at the plant to address the American people from the lectern.

Dustin Stevens from Kentucky told 25 million TV viewers:

Right now, we're running at 40 per cent capacity. Two years ago, we shut down 60 per cent of capacity when we had a downturn in the market. My father worked in the industry and worked at that plant for forty years, so this hits home for all of us. With these tariffs going into place, this gives us the ability to come at 100 per cent capacity and invest $100 million in our plant and over 300 some-odd jobs will be brought back to the communities so I would like to say thank you.[21]

For another worker, Ron Davis, it was already too late.

In 2009, my plant supplied a majority of the armour for the Humvees and all the vehicles in theatre. It's sad to say, because all these imports coming in our country, our plants will be idled in September. So, at one time our plant had 400 members. We will be down to about seventy-one. These tariffs definitely have an impact and maybe not for our plant but for the other plants out there. So, appreciate what you're doing.[22]

In a characteristic theatrical flourish, the President even challenged one employee to an arm wrestle – although the real wrangle he had just initiated was with one of the most powerful nations on earth.

It was too much for Cohn, Trump's director of the National Economic Council, who tendered his resignation. What came next was a full-blown tit-for-tat trade war, just as Cohn and others had feared. Less than a month after the steel tariffs, China imposed 25 per cent tariffs on 128 US products; the US responded the next day with 25 per cent tariffs on $50 billion of Chinese products, and so it went on. Eventually there were tariffs on over $550 billion of China's goods and on $185 billion of products from the US.

Experts lined up to warn Trump of the price ordinary Americans would pay. White House aides took to showing the President apocalyptic graphs and tables of economic indices in the hope of frightening him into changing course. To their exasperation, the President refused to be cowed. He was determined to force China to the table, however much it hurt. He firmly believed that the only way to do that was to use America's multi-billion-dollar consumer market as the bargaining chip.

Though Singham had reservations about Trump's strategy, he believes the President deserves credit for recognising that tariffs were the most powerful tool available to the US in its dealings with China. He said:

> What the Trump administration did understand was that you need to have a serious tariffication of distortion. You need to *use the tariff*. Because that's what the Chinese want – they want access to your market. It's the only thing you have that's leverage, and you need to deny it to them when they behave badly.[23]

The trade war is estimated to have cost the US between 0.3 and 0.7 per cent of GDP. However, for short-term pain, there was long-term gain. In January 2020, after a two-year trade war, the Chinese were ready to negotiate. Under a 'Phase One' deal they committed to buy an additional $200 billion-worth of US goods by 2021 and would begin to reduce tariffs on US products, while most US tariffs remained on $360 billion of Chinese goods. China also made a number of commitments to try to cut intellectual property theft, though whether these undertakings were worth the paper they were written on, given allegations of the regime's long history of dishonesty on this front, is doubtful.

Hot off signing the deal, Trump arrived in Davos for the fiftieth anniversary of the World Economic Forum, declaring that America's relationship with China was now all sweetness and light. 'Our relationship with China right now has probably never been better. We went through a very rough patch, but it's never ever been better. My relationship with President Xi is an extraordinary one. He's for China, I'm for the US, but other than that we love each other,' he told the gathered global elites.[24] The intention was to begin a second stage of talks with China for a more comprehensive deal, likely after the forthcoming election. Within weeks, all that would be derailed by 'the China virus'.

Amid the chaos of the pandemic, the international community began to wake up to the dangers associated with sticking your head into the dragon's jaws. When the Australians called for an independent inquiry into what happened in Wuhan, where the virus is thought to have originated, China threatened to boycott Australian goods. They had tried the same with Norwegian salmon in 2010, after the Nobel Peace Prize was awarded to the political prisoner Liu Xiaobo 'for his long and non-violent struggle for fundamental human rights in China'.[25]

Among world leaders, there was a belated realisation that anyone who crossed the Chinese state might find that supplies of vital imported goods, including medicines, dried up. In the UK, Prime Minister Boris Johnson launched 'Project Defend' in late May 2020, designed to ensure that the country would no longer be dependent on China for goods linked to the UK's critical national infrastructure. Others including Japan and India began exploring financial incentives to bring their manufacturing industries home.

At the time of writing, it is difficult to assess whether Trump's trade war had any positive long-term impact on the behaviour and ambitions of the Chinese regime. The US trade deficit has slightly worsened since the 2016 figure of $394.8 billion, to $480.2 billion, although with China it remained level at just under $330 billion. The figure is not as bad as it looks: as a percentage of GDP, it is around -2.2 per cent of GDP. It remains to be seen whether the new trade deal has had a significant effect on the deficit. What has very clearly changed is political attitudes towards China around the world. The Indian government, for example, announced that it was making 461,589 hectares of land available, an area double the size of Luxembourg, for businesses that wanted to leave China. Not only was it an easy opportunity for foreign direct investment for India but it would also reduce India's own dependence on its neighbour. In July 2020, the Japanese Ministry of Economy, Trade and Industry announced that eighty-seven businesses would receive just over $500 million to help them move their production lines from China in order to secure their supply chains. Thirty of the firms would move production to south-east Asia, while the remaining fifty-seven would return home to Japan.

Trump's recognition of the Chinese regime as a threat to US interests will outlast his presidency. Not only are other nations starting to wean themselves off Chinese supply chains but there is also a growing bipartisan consensus on the issue in the US. During the Democrats' primaries in 2020, presidential hopeful Senator Cory Booker exclaimed, 'The Chinese have been taking advantage of this country and other nations on Planet Earth … We need to take them on. We need to fight them.'[26] Even Joe Biden took to standing behind a podium that read 'Buy American' during his election campaign.[27] They had derided Trump's economic nationalism in 2016. By 2020, imitation had become the sincerest form of flattery.

11

BLITZKRIEG – TRUMP AND CHINA, PART TWO

Billionaires and businesses with bottomless pockets often make wacky investment decisions. The rapper Kanye West bought his wife Kim Kardashian a hologram of her deceased father. Mike Tyson acquired three white Bengal tigers, and Michael Jackson built his Disney-themed Neverland Ranch, filling it with fairground rides. When the CEO of telecommunications giant Huawei, China's largest privately owned company, sat down to think about how the firm's spanking-new headquarters in Guangdong Province might look, he let his imagination run wild. With a budget of $1.5 billion, this would be a company headquarters like no other. The new office buildings for 25,000 workers would be in the form of twelve replica European cities, linked together by a Swiss-style tram system. One minute workers could be in Paris, the city of love, the next they could cross a replica of Hungary's Freedom Bridge and enter the Italian cities of Verona or Bologna. As these lavish plans demonstrated, Huawei, a company that had started small and expanded by drastically undercutting rival telecoms firms, was flying high. Thanks to hefty state subsidies, and an allegedly flexible attitude to intellectual property, it had become the world's largest mobile phone supplier. As global mobile networks transition from the 4G mobile network to 5G, it was in prime position to exploit the opportunity. In short, it seemed unstoppable.

Then Trump became President, and Huawei had a spectacular problem on its hands. Trump was under no illusion about how the Chinese state might benefit from Huawei's involvement in the roll-out of 5G, and he was not going to give the company a free pass.

The new generation of wireless technology was very different to 3G, which had paved the way for smartphones, and 4G, enabling faster browsing. 5G was far more ambitious. At a basic level, it was around ten times faster than its predecessor, and more than 1 million devices could be supported in one square kilometre, compared to just 60,000 under 4G.

The most exciting opportunities it presented related to the scope for connectivity with other devices, with all the associated implications for artificial intelligence. With 5G, multiple devices would be able to interact with each other: fridges would be able to order food on their own; autonomous cars would become a reality as vehicles could transmit to antennae on traffic lights; and drones would be able to deliver goods straight to front doors. It promised to unlock the full potential of the so-called 'Internet of Things': the ability to transfer data without requiring human-to-human or human-to-computer interaction.

All this raised huge privacy, and indeed security, questions. Within a very short space of time, businesses responsible for the new infrastructure would have access to a wealth of highly sensitive data, as well as the power to cripple other organisations – or even whole countries – by disabling parts of the network. That information and power could fall into the wrong hands. Hostile states and non-state actors were already capable of using the internet and mobile phone network as a hybrid warfare tool. The switch to 5G dramatically increased this liability – especially if one company had too much of the market.

This, in a nutshell, was what worried Trump, and many others all over the world, about Huawei, which was set to dominate the 5G market. 'Very dangerous,' was the President's verdict.[1] What worried him was that other political leaders did not seem to get it.

Central to the security concern was China's National Intelligence Law. It stipulates that any organisation or citizen must 'support, assist and cooperate with the state intelligence work in accordance with the law'.[2] The fear was that this would allow a regime's spy agencies to exploit Huawei technology to build backdoors into the critical infrastructure of other nations. Huawei's CEO, Ren Zheng-fei, has categorically denied that any of this will happen, but among those familiar with the regime's modus operandi, such assurances carry no weight.[3]

After all, when the government of Pakistan hired Huawei to set up its surveillance systems, the company found a way to sneak Wi-Fi-transmitting cards into CCTV units. Republican Senator Tom Cotton, a Trump ally, has spelled out what this could mean for American forces based in countries where Huawei has tentacles in critical national infrastructure. Speaking to the Commons Defence Select Committee, he explained:

Our fighters in England are armed with precision-guided munitions by ground crews using special lanyards shipped from the United States. Those lanyards are transported by shipping companies operating on standard commercial networks. If that network includes Huawei 5G equipment, it could give PLA [Chinese state] hackers a window into our military logistics operations, including shipping manifests for those lanyards. Hackers could then redirect or cancel the shipments, making it impossible to load these weapons and putting fighter crews in our missions at dangerous risk.[4]

In other words, through Huawei, the Chinese could hamper a British war effort.

A second concern relates to theft of intellectual property. Chinese companies were notorious for this criminal activity, routinely crushing competitors by stealing and copying their designs. This saved a fortune in research and development, allowing Chinese companies to sell goods cheaper. So far from frowning on such behaviour, the Chinese state actively encouraged corporate espionage. Overseas companies hoping for a slice of China's 1.4-billion consumer market were quite likely to be required to enter 'partnerships' with Chinese firms, which involved handing over their intellectual property, before being allowed to operate in China.[5] Trade secrets were also acquired through cyber-attacks and old-school espionage. The associated costs of IP theft to the US economy were phenomenal: at least $250 billion a year and perhaps as much as $600 billion in counterfeit goods, pirated software and the theft of trade secrets.

Huawei itself had acquired 5G technology with suspicious speed and ease. Indeed, the US Department of Justice has accused it of running a bonus scheme to reward employees who obtained confidential information from competitors. At the time of writing, US prosecutors are investigating evidence that the company has stolen technology from no fewer than six rival firms since 2000.

Proving all this will not be easy, not least because the victims of Chinese intellectual property theft are often more afraid of the consequences of speaking out than they are of the hit to their business.

While Trump wanted to take this on, his personal rapport with Xi sometimes threatened to throw him off course. According to Bob Woodward's *Fear*, in August 2017, on the eve of the announcement of a US crackdown on industrial espionage, the President suddenly demanded the removal of all references to China from the text. Bewildered officials eventually managed to find a form of words that was both acceptable to him and did not make a nonsense of his own policy.[6] This was the flip-side of his ability to do business with almost anyone. The tendency to make it personal could be a strength, but it could also weaken his hand.

As Sino–US relations deteriorated over the coronavirus crisis, the line from the Trump administration began to toughen. 'If you are an American adult, it is more likely than not that China has stolen your personal data,' warned FBI director Christopher Wray at the Hudson Institute in early July. 'We've reached a point where the FBI is now opening a new China-related counterintelligence case every ten hours. Of the nearly 5,000 active counterintelligence cases currently under way across the country, almost half are related to China,' he added.[7] A fortnight later, Secretary of State Mike Pompeo would order China to close its consulate in Houston for 'stealing' intellectual property.[8] There were particular fears that China-linked hackers were targeting American laboratories researching Covid-19.

Workers at the consulate were given just seventy-two hours to clear the premises. In scenes reminiscent of the Cold War, they were seen emptying their files into bins in the courtyard and setting them alight. Asked if more embassies would close, Trump replied, 'It's always possible.'[9] In response, the Chinese ordered the US to close its consulate in Wuhan.

As much as all this was about money, it was also about power. 'We cannot allow any other country to out-compete the United States in this powerful industry of the future,' the President proclaimed in a press conference about 5G in April 2019. 'The race to 5G is a race America must win, and it's a race, frankly, that our great companies are now involved in. We've given them the incentive they need. It's a race that we will win.'[10]

The Chinese President saw the issue in similar terms. His 'Made in China 2025' initiative is a state-led industrial policy designed to make China dominant in global high-tech manufacturing. To US Attorney-General William Barr, the Chinese were pursuing a form of 'economic blitzkrieg ... an aggressive, orchestrated, whole-of-government (indeed, whole-of-society) campaign to seize the commanding heights of the global economy and to surpass the United States as the world's pre-eminent technological superpower'.[11]

Speaking in Michigan, Barr said that 'Made in China 2025' seeks to put China in the lead in the air, on land, in the sea, in robotics, in aviation, in electric vehicles and in many other technologies. Backed by hundreds of billions of dollars in subsidies, it poses a real threat to US technological leadership. 'It is clear that the PRC [People's Republic of China] seeks not merely to join the ranks of other advanced industrial economies, but to replace them altogether,' he said.[12]

Under Trump, as Mike Pompeo has put it, the US has 'stopped pretending Huawei is an innocent telecommunications company that's just showing up to make sure you can talk to your friends'. In a series of speeches designed to warn US voters about the nature of the threat, in summer 2020, Pompeo said, 'We've called it what it is – a true national security threat – and we've taken action accordingly.'[13]

In May 2019, Trump used an executive order to prevent the use of Huawei equipment by US companies. Across the Atlantic, however, the UK government did not seem to grasp the risk. Anxious about the cost of falling behind in the race to roll out the new technology, first Theresa May and then her successor, Boris Johnson, were ready to let the firm in. Dozens of Tory MPs repeatedly tried to make the government see sense, but ministers continued to argue that the increased productivity that the Chinese telecoms supplier offered – purportedly worth as much as £126 billion to the economy – offset any danger.

Only when Trump stepped in did that change. In a dramatic raising of the stakes, he signalled that the future of the so-called Five Eyes intelligence sharing network, between the US, the UK, Australia, Canada and New Zealand, was in question. Australia and New Zealand fell into line fairly quickly. While the UK government dithered, Trump ratcheted up sanctions on Huawei, introducing measures to prevent companies using US technology to produce components for the Chinese firm. It hit Huawei's semiconductor supply chain and raised fears in the UK that the company would turn to less secure suppliers of mobile chips. A Whitehall source conceded:

> We think the new sanctions slapped on Huawei by the US basically mean that no US intellectual property can be used in the

manufacture of Huawei's chips. This means the bits of kit they get from Taiwan and elsewhere, which we think are full of good US stuff, will be cut off from them from the autumn. They're likely to turn to cheaper, less secure, local stuff instead. There's next to no chance we could say it's safe enough to use in 5G. It changes the calculation completely.

Trump's new sanctions did the trick. In London, Culture Secretary Oliver Dowden admitted that the measure would hamper Huawei's ability to supply new equipment to the UK.

'It is a fact that the US has introduced additional sanctions on Huawei and as the facts have changed, so has our approach,' a sheepish Dowden admitted, adding that the government had taken the decision that there should be no new Huawei equipment from the end of 2020. The UK government would also set out a timetable 'to exclude Huawei completely by 2027, with an irreversible path implemented by the time of the next election'.[14]

Huawei was out of UK 5G provision, and it was down to Trump. Standing outside the White House, the President took the credit.

We convinced many countries, many countries – and I did this myself for the most part – not to use Huawei, because we think it's an unsafe security risk. It's a big security risk and I talked many countries out of using it. If they want to do business with us, they can't use it.[15]

He was right. He had forced the British government into a humiliating climbdown. Huawei had lost another international partner.

• • •

The USS *Decatur* is a 505ft destroyer that sails under the motto 'In Pursuit of Peace'. On 30 September 2018, she was making her way through the South China Sea on freedom of navigation exercises close to the Gaven Reef of the Spratly Islands, when an equally large ship appeared on the horizon. It was a Chinese destroyer. It crept closer and closer, until it was right alongside the USS *Decatur*. Then, the Chinese vessel surged ahead to a distance of just 45 yards from the *Decatur*'s bow.

The *Decatur* was forced to manoeuvre to prevent a collision. Had the two ships collided, many sailors could have been killed. This was a highly aggressive show of Chinese naval strength.

China's military power is growing exponentially to match the country's economic might and technological prowess. Trump's National Security Strategy acknowledged that the state is building the most capable and well-funded military in the world, 'after our own'.[16]

While the People's Liberation Army has long been one of the biggest employers in the world, historically, the Chinese Navy has been weak. Now, the fleet is growing. In the first three years of the new millennium, China launched only 31,800 tons of new naval vessels, a fraction of the 229,200 tons launched by the United States. By 2015–17, there had been a dramatic shift. For the first time, Chinese production of new naval ships overtook that of the US. To the alarm of US naval chiefs, new Chinese tonnage increased to 374,200 tons during that period, relative to 181,300 tons for the US. In other words, China had made almost double the amount of new ships by weight, or 'displacement', as it is known.

The incident involving the USS *Decatur* was just one among many acts of Chinese naval aggression in the South China Sea. Armed with torpedoes, the *Decatur* was able to get by relatively unscathed – weapons were never likely to be fired – but other ships have been less fortunate. Defenceless Vietnamese fishing boats are known to have been rammed and sent to the seabed. Such behaviour is linked to China's spurious claims to sovereignty over 90 per cent of the crowded sea lanes of south-east Asia, in what is known colloquially in the region as the 'Cow Tongue' and in the international community as the 'Nine-Dash Line'. The strange name is an allusion to the shape of the territorial claim, which sweeps as far as 1,200 miles southwards from China's shores. It encompasses the contested Spratly Islands and Paracel Islands and brazenly ignores the 200-nautical-mile Exclusive Economic Zones of the surrounding nations of Vietnam, Brunei, Malaysia, Indonesia and the Philippines.

In September 2015, President Xi stood in the White House Rose Garden alongside Barack Obama and hotly denied that China was trying to commandeer huge stretches of water over which it has no justifiable claim. 'China does not intend to pursue militarisation. China and the United States have a lot of common interests on the issue of South China Sea. We both support peace and stability of the South China Sea,' he claimed.[17]

This was nonsense. Despite a judgment handed down by the Permanent Court of Arbitration in The Hague, ruling that China's occupation of the Spratly and Paracel islands contravened the UN Convention of the Law of the Sea, the regime proceeded full speed ahead with the development of military infrastructure on artificial islands. The Asia Maritime Transparency Initiative, which monitors these developments, noted that at some point between September and November 2016, China also began to construct surface-to-air missiles on the Subi Reef. Similar installations have also appeared on Mischief Reef, the largest of the seven artificial islands in the Spratlys and the one nearest the Philippines, and on Fiery Cross Reef. A total of 1,379 acres have been reclaimed by China at Mischief, which now has a two-mile runway and hangar space for at least twenty-four combat aircraft, all completed in 2016. Just a year earlier, the reef had been underwater. Now it is a fully functioning military outpost.

Amid mounting tensions between the Chinese Communist Party and the West over Covid, US Secretary of State Mike Pompeo released a statement labelling Chinese actions in the South China

Sea illegal. For the first time, he spelled out America's position on China's 'Nine-Dash Line'. 'We are making clear: Beijing's claims to offshore resources across most of the South China Sea are completely unlawful, as is its campaign of bullying to control them … The PRC's predatory world view has no place in the twenty-first century.'[18]

That evening, *The Times* reported that the UK was drawing up plans to send an aircraft carrier through the South China Sea, exercising international freedom of navigation rights. Two squadrons of F-35B Lightning II jets, two Type 45 destroyers, two Type 23 frigates, two tankers and helicopters would make up the rest of the carrier strike group. The double announcement from the US and the UK was a warning but did not amount to anything that would encourage the regime to alter its behaviour. It seems unlikely that anything other than sanctions will work, and even those may have limited effect. To date, the US has only targeted a small number of companies and individuals that have supported the Chinese military in the construction of artificial islands.

Of course, Chinese territorial aggression is not confined to the South China Sea. While the world was distracted by the coronavirus pandemic, the regime was quietly pushing into the north-western Indian province of Ladakh. The move attracted little attention, unlike the regime's crackdown on democratic protests in Hong Kong. The concern for the US is that Taiwan is next on the list. Sitting roughly 100 miles off China's eastern coastline, the island represents the final safe haven for the Chinese nationalists who had fought and lost to the Communists in the 1949 civil war for control over China after the Second World War. The Communists of the People's Republic of China claim Taiwan as rightfully theirs under the 'One China' policy. This is grudgingly accepted by most world leaders. Not Trump. He was ready to risk a diplomatic rift with China by underlining his support for the Taiwanese regime. In a highly symbolic move, as President-elect, he took a call from the

Taiwanese President, becoming the first occupant of his position to talk to Taiwan's President since Jimmy Carter broke off diplomatic ties in 1979. When David Cameron met the Dalai Lama in 2012, bilateral relations were frozen for over a year. But China's response to what Trump knew was a very provocative move was surprisingly measured. In an act of deference to the new President, a mere 'official complaint' was registered by the Chinese regime.[19]

Trump did not consistently match his principled resistance to the One China policy with sustained measures that might have proven a real impediment to the regime. Nonetheless, he was considerably more favourable towards Taiwan than previous administrations had been. Congress passed a number of pro-Taiwan Bills, and the US sold some $22 billion-worth of weapons to Taiwan across the four years. In August 2020 Alex Azar, Secretary of Health and Human Services, became the most senior US official to visit the island in four decades. These gestures were well received by the Taiwanese, with more than 40 per cent expressing support for a second Trump term, versus 30 per cent hoping for a Biden victory. Subsuming Taiwan remains a key strategic objective for the Chinese regime. If they succeed, their growing navy can divert resources from the 100 miles that make up the Straits of Taiwan and can look straight across the Pacific at the US.

'China must and will be united,' President Xi told Chinese Communist Party members in the Great Hall of the People. It was January 2020. Within three weeks, Wuhan, a city of 11 million people, would be sealed off from the world in a frantic attempt to contain the spread of a deadly new respiratory virus. It was no surprise to China observers that the country that inflicted this disaster on the rest of the world recovered from its effects far faster than its competitors, and the regime has been able to pursue its geopolitical agenda under the cover of Covid to full effect.

Xi does not hide the scale of China's geopolitical ambitions, nor the state's readiness to realise its vision by force. Reuniting China is, Xi claims, 'an inevitable requirement for the historical rejuvenation of the Chinese nation in the new era'. He has said, 'We do not promise to renounce the use of force and reserve the option to use all necessary measures.'[20]

When Trump entered the White House, liberals had dismissed him as an 'isolationist' and 'economic nationalist' who would represent a danger both to the US and to global stability. In fact, he can claim the moral and political centre ground on China. His economic nationalism stood in the way of theirs, at the very least slowing the pace of the great Chinese takeover. He had correctly identified the most pressing threat to global stability – a menace shrugged off or ignored by previous administrations. In an interview with *Frontline*,[21] Steve Bannon concludes, 'Trump will be known, I think, in hindsight, for China and the courts.'*

In just four years, he changed the global narrative on China. When he failed to win a second term, of all those who celebrated, the Chinese state had most reason to be delighted and relieved. He had challenged unreasonable Chinese trading practices; curbed the expansion of Huawei; and challenged China's flagrant violations towards the international rules-based order, particularly in the South China Sea. As we have seen, other nations are now following America's lead by excluding Huawei and bringing supply chains home – or, at least, out of China's clutches. If Biden keeps up the pressure, the race for global pre-eminence will no longer be a coronation and the US may be able to maintain its stature as the world's leading superpower.

Under Trump, an unpredictable US President who had underlined his support for the Taiwanese, President Xi did not throw caution to the wind. Under Biden, annexation does not seem beyond the realms of possibility. For now, the US can continue to use Taiwan as a thorn in China's side.

---

* This is a reference to Trump's appointments to the Supreme Court.

12

LEAVE NO MAN BEHIND – TRUMP'S ATTITUDE TO NATO AND THE MILITARY

When a new CEO takes over a business, they will always look for low-hanging fruit – quick wins, if you like. Trump saw very early on that defence procurement was the lowest-hanging fruit of all: huge sums of money being spent on long-term contracts, and therefore huge potential savings. Deals made years ago, which had survived purely as a result of inertia, were ready to be ripped up and renegotiated. It played right into his skillset. His approach to defence was not just about saving money; it was about patriotism and making sure allies shared the burden of making the world a safer place. All this played into the great respect American voters have for their servicemen and women – a beautiful added bonus.

When Greece was on the verge of bankruptcy, the Prime Minister was forced to abandon all pride and beg other European nations for help. Standing by the sea in a remote Aegean fishing village, George Papandreou made a desperate plea. His country's economy was a 'sinking ship', he said, and he no longer had any other option than to seek an international bailout. 'It is vital for our nation to submit an official request to our partners in the European Union to provide us with financial support,' he announced bleakly.[1]

It was April 2010, and Greece's budget shortfall stood at a

catastrophic 15.6 per cent of GDP – more than five times the EU limit. The financial package that would be required to keep the country afloat was in the order of $330 billion. To secure the cash from Brussels and the IMF, the Greek government would have to impose drastic austerity measures in almost all areas of government spending.

Facing crippling tax rises, wage cuts and a critical shortage of essential goods, including medicines, people were already rioting. In the months that followed, there would be mass protests and violent clashes between demonstrators and police. The government had no choice but to press ahead with swingeing cuts. One area remained relatively unscathed, however: defence. For all the nation's woes, ministers were determined not to slash the budget for the armed forces. Reflecting on all this from afar, what annoyed Donald Trump was the fact that so few other European countries had the same attitude to defence spending.

Greece has a long history of investing in its armed forces, not least because defending 227 inhabited islands is expensive. Nazi occupation during the Second World War left long-lasting scars, contributing to a profound sense that the nation must never again allow itself to become vulnerable. On Crete, the largest island in Greece, gun ownership is rife. It is not unusual for Cretans to declare proudly that their antique weapons 'killed real Germans' during the war. The perceived threat from Turkey is a particular source of anxiety, because of the proximity of a number of Greek islands to the Turkish coastline. Kastellorizo in the Dodecanese is considered most vulnerable. Lying just a mile from the Turkish shore, it is within easy grabbing distance and has long been a source of tension between the two countries.

At the time of the Greek financial crisis, the government was spending 2.6 per cent of GDP on defence – considerably more than most European countries. Indeed, to its great credit, the government never let defence spending drop below the 2 per cent of GDP recommended by NATO throughout its economic troubles. At the time, it was one of just four countries out of twenty-eight member states to meet or exceed the minimum recommended amount.

The 2 per cent target had been set by NATO members in 2002. Though the figure was non-binding, the idea was to ensure that each state contributed fairly to collective defence systems. Article 5 of the NATO Treaty, which states that an attack on one member state should be treated as an attack on all member states, was a kind of insurance policy, and the 2 per cent spending on defence was the premium. In theory, leaders of all member states recognised that it would be unfair to expect one or two countries with strong armed forces to underwrite the protection of nations that did not bother investing in their own defence. In practice, however, there were plenty of free riders: by 2010, the only other nations meeting the 2 per cent pledge were France, the UK and the United States.

By 2014, this was starting to rankle. At a NATO summit in Wales, member states reaffirmed their commitment to achieve the 2 per cent pledge by 2024 – a time frame that was too generous to act as a spur for change. By the time Trump was elected, Greek defence spending stood at 2.41 per cent – higher than such spending in the UK. France had fallen below the threshold but had been replaced by Estonia and Poland, two countries that were becoming increasingly nervous about Russia's aggression. While the number of nations now meeting the minimum recommended commitment had risen by one since 2010, the overall percentage of GDP being spent on defence by European nations had fallen from 1.63 per cent to 1.44 per cent. Despite Russia's brazen annexation of Crimea from Ukraine in 2014, most NATO member states continued to assume that future wars would be discretionary, and that they could simply opt out. For decades, conflicts had only been in far-flung places like Iraq and Afghanistan, and political leaders in many NATO member states struggled to make the connection between sporadic terror attacks in their countries and the malign activities of rogue states and their proxies in the Middle East.

Trump did not share this analysis. He recognised the changing nature of warfare and the growing threat to the West from hostile regimes, and he could see that the failure of other political leaders to take this seriously was significantly weakening the alliance. His view – shared by defence chiefs and military experts across the West – was that NATO, which was established in the aftermath of the Second World War to protect members from the Soviet Union, needed to adapt to stay relevant and effective in an era of cyber-attacks, suicide bombers and the weaponisation of space. While he was determined to boost US military spending, he did not see why American taxpayers should be expected to subsidise others who were not paying their way. 'President Obama and Hillary Clinton have also overseen deep cuts in our military, which only invite more aggression ... from our adversaries ... Our adversaries are chomping at the bit,' he warned on the campaign trail in September 2016.[2]

As the leading economy in Europe, Germany was one of the worst offenders. Not only was the government failing to spend the recommended amount, but defence spending as a percentage of GDP had actually fallen from 1.35 per cent in 2010 to 1.2 per cent in 2016. With some 36,850 US soldiers still stationed in the country, a throwback to the Second World War, successive German governments simply did not see the need to provide their own manpower.

By contrast, America continued to prioritise the defence budget. In 2016, the federal government spent $656 billion – some 3.56 per cent of GDP – funding an armed forces of 1.35 million servicemen and women and a further 865,000 in reserve. In an indication of its firepower, the US has some 6,000 battle tanks (at the time of writing, the UK only has 227, around half of which are in storage and could not immediately be deployed) and ten aircraft carriers. Other NATO members spent a combined total of $255 billion and an average of 1.44 per cent of GDP on defence. The US was therefore spending 2.5 times more than everyone else put together.* With

---

* Defence spending figures for the US and NATO are at 2016 prices and sourced from NATO's database.

its tiny population, Iceland does not even have an armed forces. Trump's view was that this state of affairs was patently unfair.

As the Republican primary contest drew to a close in March 2016, he posted a shocking message on social media: 'NATO is obsolete,' he declared.[3] The tweet sent European military chiefs into a tailspin. Trump had hung a giant question mark over the future of the system that acted as the single greatest deterrent to the territorial ambitions of hostile and rogue states. Did he really believe that the most successful defence alliance in history was no longer fit for purpose? If so, what did that mean? Might America even withdraw from NATO? At this stage of his presidential campaign, Trump was still a relatively unknown quantity: anything seemed possible. The best hope among military planners in NATO member states was that this most unusual of presidential candidates, whose many qualities did not include great eloquence, had – to put it diplomatically – 'misspoken'.

A week before his inauguration, Trump clarified his comments. 'I said a long time ago – that NATO had problems. No. 1 it was obsolete, because it was, you know, designed many, many years ago. No. 2 – the countries aren't paying what they're supposed to pay. I took such heat, when I said NATO was obsolete,' Trump told the *Times* newspaper. To the relief of defence chiefs across Europe, however, the President-elect went on to stress that NATO was still 'very important' to him.[4] A few months later, in April 2017, he came full circle, declaring in a meeting with NATO Secretary-General Jens Stoltenberg at the White House that the alliance was in fact 'no longer obsolete'. The pair had had what Trump called 'a productive discussion about what more NATO can do in the fight against terrorism' – one of the President's chief concerns – and he had emerged satisfied.[5]

The immediate crisis was over, but Trump was not retreating from his basic position on the iniquity of American taxpayers bankrolling European defence. This made for one of the most awkward

– but arguably productive – NATO summits in the recent history of the alliance.

In the run-up to the gathering in Brussels in late May 2017, there was continuing concern over the President's failure to endorse the principle of Article 5. Speculation mounted that he would finally express his commitment to the mutual-aid pledge at the event, providing nervous military planners with some comfort as to his position. Instead, as he put it himself, he was 'very, very direct' with European political leaders. In place of the usual public platitudes and highly choreographed 'family photos', Trump barged in – literally elbowing the Prime Minister of Montenegro out of his way in his haste to position himself front and centre of the group snapshot – and proceeded to publicly berate the twenty-three member states that did not pay their way.[6] They owed 'massive amounts' as a result of their long-term failure to contribute their fair share, he declared, and it was simply not fair on American taxpayers.

Standing outside the gleaming NATO headquarters, European political leaders looked stony-faced as he took them to task. He declared:

> Over the last eight years the US has spent more on defence than all other NATO countries combined. If all NATO members had spent just 2 per cent of their GDP last year, we would have had another $119 billion dollars for our collective defence and for the financing of additional NATO Reserves.[7]

Despite his stark warning, he did not impose any deadlines – allowing some countries to hope that the problem would go away. Some political leaders even sought to blame him for the collective failure to reform the alliance. 'What we are currently experiencing is the brain death of NATO,' argued France's President Emmanuel Macron ahead of NATO's seventieth anniversary in November 2019. Annoyed that Washington had failed to tell its European partners that the US was withdrawing from north-eastern Syria, Macron told *The Economist* that Europe needed to start considering itself as a geopolitical power or risk losing control of its destiny.[8]

His intervention backfired. Trump himself labelled the comments 'nasty' and 'very disrespectful', and NATO Secretary-General Jens Stoltenberg leapt to his defence.[9] 'The US is increasing investments in Europe with more troops, more exercises. The reality is that we do work together. We have strengthened our collective defence. Any attempt to distance us from North America risks not only weakening the alliance, the transatlantic bond, but also weakening Europe,' Stoltenberg said. Turkey's President Erdoğan went so far as to claim that it was in fact Macron who was 'brain dead'.[10]

In the end, Trump's uncompromising message got results. Delivering such a stark speech to allies at his first NATO summit cannot have been a comfortable experience, but as a direct result of his intervention, European countries are now contributing billions more dollars to collective defence. Since 2016, every single NATO member has increased its defence spending as a percentage of GDP. When the US is excluded, spending among other member states increased from 1.44 per cent of GDP in 2016 to 1.78 per cent in 2020. The number of members meeting or exceeding the 2 per cent commitment now stands at ten out of thirty. Even Germany has increased its budget to 1.57 per cent in 2020.

'The reality is that – not least because it has been so clearly conveyed from President Trump that we need fair burden sharing – Allies are stepping up,' Jens Stoltenberg acknowledged, at NATO's seventy-year celebrations in London.[11]

Moreover, the existential threat that hung over the alliance after he labelled it 'obsolete' reinforced the urgent need to modernise the organisation. Defence chiefs already knew that it was hopelessly ill-equipped to deal with modern threats. Trump's call to arms accelerated plans to strengthen its defence and deterrence posture, with significant progress made in recent years.

'NATO today remains more capable of defending its members from Russian aggression than it was in the fifteen years before Trump took office,' argues Robert Blackwill in an assessment of Trump's foreign policy written in his capacity as the senior fellow for US foreign policy at the Council on Foreign Relations.[12] Heather Conley, a European foreign policy expert at the Center for Strategic and International Studies, has described Trump's 'laser-like focus on NATO's defence spending' as an 'important catalyst' for NATO countries to move towards their 2024 commitment.[13]

In the unfortunate event that a member state needs to call on the protection available under Article 5, perhaps the President will get the credit he deserves.

• • •

It may sound like a new brand of razor blade, but the Common-Hypersonic Glide Body (C-HGB) is a cutting-edge weapons system designed to give warfighters the edge over the enemy. Travelling at more than five times the speed of sound, highly manoeuvrable and capable of operating at varying altitudes, it can strike targets that are hundreds or even thousands of miles away in a matter of minutes. Successfully tested at the Department of Defense's Pacific Missile Range facility in Hawaii in March 2020, it represents the future of American military capability.

At around $17 million apiece (defence company Dynetics was awarded a $351.6-million contract to build twenty), these weapons don't come cheap, but, then again, the Department of Defense can afford it. In 2020 alone, it set aside some $2.6 billion to develop such missiles, a budget that would rise to $3.2 billion the following year. A further forty tests are planned for C-HGB, with a view to bringing the new weapons system into operation by 2023.

Surrounded by allies and two great oceans, the US has always been at a great geographic advantage when it comes to security

– save for during the Cuban Missile Crisis. 'If you won the lottery, and were looking to buy a country to live in, the first one the estate agent would show you would be the United States of America,' is how writer Tim Marshall describes the prime location in his best-selling book *Prisoners of Geography*.[14] Nonetheless, defence chiefs in less friendly nations are also investing in hypersonic weapons and other revolutionary warfighting technology that threatens to erode American military superiority. Huge armies, tanks and aircraft carriers are no longer enough.

Early in his presidential campaign, Trump expressed concern over the type of weapons potentially hostile regimes, including Russia and China, are acquiring and pledged to ensure the US military was properly funded. 'I'm going to build a military that's going to be much stronger than it is right now. It's going to be so strong, nobody's going to mess with us,' he proclaimed on the campaign trail in October 2015.[15] His foreign policy would be 'peace through strength', he said, three words that should always be 'at the center' of America's approach to an uncertain world.[16]

In an uncharacteristically sobering speech at a campaign rally in Greenville, North Carolina, in September 2016, Trump set out his defence priorities, from a roadmap to beat ISIS to securing America's border. However, his greatest emphasis was on the state of the country's armed forces. 'It is so depleted. We will rebuild our military.'[17]

He didn't hang about. On entering the White House, he boosted the defence budget by an extraordinary 10 per cent – several times the budget increase typically secured by the most effective defence secretaries in the UK. 'I am sending Congress a budget that rebuilds the military, eliminates the defence sequester, and calls for one of the largest increases in national defense spending in American history,' was how he put it, in his first State of the Union address to Congress in February 2017.[18] The extra money took the defence budget to $700 billion, allowing the armed forces to grow for the first time in seven years with an extra 20,300 personnel. There was also a 2.4 per cent pay rise for America's servicemen and women, and some $23.8 billion was set aside to build fourteen new ships. 'Our Navy is at about the lowest point in terms of ships that it has been in over 100 years,' Trump had argued.[19] In 2020, the last request for defence spending under Trump reached $738 billion, with $34.7 billion directed towards shipbuilding – the largest maritime spending investment in twenty years.

Trump's investment in the armed forces marked the end of a long era of cuts under Obama, who had continually slashed the budget since 2010. 'Obama shortchanged our military; this fixes us,' was how Speaker of the House Paul Ryan summed it up.[20] Trump's commitment to revitalising America's armed forces was enshrined in the 2018 National Defense Strategy. It had a three-pronged approach: strengthening alliances and attracting new partners; reforming the department for greater performance and affordability; and building a more lethal force. Defense Secretary Mark Esper, who succeeded General Mattis, promised to invest in 'game-changing' technologies to allow the US to maintain its 'long-held battlefield overmatch, which is more important than ever, as China and Russia continue to modernize their militaries and pursue advantages in emerging technologies like artificial intelligence and 5G'.[21]

During the Trump administration, spending on research and development by the Pentagon increased by 50 per cent. Money was ploughed into eleven modernisation initiatives, from the hypersonic missiles to a transition towards greater use of artificial intelligence. 'From hypersonic weapons to multi-domain warfare to soldier lethality, Trump has done more to rebuild US warfighting capabilities than any president since Reagan,' writes Loren Thompson, the COO of the Lexington Institute.[22]

While Trump was ready to give the military the funds it required, he was determined that defence companies did not exploit his largesse. He took a particular interest in a contract with defence giants

Lockheed Martin for hundreds of F-35 stealth jets, the single biggest weapons procurement programme in the world. Trump fully appreciated the capabilities of the fighter jets, describing F-35s as 'the most sophisticated aircraft in the world', but he never liked the trillion-dollar price tag, vowing well before he entered the White House to drive down the cost. The F-35 programme was 'out of control', he tweeted in December 2016; billions could, and would, be saved on this 'and other' military purchases.[23]

Trump was as good as his word. In a highly unusual move for a US President, he personally led renegotiations over the contract, inviting Lockheed CEO Marillyn Hewson to his Mar-a-Lago resort to explain why the aircraft were so expensive. As a direct result of his intervention, Lockheed knocked hundreds of millions of dollars off the price.

Writing about the episode in *Forbes* magazine, Thompson says:

> Trump was convinced he could do better than the Obama administration had done, because he thought he was a better negotiator. It turns out he was right. In the first production lot that his team negotiated, Lot 10, the price-tag for the Air Force version fell nearly 8 per cent to $94 million. The cost of other variants for the Navy and Marine Corps fell too, cumulatively saving taxpayers $500 million on just that one production lot. Lockheed Martin hadn't been planning to cut the price that far that fast, but after Trump's criticism of the program it decided to sharpen its pencils and find savings fast.[24]

Thanks to what Thompson describes as 'a skillful combination of threats, persuasion and compromise', Trump pushed the cost of each F-35 below the list price for an empty jetliner. 'The president promised he would deliver billions of dollars in savings, and that is what he has done', Thompson writes, arguing that Trump deserves much more credit for this effort.

•   •   •

When American troops left Somalia in 1994, it seemed vanishingly unlikely they would return. A well-intentioned effort to intervene in the civil war of a famine-ravaged country thousands of miles away had ended in catastrophe and the loss of many US soldiers, prompting weeks of soul-searching about the wisdom of non-essential, risky military operations in far-flung places.

The terrible events of 3 October 1993 were dramatised in the blockbuster Ridley Scott movie *Black Hawk Down*, which showed how a mission in the Horn of Africa went horribly wrong. During an attempt to capture two senior aides to a local warlord who had been terrorising UN peacekeepers in the area, Somali forces shot down two American helicopters, prompting a desperate battle to rescue the survivors. A total of nineteen US soldiers were killed in the crash and ensuing firefight, and a further seventy-three were wounded. In a cruel humiliation for the United States, the bodies of some of those killed in the so-called Battle of Mogadishu were dragged through the streets by baying local civilians. In one of the most memorable scenes in Scott's film, US troops file out in convoy to rescue comrades from the crash site, to a soundtrack entitled 'Leave No Man Behind'. The episode shocked American voters, leading to the withdrawal of troops months later and a period of retreat from overseas military engagement, including during the Rwandan and Balkan genocides.

In March 1994, the front page of the *New York Times* declared that the 'Last of the US Troops' had left Somalia. Fast-forward to the Obama administration, and US troops were back again as part of the war on terror. Several countries, including the UK, were supporting an allied campaign to combat the rising threat posed by Islamic extremists al-Shabab, which in 2013 had launched a deadly terror attack on a shopping mall in the Kenyan capital, Nairobi. By 2020, the number of 'official' US troops in Somalia had reached 700, and drone strikes were on the rise. In one of his final acts as President, Trump ordered these troops to be brought home, or removed from the direct line of fire to neighbouring countries, by 15 January 2021. The deadline was just five days before Biden's inauguration, symbolising his own determination to 'leave no man behind' when he left the White House.

His decision came less than a fortnight after the death of a veteran CIA officer in Somalia. The agent had been a member of the CIA's paramilitary division. Announcing the withdrawal, the Department of Defense declared that the US would still be able to conduct targeted counterterrorism operations in Somalia but would be based elsewhere in the region, where they would work with partner forces 'to maintain pressure against violent extremist organizations operating in Somalia'.[25] Trump preferred the surgical precision of drone strikes to risking American lives.

Somalia was the last of a series of US troop withdrawals during the Trump administration, from Afghanistan and the Middle East. In December 2018, he began scaling back the US presence in Syria where 2,000 troops had been based. At the time of writing, only around 500 remain to guard oil wells. In Afghanistan in February 2020, a historic peace deal between the US and the Taliban saw the US committing to scale back the American troop presence from 14,000 personnel to 8,600 in the first 135 days after the deal, with the intention to undertake a complete withdrawal within fourteen months. At the time of writing, just 5,000 troops remain. Finally, in Iraq, the US maintained a presence of around 5,200 troops in order to help the Iraqi government manage ISIS. In September 2020, it was announced the US would be handing over their military base in Taji to the Iraqi security forces, allowing 2,000 US soldiers to leave the country.

Frustrated with Germany's continuing reluctance to meet NATO's recommended defence spending, in summer 2020, Trump also announced the withdrawal of nearly 12,000 US troops from

German bases. 'We don't want to be the suckers anymore … We're reducing the force because they're not paying their bill. It's very simple,' Trump declared in justification, describing the country as 'delinquent'.[26] Some 6,400 troops would return to the US, and a further 5,400 would be redistributed across other NATO members, including Italy, Poland, Belgium and Spain.

Trump's announcement triggered a storm of protest in both the US and Europe. Defence experts claimed the move would weaken NATO; weaken America's position in Europe; and damage US relations with an important ally. Critics pointed out that several US military bases in Germany act as staging posts for operations in the Middle East, eastern Europe or Africa. Towns around US military bases in Germany stood to suffer a huge financial hit: in Grafenwöhr in Bavaria, the presence of American troops is estimated to be worth $800 million. Nearly half of the town's 6,500-strong population have jobs dependent on the base.

Swayed by these arguments, as Trump prepared to leave office, Congress blocked the withdrawal. It remains to be seen whether Biden will reverse the plan. Either way, Trump had sought to honour his pledge to put America First. Bolstering the German economy was never part of the remit.

Faced with a rising China, a resurgent Russia, a nuclear North Korea, irate Iranian mullahs and potential threats that are completely unknown, a wake-up call was required. Through a reinvigoration of NATO and investment into key military technologies, Trump has ensured that the US and the Western world are as prepared as they possibly can be for the challenges that lie ahead.

PART THREE

OVERSEAS MISSIONS

13

PEACE, MAN
– NO NEW WARS

Former Republican Senator Bob Corker said Trump is 'setting the country on the path to World War III'.[1] He wasn't the only one sounding dire warnings.

Stands to reason, right? Trump, the hard-nosed businessman who didn't care who he offended and deployed bully-boy tactics, would surely bring about the apocalypse. Stands to reason that other countries would want to start a war with him and, of course, vice versa. The thing is it never happened. Indeed, Trump was the only President for forty years who didn't bring the country into a new war. He also pulled troops out of various conflict zones and somehow managed to negotiate peace agreements across the Middle East with Israel. Even Little Rocket Man Kim Jong-un came to the table. Why did Trump do all this? Simple really – wars are not just bad and sad; they are really expensive. They are not good business.

Behind the Oval Office desk, looming over Trump's left shoulder like a *consigliere*, hung a portrait of former President Andrew Jackson. Within weeks of arriving in office, Trump travelled to Nashville, where he laid a wreath at Jackson's grave to honour what would have been his 250th birthday. Along with Churchill, here was a historic figure Trump admired. Why? Because this early-nineteenth-century politician was a bit like Trump himself. Jackson was America's seventh President and the first who appealed directly to the masses in an election. In 1824, he had won the popular vote by 10.2 per cent, securing fifteen more electoral college votes than his nearest rival John Quincy Adams. However, two other candidates, William H. Crawford and Henry Clay, prevented him from achieving the majority he required. It was put to the House of Representatives to decide who should become President. The Speaker of the House just happened to be Henry Clay, and, in a series of murky backroom deals, he secured John Quincy Adams the presidency, in return for which he was appointed Secretary of State.

Like Trump, Jackson had been seen as an outsider, as a result of his heritage as the son of Scotch–Irish immigrants in South Carolina – a background that marked him out from the usual north-eastern political elite. Jackson's supporters labelled the outcome of the election a 'corrupt bargain' struck in the Washington political swamp. Next time round, in 1828, Jackson's campaign slogan would be 'Andrew Jackson and the Will of the People'. This time, he beat Quincy Adams in a landslide, with 178 electoral votes to eighty-three.

It was Steve Bannon who told Trump about this early populist. Recounting his first ever meeting with the future President in 2010, Bannon said: 'I give him the history of populism with Andrew Jackson, William Jennings Bryan, and bring him up to date with Ross Perot, everything like that. He turns to me and goes, "That's what I am."'[2] Bannon's own interest in Jackson's influence originated with the work of academic Walter Russell Mead, whose book, *Special Providence*, identifies four types of American foreign policy practised by US statesmen. Russell Mead called his four schools of foreign policy 'Wilsonian', 'Hamiltonian', 'Jeffersonian' and, last but by no means least, 'Jacksonian'. At an event at the London think tank Chatham House, Mead described Jacksonians as

nationalists who are not interested particularly in converting the

rest of the world, whether it is to Christianity or democracy or
anything else, they would like to leave the rest of the world alone,
as long as the rest of the world doesn't bother the United States.
Jacksonians were horrified by the threat that the Soviet Union
seemed to pose to the American way of life and to American security. So, they were ready to fight the Cold War, they were ready
to pay taxes, they were ready to be drafted, they were ready to
fight wars. This was Trump's base.[3]

Bannon would subsequently send a text to Mead saying that he was
the reason that Jackson hung in the Oval Office.

Jacksonians are still ready to fight wars, but only if such wars
are clearly in the interests of the United States. If the real mission
is regime change to promote ideological reform, count them out.
These were the principles that underpinned Trump's foreign policy
– as a result of which, he would become the first President since
Carter not to start any new wars.

• • •

The President of the United States is widely seen as the most powerful person on earth, but he does not have the free rein that many
imagine. It comes as something of a shock to new occupants of the
White House to discover just how little they can do, particularly
in relation to domestic policy. America's Founding Fathers had
worried about the effects of an overbearing central government and
deliberately constrained presidential power. Enshrined in the US
Constitution are checks and balances between the executive (the
presidency), the legislature (Congress) and the judiciary (the Supreme Court), which frequently combine to frustrate a President.
Congress has sole power to legislate, though some of its powers are
devolved to state level. Meanwhile, in the domestic arena, Presidents
are limited to attempting to influence the passage of legislation via

allies in Congress, or to deploying the presidential veto to stop bills they dislike. If the White House and Congress are controlled by the same party, they generally seek to co-operate. However, it is not unusual for the House of Representatives and the Senate to be controlled by the opposition party to the presidency, creating a divided government. In the 2018 mid-term elections, for example, the Republicans lost control of the House to the Democrats, further limiting Trump's room for manoeuvre. It tends to be the case that the President loses control of both the House *and* the Senate in the mid-term elections of their second presidential term. The last President to have Congress on their side for their entire time in office was Jimmy Carter in the 1970s. What this means is that Presidents can arrive in the White House with all sorts of grand visions, but Congress has a habit of ensuring the grand visions remain nothing more than that. A classic way for the House of Representatives and Senate to frustrate the White House is to refuse to pass funding for the federal government. Lose the House, and you lose the money. When disagreements arise, this can cause a government shutdown where federal employees are furloughed and public services grind to a halt.

Where Presidents can flex real muscle is over foreign policy. The President represents the United States abroad and, as 'Commander-in-Chief', is the ultimate chief of the US military. When it comes to military matters, Congress tends to follow the President's lead. The last time Congress officially declared war was to join the Second World War in 1941 and 1942. Instead, it now agrees to resolutions authorising military force. As Commander-in-Chief, the President can unilaterally authorise military action for a maximum period of ninety days. Thereafter, they require permission from Congress. Given the constraints associated with domestic policy, Presidents often shift their focus abroad. George H. W. Bush launched Operation Desert Storm to retake Kuwait from Saddam Hussein and sent troops into Somalia. Bill Clinton provided military assistance in Kosovo. Bush Jr went further, with long campaigns in Iraq and Afghanistan. Despite his Nobel Peace Prize, Obama increased troop numbers in Afghanistan (though would later bring some troops home); launched military strikes in Libya; and called on Hosni Mubarak and Bashar al-Assad to stand aside in Egypt and Syria, respectively.

Some commentators have gone so far as to suggest that to win a presidential election in America, you need to start a war for a 'rally round the flag' effect. James M. Lindsay of the Brookings Institution wrote in 2003, 'The invasion of Iraq has validated a basic rule of American politics: Americans rally round the president in times of national crisis.'4 Bush received a thirteen-point poll rise in the first month of the Iraq War, and there was a 24-point increase in people who were satisfied in the direction the country was going. Since US independence in 1776, the country has been embroiled in some military engagement or other for 225 out of 244 years.

Trump was different. On the campaign trail in 2016, he repeatedly argued that 'great nations do not fight endless wars'.5 He was determined to bring an end to what he saw as 'disastrous' foreign adventures. The rallying cry was 'America First'. This President would not waste any more time pitching up in the world's worst trouble spots and trying to sort out other people's problems.

His attitude resonated with many American voters, particularly the families of the 1.4 million men and women who serve in the US armed forces, many of whom could not see why so many resources continued to be directed at seemingly hopeless foreign adventures. They might not have been able to put a figure on it, but most knew that, since 2001, wars in the Middle East had cost American taxpayers trillions. (A study by Brown University put the figure at $6.4 trillion.) They were also keenly aware of the number of American lives lost on these missions: a total of 4,431 American fatalities in the Iraq War and a further 31,994 wounded in action. The war in Afghanistan resulted in the deaths of another 2,219, with some 20,093 wounded in action. None of these conflicts ever seemed to be fully over, and the number of dead and wounded Americans continued to mount. Since the initial operations in Iraq and Afghanistan were wound up in 2010 and 2014 respectively, an additional 194 US servicemen and women had been killed and 803 wounded. Voters wondered what it had all been for.

According to Mead, these wars were the legacy of 'Wilsonians' and 'Hamiltonians':

> At the end of the Cold War in 1990, the American schools of foreign policy split. Hamiltonians and Wilsonians are all excited about the opportunity to build a new world order. Now that the bad guys have gone, the Soviets are off the field, now we can really build a global commercial system based on free trade, now we can really push democracy around the world. I think it is fair to say that the George H. W. Bush administration, the Clinton administration and the George W. Bush administration all shared this basic world view and saw American foreign policy as attempting to build a global order on these fundamental principles.[6]

Such objectives were well intentioned, but Trump's view, widely shared among his base supporters, was that it only left chaos and devastation.

Trump's early experiences dealing with the consequences of high-risk overseas military operations reinforced his aversion to any unnecessary military engagement. Just nine days into his presidency, US Navy special operator senior chief William 'Ryan' Owens became Trump's first war casualty, following a botched operation in Yemen. A month later, Ryan's wife Carryn was invited to attend the State of the Union Address. Genuinely moved by the agony of the Owens family, Trump paid glowing tribute both to the lost serviceman and to the wider armed forces.

'The challenges we face as a nation are great. But our people are even greater, and none are greater or braver than those who fight for America in uniform,' he said. 'Ryan died as he lived: a warrior, plus a hero battling in opposition to terrorism and securing our country … Ryan's legacy is etched into eternity.'[7] The applause among the Congressmen lasted nearly two minutes. To lighten the mood, Trump joked, 'And Ryan is looking down right now, you know that, and he is very happy because I think he just broke a record!' The cost of conflict had a human face. Ryan and Carryn Owens were *not* just numbers on a Department of Defense spreadsheet. Trump ended by saying, 'We will never forget Ryan.' It was more than just a platitude.

Three years later, at the 2020 State of the Union Address, Trump invited Amy Williams, the wife of another serviceman, and her two young children to attend the speech as guests of honour alongside First Lady Melania. Amy's husband, Sergeant First Class Townsend Williams, was seven months into his fourth deployment to Afghanistan, and Trump wanted to acknowledge the sacrifice he and his family were making.

War places a heavy burden on our nation's extraordinary military families … Amy works fulltime and volunteers countless hours helping other military families … Amy's kids haven't seen their father's face in many months. Amy, your family's sacrifice makes it possible for all of our families to live in safety and at peace and we want to thank you.[8]

The President had a surprise for the family. In the kind of theatrical flourish Trump understood well after years of working on the hit TV series *The Apprentice*, Sergeant Williams came bounding down the stairs to his waiting family, a moment that moved even the most hardened Congressmen and women in the room.

All this was more than just showmanship: Trump was inconsistent on many issues but not when it came to the folly of foreign wars.

Despite numerous provocations from hostile states, he managed to avoid committing more US lives and additional taxpayers' money to new foreign interventions. To some, this is his greatest achievement. As Tim Stanley of the *Telegraph* has written, 'Trump, we were told, was a reckless lunatic. He turned out to be more peaceful than Obama.'[9]

Of course, these days, wars are not just fought by soldiers, sailors and fighter pilots using conventional weapons; as we have seen, Trump was not averse to starting trade wars and propaganda wars. What he gets precious little credit for is the positive contribution he made on the world stage. Since leaving the White House, Bannon has been at pains to correct widespread misunderstanding about Trump's approach to foreign policy.

In May 2018, he told a security conference in Prague, 'They've claimed that President Trump is an isolationist, and one of the big worries in Europe among our allies and our partners is a retreating America. Nothing could be further from the truth.' Under Trump, Bannon stressed, America was ready to step into overseas conflicts 'where it is in the vital national security interest of the United States; let's underline vital.'[10]

As we shall see, Trump did consider it vital to continue the war on terror; to bear down on the development of nuclear weapons in Iran and North Korea; to play an active role in improving stability in the Middle East; and to reinforce totemic 'red lines' on the use of chemical weapons. His very tangible contributions to these international efforts are routinely glossed over and ignored by those who find it impossible to imagine that anyone they instinctively disliked so much might be capable of doing anything positive on the world stage.

14

RED LINES – TRUMP'S RECORD IN SYRIA

The bloody war in Syria is now all but over, after President Bashar al-Assad's regional allies helped crush opposition to his regime. In the course of the conflict, some 400,000 people were killed and another 70,000 died due to a lack of basics such as food, clean water and healthcare. A further 1.9 million were wounded. As Assad's forces murdered their compatriots and obliterated Syria's wealth, institutions and infrastructure, the West largely stood by.

Agonising as it was to watch, the decision not to get involved was probably wise. I am not sure that adding Western firepower to the mix would have made anything better, and it might well have made things considerably worse. However, as Trump recognised, there is no point in the international community laying down 'red lines' if they are never enforced. Personally, I think he got the immensely difficult balance between the principle of non-intervention on the one hand and the responsibilities associated with being the most powerful country in the world on the other just about right.

In the early hours of 21 August 2013, rockets began raining down on the Syrian suburb of Ghouta in eastern Damascus. This was not unusual in a civil war that had been raging for two and a half years. What was strange was the sudden warning from loudspeakers on local mosques, urging residents to evacuate their homes immediately. Many had gone to sleep that night fearing they might not wake up the following day. Those who were too frightened to drift off were the fortunate ones: they were able to make a quick exodus. Many of those who did not get out paid a terrible price.

The surface-to-surface Soviet rockets slamming into the Ghouta suburb that morning contained the deadly nerve agent sarin. It is twenty times more lethal than cyanide and was the chemical of choice for the cult that targeted a Tokyo subway in 1995, gassing thirteen people. Being heavier than air, the nerve agent sinks to the ground, making it particularly lethal to victims who are literally lying low. In Syria, those who ingested the deadly substance started foaming at the mouth, and their organs began to disconnect from their central nervous system. Toxic nerve agents don't discriminate: fighter, father, mother, grandparent, baby – it didn't matter. The gas got them in the same way.

Nobody knows quite how many Syrians died that morning, which is of course how the perpetrators wanted it. While estimates range from a couple of hundred people to just under two thousand, US intelligence suggests the figure was around 1,400. Médecins Sans Frontières, a medical NGO, reported that at least 3,600 were treated for symptoms in the three nearby hospitals. Not content with presiding over hundreds of thousands of civilian deaths by barrel bombs, shelling and machine-gun fire, President Bashar al-Assad of Syria had – not for the first time – resorted to the use of chemical weapons against his own people.

Exactly a year earlier, on 21 August 2012, Obama had warned the Syrian regime that such behaviour was an atrocity too far. The systematic murder of innocent people by conventional means had not been enough to persuade Western leaders to get embroiled in the desperate civil war, but the use of chemical weapons was a 'red line', Obama declared, and would change his calculus if used.[1] If nobody did anything, dictators around the world would know America was ready to turn a blind eye to such crimes. The credibility of the international rules-based order was at stake.

Across the Atlantic, David Cameron was appalled by the evidence emerging about the scale and impact of the 2013 attack and was keen to confer with Obama over how to respond. For his own part, he was ready to support the US in a joint show of strength, launching ballistic missiles from submarines in the Mediterranean. He could use executive powers to do so without consulting Parliament, sending a short, sharp message to Assad – though it would not make him popular with MPs. The alternative was to gather more evidence against the Syrian regime, attempt to drum up international support and invite MPs to endorse military strikes. Both leaders knew that anything involving the United Nations was likely to be hopeless. With Russia a permanent member of the Security Council with the right to a veto, the idea of securing a UN resolution was wishful thinking.

In his memoir, Cameron angrily recalls how Obama left him hanging as he dithered over how to respond to the attack. 'For four days I waited for him to call back. Four days. A large-scale chemical attack happened mid-week, and the leaders of two of the world's biggest military powers and the world's (supposedly) strongest two-nation alliance didn't speak until the weekend,' Cameron writes, testily.[2]

As the clock ticked, the window for an early strike closed. While a frustrated Cameron was waiting for Obama's call, the President was trying to persuade UN Secretary-General Ban Ki-moon to extricate his twenty chemical-weapons inspectors from Syria. They had arrived three days earlier to investigate another incident, and there was a concern that if the situation escalated, their safety could not be guaranteed. Ban Ki-moon dug in, and they stayed until 31 August.

Meanwhile, Labour and Conservative MPs, nervous about the UK's potential participation in military action, were becoming increasingly vociferous in their demands for a parliamentary vote. As pressure from the Labour Opposition and his own backbenches mounted, Cameron took the drastic step of recalling Parliament from its summer break. It was a fatal error, resulting in an extraordinary humiliation for the Prime Minister. The combination of a bungled Whips operation and the skulduggery of opposition leader Ed Miliband, who had led Cameron to believe that Labour would support the strikes, resulted in the defeat of the motion to launch airstrikes in Syria by 285 to 272 votes. However Obama decided to respond to the attacks, America's closest military partner would not be adding its firepower.

US warships were now in position, but Obama was wobbling. The day before the UK vote, he had received a letter from senior Republican Congressmen arguing that engaging the US military in Syria without 'prior congressional authorization' when there was no direct threat to the US would be an abuse of his position.[3] A separate letter from John Boehner, Speaker of the House of Representatives, urged Obama to 'make the case to the American people and Congress for how potential military action will secure American national security interests, preserve America's credibility, deter the future use of chemical weapons, and, critically, be a part of our broader policy and strategy'.[4]

Obama did have the necessary powers: as we have seen, under the War Powers Resolution of 1973, US Presidents have the authority to launch military action for a period of ninety days* without congressional sign-off. However, the President was nervous.

Spooked by Cameron's defeat in the House of Commons and facing pressures of his own, he pivoted, telling aides it was probably right to seek authorisation for military action from Congress. For too long, Presidents alone had jumped from war to war, he argued, and if Congress endorsed strikes, everyone would have a stake and military actions would have greater credibility. Obama's national security adviser, Susan Rice, was appalled. She knew that

---

* Sixty days of military action and thirty days to withdraw.

Congress would never vote in favour. She could see that the President risked undermining himself and setting a dangerous precedent by voluntarily relinquishing the power associated with his status as Commander-in-Chief. Obama had made up his mind, however. On 31 August, he stood in front of the White House in the Rose Garden and told the American people, 'While I believe I have the authority to carry out this military action without specific congressional authorization, I know that the country will be stronger if we take this course, and our actions will be even more effective.'[5]

As Cameron recalls in his memoirs, 'A British PM had lost a vote, and an American President had lost his nerve.' He would later describe Obama's handling of Assad as 'the thing I regret most about his entire presidency'.[6]

• • •

In the days that followed, the Obama administration tried to win over Congress, but it was increasingly apparent that securing support for strikes would require expending huge political capital. It was against this backdrop that Obama made what, with the benefit of hindsight, seems an elementary mistake. Desperate to be seen to be doing something in response to Assad's outrage, he did a deal with the Russians that would all come to naught.

The opportunity arose at the G20 summit in St Petersburg, which took place on 5 September. There, Obama had a private conversation with Vladimir Putin, in which the Russian President agreed to throw his weight behind moves to reduce Assad's chemical-weapon stockpiles. Keen to establish a warm-water port at the Syrian coastal city of Tartus, to house a Russian fleet in the open Mediterranean, Putin had been cultivating Assad, and there was an increasing Russian military presence in Syria.

In his memoir, Ben Rhodes, Obama's deputy national security adviser, tells how Obama suggested they co-operate:

For years, Obama had proposed that the United States and Russia work together to address the threat from Syria's chemical weapons stockpile; for years, Russia had resisted. This time, Obama again suggested working together to remove and destroy Syria's chemical weapons. Putin agreed and suggested that John Kerry follow up with his Russian counterpart.[7]

With this new way out, on return from St Petersburg, Obama abandoned his attempt to secure Congressional approval for military strikes, telling the nation that he preferred to pursue a 'diplomatic path'.[8] Kerry, then Secretary of State, was subsequently dispatched to meet his Russian counterpart, while Obama continued talking direct to Putin.

On 14 September, the deal was revealed. Syria's chemical weapons would have to be destroyed or removed by mid-2014. The White House claimed it represented an 'important, concrete step toward the goal of moving Syria's chemical weapons under international control so that they may ultimately be destroyed'.[9] Kerry later suggested that the deal involved the elimination of '100 per cent of chemical weapons' in Syria.[10]

The regime duly opened the door to chemical-weapons inspectors from the Organisation for the Prohibition of Chemical Weapons. The team discovered 1,000 tons of Category One chemical weapons and an additional 290 tons of Category 2 material across twenty-one different sites. The substances were transported to the port of Latakia before being shipped to the Italian port of Gioia Tauro, where they were destroyed on a container ship owned by the US maritime administration.

It sounded too good to be true – and it was. The regime still had weapons stockpiles. Six months later, Putin, too, thumbed his nose at the international rules-based order with the annexation of Crimea from Ukraine. He too had no truck with 'red lines'.

• • •

Having sailed perilously close to the wind, Assad had got away with it – and it would not be very long before he did it again. This time, it was Trump's resolve that would be tested.

On 4 April 2017, Syrian warplanes dropped more sarin on the town of Khan Shaykhun in Idlib province. Between eighty and ninety people were killed and many hundreds injured. Those caught in the path of the chemical attack showed symptoms of redness of the eyes, foaming from the mouth, constricted pupils, blue facial skin and lips, severe shortness of breath and asphyxiation.

It was all horribly familiar. Evidently, the much-trumpeted elimination of chemical weapons from Syria had been a sham. Reluctant as he was to embroil America in foreign wars, Trump would not make the same mistake as Obama. According to numerous insider accounts of the White House during this period, he was galvanised by his daughter Ivanka. She was appalled by images of dying children and insisted he act. 'Years of previous attempts at changing Assad's behaviour have all failed, and failed very dramatically,' Trump declared, stressing that the resulting refugee crisis and destabilisation of the region posed a threat to America.[11] It was time to show Assad, and other tyrants who might consider gassing their own people, that the US would take a stand.

Trump's instinct was simply to take out Assad. According to Watergate journalist Bob Woodward, in a dramatic telephone call, the President told Secretary of State Jim Mattis the military should 'go in' and 'fucking kill' Assad, 'kill the fucking lot of them'. Mattis is said to have indicated his assent, before turning to a senior aide and saying, 'We're not going to do any of that.'[12]

Instead, defence chiefs drew up a range of possible responses. Back in 2013, when Trump was a private citizen and Obama was wrestling with the same situation, Trump had been scathing about the prospect of America 'going in'. Taking to Twitter, he labelled Obama 'very foolish' for considering an attack. 'If you do many very bad things will happen and from that fight the US gets nothing!'[13]

Now it was his responsibility, he felt very differently. The chemical attacks weighed heavily on him, and he took an uncharacteristic interest in the detail of the effects of nerve agents. There was a limit to how far he could go, however. Assassinating Assad would put the US on collision course with Russia and potentially other nations, including China and Pakistan. Trump had promised not to drag America into situations like this: he knew voters were sick of 'regime change' wars.

Instead, military chiefs suggested targeting the airbase from which the chemical-weapon attack had been launched. It would be struck by fifty-nine Tomahawk Cruise missiles, taking out Syrian jets, aircraft shelters, radar stations, air defence systems and fuelling stations. This was far more than Obama did in 2013, but, assuming sufficient care was taken to avoid harming any Russians in the process, it was not going to start a war. Caution was paramount: the Russians had a significant presence on the ground.

Fortunately, the operation went to plan. Following a successful strike with no Russian casualties, Secretary of State Rex Tillerson issued a statement declaring that the strike had been necessary to protect US national security:

> We do not want the regime's uncontrolled stockpile of chemical weapons to fall into the hands of ISIS or other terrorist groups who could, and want to, attack the United States or our allies. Nor can we accept the normalization of the use of chemical weapons by other actors or countries, in Syria or elsewhere.[14]

Tillerson also took aim at Russia, accusing Putin's regime of failing in its responsibility to uphold the letter and spirit of their joint deal in 2013. 'It is unclear whether Russia failed to take this obligation seriously or Russia has been incompetent, but this distinction doesn't much matter to the dead. We can't let this happen again.'

Trump's firm response was praised across the political divide.

It was, according to Democrat Senate Minority Leader Chuck Schumer, an 'appropriate', 'pinpointed, limited action to punish and hopefully deter Assad from doing this again'.[15] Nancy Pelosi, the Democrat House Minority Leader, echoed these views, describing it as a 'proportional response to the regime's use of chemical weapons'.[16] Trump was also supported by rival Republicans who had challenged him for the Republican presidential nomination, including Senator Marco Rubio, who said, 'President Trump has made it clear to Assad and those who empower him that the days of committing war crimes with impunity are over.'[17] GOP grandees, Senators Lindsey Graham and John McCain, who had been hostile to Trump in the past, made a joint statement, reading: 'Unlike the previous administration, President Trump confronted a pivotal moment in Syria and took action. For that, he deserves the support of the American people.'[18] Even Trump's staunchest media detractors were full of praise, with CNN host Fareed Zakaria describing it as a watershed moment. 'I think Donald Trump became president of the United States last night ... For the first time really as president, he talked about international norms, international rules, about America's role in enforcing justice in the world.'[19]

The decision to strike Syria had been made while President Xi Jinping of China was visiting Trump at Mar-a-Lago. Over the 'most beautiful piece of chocolate cake' that he had ever seen, Trump told Xi about the military action. 'Good, he deserved it,' Xi is said to have replied.[20] The red line that had been washed away by a vacillating Obama had been firmly reinstated.

• • •

For the purposes of this book, it would have been nice to be able to claim that thanks to Trump's decisive action, the Syrian regime never dared use chemical weapons again. Unfortunately, it's not as simple as that. Exactly a year after the first set of US strikes on

Syria, another attack on innocent civilians took place, this time in the city of Douma, which was assaulted by two Syrian helicopters with barrel bombs filled with chlorine. Approximately four dozen people were killed and hundreds more showed symptoms from the chemicals. Trump was appalled, describing the attack as 'SICK'. He tweeted:

> Many dead, including women and children, in mindless CHEM-ICAL attack in Syria. Area of atrocity is in lockdown and encircled by Syrian army, making it completely inaccessible to outside world. President Putin, Russia and Iran are responsible for backing Animal Assad. Big price to pay. Open area immediately for medical help and verification. Another humanitarian disaster for no reason whatsoever.[21]

It happened at a time of upheaval in the White House: the federal government was without a Secretary of State. Mike Pompeo was preparing for his confirmation hearing ahead of replacing Rex Tillerson, who Trump had fired via tweet on the 13 March: 'Mike Pompeo, director of the CIA, will become our new Secretary of State. He will do a fantastic job! Thank you to Rex Tillerson for his service! Gina Haspel will become the new director of the CIA, and the first woman so chosen. Congratulations to all!'[22] An aide had to inform Tillerson that he had been fired, the Secretary of State not being a Twitter user himself. H. R. McMaster was also on his way out, after it was announced nine days after Tillerson's firing that he would be leaving. His replacement as national security adviser, John Bolton, arrived just two days after the Syria attack. Adding to the chaos, Trump's personal lawyer, Michael Cohen, had his office raided by the FBI, while former FBI director James Comey was about to release a book that was likely to fuel the Russian conspiracy theory. Trump had more than enough to manage.

Trump's response this time round would be markedly different to 2017, not least because the UK and France were ready to help. This time, the strikes would be heavier, directed at three targets as opposed to one. They were a scientific research centre in Damascus, where it was believed chemical and biological weapons were developed, and two storage facilities west of the city of Homs. The total number of missiles fired was also increased from fifty-nine to 105. Neither Trump nor Theresa May, who had succeeded David Cameron as Prime Minister in 2016, would repeat the mistakes of their predecessors by seeking permission from legislators to act.

According to John Bolton, Trump was given five different options. He said Mattis presented his favoured options by categorising the options as 'low' and 'high risk' and then indicating his preferred low-risk options as 'ready to go'.[23] Bolton wanted to go further, arguing that, this time round, they should target other military assets or even destroy one of Assad's palaces. He believed the very reason everyone was back in the Situation Room was because the 2017 strikes 'had failed to establish conditions of deterrence in Assad's mind sufficiently powerful that he never used chemical weapons again'.[24] Mattis argued that preparations for more drastic action of this kind would take too long.

Once again, the missiles evaded Syria's air defences and hit their intended targets. America's allies had been brought into the fold to underline the importance of the international rules-based order. 'A perfectly executed strike last night. Thank you to France and the United Kingdom for their wisdom and the power of their fine Military. Could not have had a better result. Mission Accomplished!' was Trump's response.[25]

• • •

There was a limit to what Trump could have been expected to achieve in Syria. Taking office in 2008, three years before the civil war began, Obama had far more scope to change the course of events. By the time Trump became President, the situation in Syria had deteriorated beyond repair. It was estimated by the UN Special Envoy for Syria that around 400,000 had been killed by that point – nearly 2 per cent of Syria's pre-war population. A further 6.6 million civilians had fled the country and another 6.7 million were internally displaced. The only thing that would have made the situation much worse was direct conflict in Syria between two other states with a capable war-fighting ability. There was one policy, no-fly zones, that could have provoked exactly that. Who backed it? Hillary Clinton.

In the run-up to the presidential election in 2016, Clinton suggested that if she won, she would seek to impose so-called 'no-fly zones' over Syria. Seeking to big up her foreign policy credentials, in the third presidential debate, she said:

> I'm going to continue to push for a no-fly zone and safe havens within Syria, not only to help protect the Syrians and prevent the constant outflow of refugees, but to frankly gain some leverage on both the Syrian government and the Russians so that perhaps we can have the kind of serious negotiation necessary to bring the conflict to an end and go forward on a political track.[26]

By now, the Russians had a significant military presence in the region, making this a very risky proposal indeed. What if a Russian plane violated the no-fly zone? Clinton was asked by Fox News anchor Chris Wallace. Would she shoot the plane down? Not surprisingly, she did not respond.

Among military and intelligence personnel there were serious fears that a no-fly zone would only turn a kind of 'Cold War' between regional powers into a hot conflict between Russia and the United States. James Clapper, Obama's director of national intelligence, told an audience at the Council on Foreign Relations that he 'wouldn't put it past' the Russians to shoot down an American plane.[27] Similar warnings were also issued by defence chiefs.

Some weeks earlier, General Joseph Dunford, chairman of the joint chiefs of staff, told the Senate Armed Services Committee that for the US to control the airspace in Syria 'would require us to go to war against Syria and Russia … That's a pretty fundamental decision that certainly I'm not going to make,' he said.[28] As for Trump, his view was that such a strategy would result in 'World War Three'.

On the campaign trail, he told a crowd, 'You're going to end up in World War Three over Syria if we listen to Hillary Clinton. You're not fighting Syria anymore, you're fighting Syria, Russia and Iran, all right?'[29] There was already a precedent that miscalculations could occur in Syria, when a Russian jet was shot down by a Turkish F-16 in November 2015. Footage has also emerged of Russian armoured vehicles chasing and ramming a US convoy out in Syria in 2020. Clinton's idea was far too dangerous.

Clinton herself had been sceptical about a no-fly zone only three years earlier. In a speech to Goldman Sachs in 2013, she told financiers that Syria had 'very sophisticated air defense systems', which were getting even better thanks to Russian imports.

> To have a no-fly zone you have to take out all of the air defense, many of which are located in populated areas. So our missiles, even if they are standoff missiles so we're not putting our pilots at risk – you're going to kill a lot of Syrians. So all of a sudden this intervention that people talk about so glibly becomes an American and NATO involvement where you take a lot of civilians … then you add on to it a lot of the air defenses are not only in civilian population centers but near some of their chemical stockpiles. You do not want a missile hitting a chemical stockpile.[30]

Trump too was quite capable of contradicting himself. Before becoming President, he had urged Obama not to shout about his Syria strategy. He criticised the then President for signalling the potential airstrikes in 2013. 'Why do we keep broadcasting when we are going to attack Syria. Why can't we just be quiet and if we attack at all, catch them by surprise?' he tweeted.[31] Yet, in December 2018, Trump was guilty of the same, broadcasting his intention to withdraw the remaining 2,000 US soldiers from north-east Syria within thirty days following victory against ISIS. 'We have defeated ISIS in Syria, my only reason for being there during the Trump presidency,' he declared.[32]

The shift in US foreign policy under Trump would see the abandonment of the Syrian Democratic Forces (SDF) and Kurds who had led the fight against ISIS on the ground. The SDF had not been fighting on behalf of the US, as was sometimes suggested, but for their own freedom. The decision to withdraw sparked an uproar among even some of Trump's closest allies, with Jim Mattis submitting his resignation the very next day. 'My views on treating allies with respect and also being clear-eyed about both malign actors and strategic competitors are strongly held and informed by over four decades of immersion in these issues,' Mattis said in his resignation letter. 'We must do everything possible to advance an international order that is most conducive to our security, prosperity and values, and we are strengthened in this effort by the solidarity of our alliances.'[33]

Others to criticise the decision included Republican Senator Lindsey Graham who said, 'Withdrawal of this small American force in Syria would be a huge Obama-like mistake.'[34] In another tweet, he added, 'The confusion surrounding our Syria policy is making life much more difficult and dangerous for Americans in the region.'[35]

Trump's view was that Syria's allies, Russia and Iran, should do whatever heavy lifting remained. He declared:

Getting out of Syria was no surprise. I've been campaigning on it for years, and six months ago, when I very publicly wanted to do it, I agreed to stay longer. Russia, Iran, Syria and others are the local enemy of ISIS. We were doing there [sic] work. Time to come home and rebuild. #MAGA[36]

In the end, Trump would climb down by decelerating the withdrawal and leaving a few soldiers to guard oil wells in north-eastern Syria. Less than a year later, 1,000 troops would be redeployed to Iraq, where America's vital strategic interests were more worthy of protection.

According to Trump's special representative for Syria engagement, there was rather more to his long-term Syria strategy (or at least the strategy pursued by his administration) than met the eye. In withdrawing American troops from north-east Syria, the White House was not just pursuing a Jacksonian 'America First' policy – though that was a driving factor. The bigger picture was to tie Russia in knots. In May 2020, Ambassador James Jeffrey told the Hudson Institute that his job was to 'make Syria a quagmire for the Russians'.[37] Putin had long meddled in international politics simply to divide and undermine the various players. Now a US President was playing Russia at its own game.

A decade after the civil war began, Syria is still in ruins. Assad remains in power; the economy is in a state of collapse; and some 83 per cent of those who survived the regime's atrocities live in poverty. Thousands of people are on the breadline in refugee camps. Trump never wanted to get involved, and he did so on a point of principle in the face of bitter opposition from his strategy chief Steve Bannon, who repeatedly argued that it was not in America's interests to do anything at all. For Trump, genuinely moved by the suffering associated with chemical attacks, there was both a moral imperative and an obligation to assert his nation's place in the world. He refused to display the same 'weakness and irresolution' as Obama had shown during his administration.[38] Dictators in other parts of the world were on notice: under Trump, America would no longer ignore appalling human rights violations in other nations.

15

SHADOWS IN THE DARKNESS – TRUMP'S RECORD IN THE WAR ON TERROR

Since 9/11 and the declaration of the 'war on terror', successive Presidents have tried and failed to defeat the Islamic terrorists hell-bent on destroying the American way of life. It took ten years to find and kill bin Laden, only to leave a void filled by ISIS. Another six years of terror and beheadings followed. ISIS was dismantled and its leader killed within three years of the Trump presidency. It would seem the war on terror, for now at least, has been won.

For fourteen long years, America's most powerful non-nuclear weapon lay waiting for a suitable target. Quite where it was stored or how it was maintained as it gathered dust is, of course, top secret. What is known is that the so-called 'Mother of All Bombs' (MOAB) was so enormous that, rather to the chagrin of its creators, it was of limited use. At 30ft long and weighing 21,600lb, it could only be launched out of the back of a cargo plane – hardly the subtlest of delivery systems. With a blast radius of one mile either side of the explosion, it was the polar opposite of a precision strike. The original plan had been to use it to blow-up bunkers during the second Iraq War, but the conditions were never quite right. As time went by, it became an extremely expensive white elephant.

Curiously, the man who designed this formidable weapon was

a devout Christian. Albert Weimorts, who worked for the US Air Force Research Laboratory in Florida, started creating 'bunker buster' bombs in the 1990s after Iraqi leaders developed subterranean defence facilities impenetrable to conventional bombs. Apparently, the God-fearing teetotaller squared his deep religious faith with his day job creating killing machines on the grounds that his munitions would be used in the fight against evil – and perhaps even save some American lives.

Weimorts never lived to see the MOAB deployed – tragically, he died of a brain tumour in 2005 – but, in 2017, his creation finally came into its own. It was perfect for targeting a nest of ISIS fighters hiding out in an isolated cave complex in the mountains of eastern Afghanistan. Amid conditions of great secrecy, defence chiefs began readying MOAB to unleash hell.

When Trump arrived in the White House, the most pressing national security issue was ISIS in the Middle East. If left unchecked, the Islamic Caliphate would continue to spread, destabilising the entire region. As its power and wealth grew, so would its influence. The terror network had already spread its tentacles out of Iraq and Syria into the Taliban heartlands of Afghanistan. US Special Forces had been tasked with hunting down and neutralising these fanatics. Trump was deeply moved when one operative, Staff Sergeant Mark De Alencar, lost his life in a firefight while trying to clear Nangarhar Province of the enemy, the first fatality in Afghanistan of his administration. The President took the time to call De Alencar's widow, describing her late husband as an 'unbelievable hero'.[1]

A week later, in the same part of Afghanistan, the US military played the highest card in its deck. MOAB was finally being used. Trump did not have to personally authorise the detonation, but he had made it very clear that there should be no mercy towards ISIS. On 13 April 2017, less than three months into his presidency, the MOAB was loaded into an MC-130 cargo plane and dropped over a cave complex in Nangarhar. The mission was a resounding success.

A provincial spokesman in Nangarhar announced that over ninety ISIS fighters had been killed, including four commanders, clearing the way for US Special Forces and the Afghan army to safely manoeuvre their operations on the ground.

MOAB isn't just about raw strength. There is also a psychological dimension. Before the weapon was tested in the run-up to the Iraq War in 2003, then Secretary of Defense Donald Rumsfeld said:

> The goal is to not have a war. The goal is to have the pressure be so great that Saddam Hussein cooperates. Short of that, an unwillingness to cooperate, the goal is to have the capabilities of the coalition so clear and so obvious that there is an enormous disincentive for the Iraqi military to fight against the coalition.[2]

With the deployment of MOAB, American airpower was on full display. It was a powerful message to ISIS that the new occupant of the White House was serious about fulfilling his campaign pledges to eradicate them 'from the face of the earth'.

In pre-election presidential debates, Trump had promised to 'knock the hell out of ISIS'.[3] 'We are going to defeat ISIS. ISIS happened a number of years ago in a vacuum that was left because of bad judgment. And I will tell you, I will take care of ISIS,' he promised.[4] On another occasion, with typical use of the vernacular, he said he would 'bomb the shit' out of them.[5] And he did.

The choice of munitions was not the only change in strategy against ISIS. Again in April 2017, military rules of engagement were relaxed to give US troops more scope to strike the enemy and support allied Afghan forces. Under Obama, military commanders had been restricted to firing when they came under attack. The changes were designed to make it easier to launch rapid raids and airstrikes. It had a dramatic impact. In 2016, Obama's last year in office, 30,743 weapons were released during sorties in Iraq and Syria. Under Trump the following year, the number of strikes rose by almost a third.

Trump rarely uses words carefully, and when it comes to the war on terror, he has always been blunt. At a rally in Alabama, he suggested mosques across America should be kept under surveillance in an exhaustive effort to root out those who would harm the US. 'I want surveillance of these people, I want surveillance if we have to, and I don't care. Are you ready for this, folks? Are you ready?' he declared.[6]

Anticipating the backlash he would face for suggesting millions of ordinary Americans be treated as terror suspects, he told the crowd:

> They're going to make it such a big deal! They're going to make it so big. 'He said something so politically incorrect!' That's why we're going to hell because we're so politically incorrect! Such a big deal ... Such a big deal ... I want surveillance of certain mosques ok, if that is ok? I want surveillance. You know what? We've had it before and we'll have it again.

Trump didn't care if bleeding-heart liberals squealed. What mattered to him and his campaign team was the message he was sending to the many Americans who worried about terrorism, particularly of the homegrown kind: we are going to rid our country of this scourge. Trump also liked using the term 'radical Islamic terrorism'. It was a phrase the Establishment hated. It had been scrupulously avoided by both the Obama administration and Hillary Clinton's campaign, for fear it would spark allegations of Islamophobia. Obama preferred expressions like 'violent extremism', while Clinton tended to talk about 'radical jihadism'.[7] She stated:

> I have clearly said many, many times we face terrorist enemies who use Islam to justify slaughtering innocent people. We have to stop them and we will. We have to defeat radical jihadist terrorism or radical Islamism, whatever you call it – it's the same. But we cannot demonize, demagogue and declare war on an entire religion.[8]

In the second debate, Clinton also said:

> It's also important I intend to defeat ISIS, to do so in a coalition
> with majority Muslim nations. Right now, a lot of those nations
> are hearing what Donald says and wondering, why should we
> cooperate with the Americans? And this is a gift to ISIS and the
> terrorists, violent jihadist terrorists. We are not at war with Islam.
> And it is a mistake and it plays into the hands of the terrorists to
> act as though we are.[9]

Trump knew these subtleties were lost on millions of ordinary
Americans and saw no reason to beat about the bush. His inaugural
speech set the tone. 'We will reinforce old alliances and form new
ones – and unite the civilized world against radical Islamic terrorism, which we will eradicate completely from the face of the earth.'[10]
Speaking at the time, Trump's former deputy assistant Dr Sebas-
tian Gorka defended Trump's choice of words. 'They expected us
to dilute the verbiage. Radical. Islamic. Terrorism. Politico, did you
hear it? *New York Times*, did you hear it? *Washington Post*, CNN,
did you hear it? The President is not backing down,' he said.[11]

Naturally, there were cries of 'racism' from the left, but Trump's
plain-speaking approach went down well with swathes of voters
bewildered by the failure of the West to stop the killings, beheadings and terror attacks perpetrated by Islamic fundamentalists.
There was a growing frustration with a cycle of candles, prayers and
landmarks being illuminated in a nation's flag each time there was
an attack. Trump's rhetoric sounded like real leadership. Finally, a
politician was articulating how they instinctively felt about the way
the world's most formidable military power should respond to such
outrages. He made it all sound so simple. The question was whether
he would deliver.

• • •

The rapid rise of ISIS had caught America by surprise. The terror group had splintered from al-Qaeda in Iraq in 2006 before being forced underground by the surge of US forces in 2007. With the withdrawal of US troops from Iraq in 2011, however, ISI, as it was then known, began regrouping, exploiting the instability of the Syrian civil war to establish a new basis. Soon, the network would be rebranded the 'Islamic State in Iraq and Syria'.[12]

The organisation began fighting other rebel groups in Syria, driving them out of the city of Raqqa, where it established dominance. It was becoming increasingly dangerous, but, outside the region, it was still not widely recognised as a grave threat. In January 2014, Obama flippantly likened the new terror network to junior varsity basketball players posing as premier league professionals. He told the *New Yorker* magazine:

> The analogy we use around here sometimes, and I think is accurate, is if a jayvee team puts on Lakers uniforms that doesn't make them Kobe Bryant.* I think there is a distinction between the capacity and reach of a bin Laden and a network that is actively planning major terrorist plots against the homeland versus jihadists who are engaged in various local power struggles and disputes, often sectarian.[13]

Amateurs they may initially have seemed, but by that summer, the so-called 'junior varsity team' had seized the cities of Raqqa, Fallujah and Mosul in Iraq and Syria. By early August, the network was capturing land in northern Iraq, including the city of Sinjar, one of the largest settlements for the Yazidi people. At Sinjar, the Yazidi men were massacred; the women were sold as sex slaves. Over 200,000 fled the city with many heading into the isolated mountains for their own safety. The risk of hypothermia and starvation was on

---

* Kobe Bryant was a Los Angeles Lakers basketball player. He was widely considered one of the greatest basketball players of all time.

balance more appealing than the risk of subjection to the barbarism of ISIS fanatics, who were crucifying, raping and beheading their way across the Middle East. There was no longer any denying the scale of the threat the new organisation posed in the region.

On 7 August 2014, US fighter jets began bombing. However, it was not until the brutal beheading, on 25 August, of American journalist James Foley that the terror network achieved the global notoriety it sought. In an appalling video of his murder, a black-clad ISIS executioner condemned US airstrikes and warned that any aggression by America would 'result in the bloodshed of your people'.[14] The group warned that it had another US hostage, journalist Steven Sotloff, who would suffer the same fate as Foley if Obama refused to stop the strikes. A few weeks later, Sotloff was also beheaded. ISIS had replaced al-Qaeda as the terror network most feared by the West. Their capacity for evil, too, was not limited to the Middle East.

A month later, ISIS spokesman Abu Mohammad al-Adnani urged 'lone wolves' to launch attacks around the world against the West.[15] The war in Iraq and Syria was now arriving on our doorsteps, in the shopping malls and on the streets of the civilised world. The years that followed saw a grim succession of appalling terror attacks on innocent civilians in the West, including a siege at a Sydney café; a mass shooting at the offices of *Charlie Hebdo* magazine in Paris, following the publication of satirical cartoons of the Prophet Muhammad; and the use of a lorry to mow down a crowd on Bastille Day in Nice. The latter attack left eighty-six people dead and a further 434 injured.

When Obama's first presidential term began in 2008, almost 40 per cent of Americans worried about being a victim of terrorism, according to Gallup polls. It was just three years after the 7/7 attacks in London and not long after the US had poured more troops into Iraq to quell renewed insurrections. By the end of 2016, the percentage of people afraid had increased to 51 per cent, the highest since the immediate aftermath of 9/11. Despite success in the killing of bin Laden, Obama had failed to grip this crisis, presenting a clear opportunity for the new President.

• • •

On the face of it, Syed Rizwan Farook and Tashfeen Malik were a normal couple in their late twenties. They had a six-month-old baby and lived quietly in Southern California. Farook was born in Chicago and earned more than twice the national median wage as an environmental health specialist at the San Bernardino County Department of Public Health. A devout Muslim, he is thought to have met his wife Tashfeen while he was in Saudi Arabia for the Hajj pilgrimage in 2013. She had grown up in the Middle East but had returned to the Pakistani province of Punjab in 2007. Having studied pharmacy, she seemed committed to making it her career, but all that seemed to change when, in 2009, she began attending a madrassa with notoriously conservative views. When she met Farook in 2013, they began to engage in increasingly extremist online chat about martyrdom and jihad. None of this was picked up by intelligence agencies, and, a year later, in 2014, she was given a fiancée visa to come to the United States to marry Farook.

On the morning of 2 December 2015, Farook and Malik dropped their daughter off with Farook's mother. The couple then drove to the Inland Regional Center in San Bernardino, where many of Farook's colleagues from the Department of Public Health had gathered for a conference. He attended the event for a couple of hours before slipping out to meet his wife. On the table where he had been sitting, he left a rucksack containing a pipe bomb. Half an hour later, during a break in the programme, Public Health workers began filing outside for some fresh air. Waiting for them were Farook and Malik, armed with semi-automatic pistols and assault rifles. They began gunning down Farook's colleagues while a Facebook post announced Malik's allegiance to ISIS. The couple then forced their way inside the conference hall, firing off more rounds at helpless attendees before making their escape. One of the attendees notified the police that they suspected Farook had been behind the attack and plainclothes officers were immediately dispatched to the couple's property. Later that day, the couple attempted to flee their home, prompting a car chase and shootout in which they both died. Between them they had murdered fourteen innocent people and injured a further twenty-one, making it the deadliest terror attack in the US since 9/11 at the time.*

The attack came as the race for the Republican presidential nomination was stepping up. There had yet to be any primaries, and the field was still crowded with some fourteen hopefuls. Trump was convincingly in the lead, with most polls giving him a twenty-percentage-point advantage ahead of his closest political opponents, Senators Ted Cruz and Marco Rubio. Five days after the San Bernardino attack, he set out how he would deal with terrorism if he were to lead the country. The vetting process at the time was clearly not robust enough. Tashfeen Malik had navigated three background checks before her arrival in the US. Trump called for a 'total and complete shutdown of Muslims entering the United States until our country's representatives can figure out what the hell is going on!'[16] It was a stark contrast to Obama's pledge a few months earlier to bring 10,000 refugees from Syria to the United States.

Trump's comments sent the Establishment into a tailspin, sparking anger across partisan divides. In a bid to appeal to more moderate Republicans, Marco Rubio, the Republican Senator for Florida and Trump's rival, tweeted, 'I disagree with Donald Trump's latest proposal. His habit of making offensive and outlandish statements will not bring Americans together.'[17] The Democrat candidate, Bernie Sanders, was equally scathing: 'The US is a strong nation

---

* This would be surpassed six months later, in June 2016, by an attack at a gay nightclub in Orlando, carried out by a homegrown terrorist pledged to ISIS, where forty-nine people were shot dead.

when we stand together. We are weak when we allow racism and xenophobia to divide us. cc: @realDonaldTrump'[18] However, Steve Bannon has since defended Trump's comments, describing the intervention as a 'necessary jolt to the system'. He told viewers of *Good Morning Britain*:

> He was trying to get people to pay attention. This is what Trump does ... he is a disruptor. One of the reasons that he is a disruptor is to break through the noise to get people's attention. That's what he did then. He had a more moderate policy going forward. He was the one that had more outreach to the Middle East, and we are more engaged there now in a peaceful way, not going in with wars in Iraq.[19]

Democrats and the moderate Republican Establishment had hoped Trump didn't really mean it, but on arrival at the White House he made clear he was serious. He began his presidency with a barrage of executive orders – a shock and awe strategy to show he was going to get things done. No President has signed more executive orders in their first hundred days since Herbert Hoover in 1929. Executive Order 13769, signed at the Pentagon on 27 January 2017, just seven days into Trump's presidency, was designed to protect the nation from foreign terrorists entering the US. The Department of Homeland Security would review existing screening and vetting procedures for foreign nationals arriving in the United States. Meanwhile, the executive order placed a ninety-day restriction on citizens from Iraq, Syria, Iran, Sudan, Libya, Somalia and Yemen entering the United States. It also put a stop to the arrival of all refugees in the United States for 120 days and Syrian refugees indefinitely. What followed was an extraordinary battle of wills in which Trump discovered that executive orders – devices that allow Presidents to instruct federal employees to do things relating to the executive branch of government – are not quite the legislative bazookas they sound.

Obama had learned the same hard lesson when he tried to close Guantanamo Bay. His executive order, signed just two days into his presidency, instructed a review of Guantanamo with a view to closure within a year. Amid resistance from Congress, Guantanamo remains open today, Trump having signed an executive order in 2018 to retain the facility. (In a statement that would have appealed to many American voters, he argued that it was time to learn from the mistakes of the past, when terror suspects had been released from detention too soon, only to return to the battlefield.) Roosevelt had more success with the confiscation of gold during the Great Depression, but in general successive Presidents had used the tool sparingly, conscious of the political backlash associated with flexing their muscles in this way.

Trump's executive order on Muslim citizens triggered a firestorm. Left-wing protestors descended on airports across the country to signal their disgust. It was chaos: the temporary ban had been implemented with so little notice that visitors were arriving in the US from the seven proscribed nations and being held in airports. Immigration lawyers were setting up shop in terminals, while some demonstrators demanded that Trump and Bannon themselves be deported. Soon #NoBanNoWall was trending on social media. In London, thousands of protestors lined Whitehall, congregating outside No. 10 chanting 'Hey, hey! Ho, ho! Donald Trump has got to go!'[20] As we have seen, a petition was also launched in the UK calling for the cancellation of Trump's state visit. It attracted an extraordinary 1.86 million signatures and the support of Labour leader Jeremy Corbyn, who described the ban as 'shameful'.

A barrage of legal challenges followed, and the measures began to disintegrate. Judges in New York and Massachusetts struck down parts of the order within hours of the ban coming into effect.[21] On 3 February, Judge James Robart of the US District Court for the Western District of Washington blocked the travel ban nationwide. An incensed Trump took to Twitter to rail against the strictures the 'so-called judge' had imposed. His opinion was 'ridiculous', Trump declared, and would be overturned. 'What is our country coming to when a judge can halt a Homeland Security travel ban and anyone, even with bad intentions, can come into US?' he continued.[22]

The Department of Justice attempted to appeal the ruling in the Court of Appeals for the Ninth Circuit in the case of *Washington v Trump* (2017) but met with dissent. State Attorney-Generals from fifteen additional states put forward amicus briefs* outlining why they thought Trump's travel ban should be blocked. In a joint statement, in which they described themselves as 'chief legal officers for over 130 million Americans and foreign residents' of the United States, they condemned what they called Trump's 'unconstitutional, un-American and unlawful' executive order.[23] The Court of Appeals backed the decision by Judge Robart, preventing the travel ban from coming into force.

Trump refused to give up, ordering lawyers to draw up a new version of the order. Among the changes was the removal of Iraq from the list of seven countries; tweaks to the rules around refugees; and the removal of the indefinite ban on Syrian refugees. Once again, a worldwide review of vetting procedures by Homeland Security was requested. In an attempt to avoid more chaotic scenes at airports, this time there would be a bit more notice.

Hours before it was due to come into force, US District Court Judge Derrick Watson from Hawaii imposed a temporary restraining order. In the judge's opinion, the measures were designed to target a certain religion (in this case, Islam) breaching the so-called Establishment Clause of the First Amendment, which states, 'Congress shall make no law respecting an establishment of religion, or prohibiting the free exercise thereof'. Hawaii's Attorney-General, Douglas Chin, was rather blunter, describing it as a 'neon sign

---

* These are documents known as 'friends of the court'. They are provided by people or organisations not involved in the case in order to provide information and expertise for the court to consider.

flashing "Muslim ban, Muslim ban".[24] This, according to Trump, was 'unprecedented judicial overreach'.[25]

It would take him a third attempt to succeed, by which point he had also added Chad, Venezuela and North Korea to his list. Following a review by the Department of Homeland Security, the severity of the bans would vary from nation to nation, with the total suspension of all travel from North Korea and Syria but a significantly more relaxed approach to Venezuela.

Once again, Hawaii's Judge Watson intervened, arguing that it suffered from 'precisely the same maladies as its predecessor'.[26] Exasperated, the White House reiterated the President's determination to 'keep the American people safe and enforce minimum security standards for entry into the United States'.[27] The dispute was finally resolved in the Supreme Court. The case of *Trump v Hawaii* (2018) was eventually heard more than a year after the initial executive order. In a tight 5–4 vote, the Supreme Court divided along ideological lines in favour of the President and judicial restraint, ruling that the executive order was a lawful exercise of the President's statutory authority. Trump had won the battle. But he had still not won the war.

•   •   •

The travel ban showed Trump was serious about keeping potential terrorists out of America, but what about their base in the Middle East? ISIS had reached its peak in late 2014 with over 100,000 square kilometres and more than 11 million people under the control of the Islamic Caliphate, stretching across the Syria–Iraq border. The terror network controlled an area of land similar in size to Iceland, South Korea or Portugal.

According to David Cohen, Obama's Undersecretary for Terrorism and Financial Intelligence in the Treasury, it was 'probably the best funded terrorist organisation we have confronted'.[28] The money came from oil: perhaps as much as $1 million to $1.5 million every day. Other revenue streams included hostage ransoms, taxation, extortion, wealthy donors and the sale of antiquities. When ISIS took hold of northern Iraq, the terror organisation also plundered half a billion dollars from Iraqi banks.

Brute force was required to destroy the rogue state they had established in the vacuum of Iraq and Syria. Boots on the ground were out of the question: voters had had quite enough of that. Instead, in mid-2014, an international coalition was formed to conduct airstrikes across Iraq and Syria, coupled with ground forces led by the Iraqi army, Kurdish *peshmerga* and Syrian rebels, which eventually became the Syrian Democratic Forces. A strictly limited number of US personnel in the region would provide training. The US mission in Iraq and Syria was codenamed Operation Inherent Resolve.

While Trump carried on Obama's strategy when he took office, it needed to be stepped up a gear. In interviews to appoint a Secretary of Defense, Jim 'Mad Dog' Mattis called for a 'war of annihilation'. 'We need to change what we are doing. It can't be a war of attrition,' he had urged.[29] Mattis had been commander of the US Central Command (CENTCOM), which oversees military operations in the Middle East, during the Obama presidency before being fired for being too bellicose towards Iran. Trump's aides hoped he and the 45th President would be more philosophically aligned.

By summer 2017, coalition forces were making tangible progress. After a nine-month slog, Iraq's second largest city, Mosul, was retaken by Iraqi forces. They fought house-to-house, street-by-street through the narrow alleyways of the ancient city where Abu Bakr al-Baghdadi, the Caliph of ISIS, had originally declared the creation of an Islamic Caliphate three years earlier. ISIS fighters had left the place riddled with booby traps. Meanwhile, a steady stream of civilians poured onto the streets waving white flags and trundling carts loaded with belongings as they tried to escape before becoming human shields for the remaining ISIS fighters. A few weeks later, the Syrian city of Raqqa, which had become the de facto capital of ISIS, also fell to the Syrian Democratic Forces.

It was not until March 2019 that the final ISIS stronghold of Baghuz, on the Syrian border with Iraq, capitulated. Trump held up a map and said:

Everything in the red, this was on election night in 2016, everything red is ISIS. When I took it over, it was a mess. Now, on the bottom, that's the exact same: there is no red. In fact, there's actually a tiny spot, which will be gone by tonight.[30]

The physical state of ISIS had finally been defeated just less than five years after the caliphate had been declared in Mosul. However, the head of the snake was still alive – and proving frustratingly elusive.

• • •

Abu Bakr al-Baghdadi was the most wanted man on the planet; one of only three people ever to have had a $25 million bounty on his head, that being the maximum reward the US government ever offers for information leading to the capture of a villain. This put him in the same dubious company as Ayman al-Zawahiri, the Egyptian leader of al-Qaeda (who many believe remains at large), and Osama bin Laden.

Al-Baghdadi was a reclusive religious scholar who had been held in the US Camp Bucca detention centre during the Iraq War, where the seeds of the ISIS leadership were sown. He became the leader of al-Qaeda in Iraq in 2010, at which point he came to the attention of the US State Department, attracting an initial bounty of $10 million. In July 2014, having eluded Western intelligence services for years, he made a brazen public appearance in Iraq to declare the creation of the Islamic Caliphate. Clad in black robes, he appeared at the Great Mosque of al-Nuri in Mosul to proclaim that the jihad, or holy war, had finally been rewarded. The man known as the 'Invisible Sheikh' and 'The Ghost', a shadow in the darkness, was cocking a snook at the West, but the defiant sermon to his disciples was a one-off. Moments later, he was gone.

In November 2016, he had a near miss when he made a radio call urging his followers to carry on fighting in the Battle of Mosul. The transmission was intercepted, and attempts were made to take him out. Once again, he was too fast.

Trump would not be able to claim any victory in the war on terror without this scalp. At a rally in Alabama during the 2016 election campaign, he declared, 'We have a situation where ISIS has raised its ugly head again and we have got to chop off that head like it is chopping off the heads of our people.'[31]

Had she become President, Hillary Clinton would also have made the Invisible Sheikh her prime target. 'I would go after Baghdadi. I would specifically target Baghdadi, because I think our targeting of al-Qaeda leaders – and I was involved in a lot of those operations, highly classified ones – made a difference. So, I think that could help,' she had said, in one of the presidential debates.[32] Clinton had been Secretary of State when bin Laden was taken out by Navy Seals in 2011. It had given Obama a significant poll boost, his approval ratings jumping nine percentage points to 56 per cent, his highest rating since 2009. Obama's handling of terrorism also reached a career high of 69 per cent.

For some time after Trump became President, it was unclear whether The Ghost was still alive. However, an audio message released in September 2019 confirmed he was still at large. Intelligence chiefs believed he was hiding out in a remote town on the Syria–Iraq border; now, it was a matter of finding him.

In a high-stakes operation, launched under cover of darkness from Iraq on 26 October, eight US attack helicopters converged over the Syrian village of Barisha, just a few miles from the border with Turkey, to finish him off. Gathered in the US Situation Room watching the special operation were Trump, Mike Pence, Robert O'Brien (national security adviser), Mark Esper (Defense Secretary), Mark Milley (chairman of the joint chiefs of staff) and Brigadier General Marcus Evans. They held their breath as Special Forces surrounded a compound, from which two adults and eleven children emerged and were taken into custody. US forces then blew their way through a wall in the compound (for fear the door would be booby-trapped), beyond which they believed Baghdadi was hiding. Wearing a suicide vest, he had attempted to make a run for it down a tunnel, accompanied by two of his children. He was chased down the tunnel by a US military dog called Conan. When he hit a dead end, he detonated the suicide vest, killing his two children and bringing the tunnel down on top of him. The compound was then pounded to dust by US forces, in order that it should not be turned into a shrine for a 'martyr'.[33]

Trump was jubilant. 'Something very big has just happened!' he tweeted excitedly – without elaborating.[34] He needed to be sure before telling the world. Thirteen hours later, he stepped out in front of the press to announce that the United States had 'brought the world's No. 1 terrorist leader to justice'.[35] Abu Bakr al-Baghdadi was finally dead.

With the destruction of the physical caliphate and the death of Baghdadi, ISIS has disintegrated, though there is every possibility that it will exploit the continuing security vacuum in the Middle East to rise again. At the time of writing, there are reports of fighters regrouping in northern Iraq. Eliminating the threat from Islamic extremists in the Middle East was never going to be possible in one presidential term and was unlikely to be achievable in two: until real stability can be established, ISIS will simply be supplanted by another militant group.

Indeed, al-Baghdadi was swiftly replaced by an equally brutal leader, known as Muhammad Sa'id Abdal-Rahman al-Mawla. Like his predecessor, he too was detained at Camp Bucca by the United

States and interrogated in the aftermath of the Iraq War. His nickname is 'The Destroyer'. In June 2020, the US State Department doubled the bounty on al-Mawla to $10 million.

One school of thought, espoused by Dr Colin P. Clarke of the Rand Corp., is that with the death of Baghdadi, affiliates of the group will begin to break away and fight their own causes. ISIS itself had emerged and grown following the death of bin Laden and the splintering of al-Qaeda in Iraq. US defence and intelligence chiefs and their allies in the war on terror know they cannot afford to let their guard down, as new threats emerge in Syria and Iraq, and further afield in Libya, Bangladesh, Nigeria and south-east Asia.

For now, however, ISIS remains a shadow of its former self – and for that, Trump can take significant credit. He raised security and counterterrorism to the top of his administration's agenda. His travel ban focused attention on the reliability of vetting at the US border. For all the outrage, Obama had done much the same, in a rather quieter way. Trump's Democrat predecessor had imposed increased travel restrictions on the very same seven countries at the centre of Trump's crackdown, and the Department of Homeland Security had labelled them 'countries of concern'. These are not stable democracies, as protestors sought to suggest: they are among the most dangerous and unstable regimes on earth. The 2016 Fragile State Index ranked Somalia, Sudan, Yemen and Syria in the highest category of state fragility: 'very high alert'. Iraq was labelled 'high alert', Libya 'alert' and Iran 'high warning'.[36]

Among those who defended the President against charges of religious discrimination was Sheikh Abdullah bin Zayed, the UAE's Foreign Minister:

> The United States has taken a decision that is within the American sovereign decision … There are attempts to give the impression that this decision is directed against a particular religion, but what

proves this talk to be incorrect first is that the US administration itself says ... that this decision is not directed at a certain religion.[37]

The ban had sent a clear message to the US federal government and Arab nations, including Saudi Arabia and the UAE, that the US was determined to put an end to radical Islamic terrorism. Events in San Bernardino had underlined the consequences of weak vetting procedures.

No US President really owns the victory when international terrorists are brought to justice, but Trump probably deserved more credit for the death of Baghdadi. Certainly, Obama had earned plenty of plaudits for the killing of bin Laden. Polls by the *Washington Post* and ABC News showed only 54 per cent believed Trump should receive a 'great deal/some' credit for killing Baghdadi, compared to 76 per cent for Obama in 2011. This was despite the fact that 26 per cent of Americans felt safer after the death of Baghdadi, compared to only 22 per cent feeling safer after the death of bin Laden. With ISIS all but destroyed – at least temporarily – under an administration that did more than just talk tough on terrorism, Americans may sleep a little safer.

16

THE LESSER EVIL – TRUMP AND SAUDI ARABIA

Saudi Arabia: a country that effectively found its wealth when Major Frank Holmes (a Brit) set up the Eastern and General Syndicate in London to develop oil ventures in the Middle East in 1920. John Paul Getty, of course, then set the bar far higher in the late '40s and beyond. The barren stretch of desert became one the richest, and therefore one of the most important, places in the world. Unfortunately, human rights leave a lot to be desired.

Trump didn't consider it his place to lecture the Saudis about that. Nor did he see the point in declining to sell them arms. His logic: if the Saudis don't buy arms from us, they will buy from China or Russia – would that be good for America? Moreover, he recognised that Saudi Arabia is an important ally against a much greater evil: Iran.

Which country should Donald Trump have visited first in his capacity as 45th President of the United States? For any new occupant of the White House, it is a hugely important question, presenting both opportunity and risk. Get it right, and it sends a powerful signal to the world about the new administration's foreign policy priorities; get it wrong, and the trip could be far more than a public relations disaster, potentially souring diplomatic relations with key allies and inflaming tensions with less friendly nations.

Under other circumstances, it would surely have been the UK, but clearly that was out: it was crystal-clear that any such trip would be bedevilled by protests. So, where else? Trump's predecessors had generally played it safe, tending to opt for Canada or Mexico. But Trump did not intend to be a President like any other, and so it was that he and his advisers chose the Middle East.

Presentationally, the Kingdom of Saudi Arabia offered many advantages. Trump's hosts could be relied upon to provide him with a spectacular reception, with no expense spared as they rolled out the red carpet. More importantly, it was an amazing diplomatic opportunity. Choosing Saudi Arabia for his first overseas engagement would show that the 'America First' rhetoric of his campaign did not mean that his administration would only look inward. Attending the Arab Islamic American summit, he would show that there was no inherent contradiction in his commitment to 'MAGA' – Make America Great Again – and working with foreign allies.

Trump's welcome in Riyadh did not disappoint. The Saudis spent a reported $68 million pulling out all the stops for their most eminent visitor. Within hours of Trump's arrival, he was bestowed with the King Abdulaziz al Saud Collar, a golden medallion representing the highest civilian honour in Saudi Arabia. Other luxurious gifts included cheetah- and tiger-fur robes, a silver dagger and a pearl-encrusted sheath. On the first night of his visit, the President was entertained with a traditional ceremonial sword dance known as the *ardah*. Trump, Rex Tillerson, Wilbur Ross (Secretary of Commerce) and other male US officials swayed somewhat uncomfortably along to the drum beat and poetry of the war dance, surrounded by Saudi dignitaries dressed in their *daghla* ceremonial robes. The entourage then proceeded to a state banquet, hosted by the ageing King Salman bin Abdulaziz al Saud, at the Murabba Palace. In this most unfamiliar culture, Trump, who was not particularly interested in diplomatic protocol, could easily have blundered. To the relief of his entourage, he did not put a foot wrong, even when he was invited to gather around a glowing purple orb to mark the beginning of a ceremony celebrating the opening of a new organisation tasked with combating 'extremist ideology'. Photographs of the President huddled alongside King Salman and President Sisi of Egypt in the lurid light prompted the Church of Satan to issue a tweet clarifying that it was nothing to do with them, but Trump took it all in his stride. After all, it was all in a good cause: while Trump regarded his main mission as drumming up huge defence contracts for America, he was also supposed to be co-ordinating efforts by the US and friendly Muslim nations to root out Islamic terrorism.

Leaders from fifty-four Muslim countries, ranging from Indonesia to Kazakhstan to Nigeria, had convened in Riyadh for the summit, with the motto 'Together, We Prevail'. Trump's message to allies at this conference was simple and seemed as tailored for his domestic audience as it was to the Middle East: 'A better future is only possible if your nations drive out the terrorists and extremists,' he said. They must 'Drive. Them. Out.' He continued, 'DRIVE THEM OUT of your places of worship. DRIVE THEM OUT of your communities. DRIVE THEM OUT of your holy land, and DRIVE THEM OUT OF THIS EARTH.'[1]

It was the sort of chant he used to whip up his supporters at rallies, and he knew it would be heard in millions of American homes. He acknowledged that while terror attacks in Boston, San Bernardino and Orlando had scarred America, it was in fact the Muslim community that bore the brunt of violent extremism around the world. Some 95 per cent of those killed are Muslim. A peaceful Middle East with Arab nations driving the change was vastly preferable to the United States expending time and energy where it was not wanted. If Arab nations could pay for it themselves, so much the better.

Justifying the visit, Steve Bannon told students at the Oxford University Union in the UK:

We went to Riyadh before Jerusalem, and before Rome, to send a message to the Islamic community. We are there for you and we are your allies, and we understand there is a problem. The problem is with radical Islamic jihad and it is as big a problem for you and your own countries as it is for us in the West. We have to party together to stop that. Stop the financing of it. Stop the spread of it because it is killing you more than it is killing us.[2]

The Saudi regime was thrilled. Foreign Minister Adel al-Jubeir publicly declared it a 'coup for peace and coexistence'.

This is a very powerful message to the Islamic world that America and the West is not your enemy. This is a very powerful message to the West that Islam is not your enemy. This visit will change the discourse and the dialogue between the Islamic world and the West in general and the US in particular. It will isolate the extremists whether they be Iran, ISIS or al-Qaeda who say that the West is our enemy.[3]

Back in the US, this was music to the ears of American voters weary of the 'war on terror' that had dragged on, to no very obvious positive effect, since 2001.

The Riyadh summit swiftly paid dividends. Less than three weeks later, Saudi Arabia, the UAE, Bahrain and Egypt cut diplomatic ties with Qatar, whose growing proximity to Iran and funding of the Muslim Brotherhood, a group that had been designated a terror organisation, was a mounting source of concern. A blockade was established around the peninsular nation. In theory, Qatar was a close US ally, with one of the largest US military bases in the region. The power play caused unease among the foreign policy and security establishment. Nonetheless, the Qataris were issued with thirteen demands, including the loosening of diplomatic ties with Iran and an end to the cash flow to organisations deemed terrorist groups by the four Arab nations and the US. This would include the Muslim

Brotherhood, ISIS and Lebanon's Hezbollah. More bizarre instructions included shutting down the news organisation Al Jazeera and achieving all of the thirteen points within ten days.

Trump felt his strategy was going well. 'So good to see the Saudi Arabia visit with the King and fifty countries already paying off. They said they would take a hard line on funding extremism, and all reference was pointing to Qatar. Perhaps this will be the beginning of the end of the horror of terrorism!'[4]

The Qataris were quick to be seen to fall into line. Soon, Secretary of State Rex Tillerson would fly to Qatar where, on 10 July 2017, he signed an agreement with his counterpart to target the financing of extremist organisations. 'The memorandum lays out a series of steps that each country will take in coming months and years to interrupt and disable terror financing flows and intensify counter terrorism activities globally,' Tillerson said.[5]

A year later, Qatar's monarch, Sheikh Tamim bin Hamad Al Thani, would also visit the White House. Trump believed Qatar had turned a corner and praised Al Thani's counter-terrorism efforts. He said, 'You've now become a very big advocate, and we appreciate that.'[6]

Here was a President co-operating with Arab nations to tackle one of the most complex and pressing issues in the world. For too long, America had blundered unwittingly into the Middle East, claiming to have all the answers. Instead, Trump was putting the onus on the Arab and Muslim nations to take the lead – though nonetheless making clear that the US would be there to support them if required.

• • •

In the arid scrubland between Israel and the Gaza Strip are a dozen or more towering structures that look like huge batteries. They have been painted a sandy colour to blend in with the sun-baked terrain, but the enormous mobile blocks are not exactly camouflaged, not least because they have flashing red lights at the top. It is a signal that they are primed for action, which means they could launch a missile at any moment.

The structures, which are constantly on the move, are part of the famous 'Iron Dome' shield that protects Israel from attacks by Palestinian militants. In one of the most sophisticated defence systems in the world, it uses radars and algorithms to strike enemy missiles out of the sky before they hit civilian or strategic targets. It is said to have intercepted more than 2,400 missiles since it was switched on in 2011.

The Saudis looked at this system with envy. As the war against the Iranian-backed Houthis in Yemen escalated, cities in the kingdom were a growing target for rocket strikes. Some missiles were even beginning to reach Riyadh. They needed the equivalent of Israel's Iron Dome – and American defence giant Lockheed Martin had the answer.

A system similar to the one defence company Rafael supplied the Israelis was among the big-ticket items Trump and his team hoped to sell to the Saudis during that first visit in 2017. Known as THAAD (Terminal High Altitude Area Defense), the system uses 20ft missiles with a range of 125 miles and is capable of reaching an altitude of almost 100 miles. They could intercept missiles flying both inside and outside the Earth's atmosphere.

For an increasingly nervous Saudi regime, the $15 billion price tag was a relatively modest price to pay. For the Americans, the sale would be a huge boost for the defence industry in general and Lockheed Martin in particular. THAAD supports 18,000 direct and indirect jobs across the United States. Soaring demand for the shield system has enabled the company to hire an additional 4,000 workers since 2018.

Trump may have come to Riyadh to talk peace, but he was also on a mission to sell the instruments of war. Peddling arms to the Saudis upset the cognoscenti, who were particularly exercised by the way American-manufactured aircraft and munitions were being used in the bloody civil war in Yemen. But it kept US defence companies in business. And as we have seen, Trump had promised to deliver jobs, jobs, jobs.

On day one of his trip, in the Saudi Royal Court, the President sat alongside King Salman bin Abdulaziz al Saud, behind a black-and-gold lacquer desk, to add their signatures to a raft of arms deals. With a certain amount of creative accounting, the figure they managed to reach for the value of these sales was an eye-watering $110 billion. Critics could argue about the fine print – and of course they did – but even if only a fraction of what was agreed on paper that day turned into real transactions, it was a huge boon for the industry. When left-wing commentators branded Trump 'one of the most aggressive arms salesmen in history' they did not mean it kindly, but it was a badge he would wear with pride.[7] For Trump, this was about keeping people in work. In fact, the President was only building on progress made by his predecessor in the White House, who, for all his Nobel Peace Prize winning, had been quite an enthusiastic hawker of weapons himself. Indeed, the Obama administration had offered Saudi Arabia what was then a record $115 billion in weapons, military training and equipment – the most of any US administration in the 71-year US–Saudi alliance.[*] As so often, Trump's critics tried to have it both ways: on the one hand, accusing him of exaggerating arms sales; on the other, accusing him of selling too much. The reality was that the US had long been Saudi Arabia's primary arms supplier and – without a long philosophical debate about the morals and ethics of the arms industry that his detractors would have liked – the President was simply reinforcing that status and doing so very well.

The bigger picture was the threat posed by Iran. Trump knew the

---

[*]   This figure is based on forty-two deals studied by the Center for International Policy. However, most of the equipment has yet to be delivered to the Saudis.

Saudis were important allies against the rogue state. He understood that the Middle East was embroiled in a tectonic collision of cultures and religious traditions seeking hegemony in the region, with Saudi Arabia as the leading Sunni nation pitted against Shi'a-dominated Iran. He understood that the latter was increasingly using proxies in the region to promote its agenda, meddling in conflicts that were frequently characterised as civil wars but in fact involved multiple external players. In Lebanon, Hezbollah dominated politics, while Shi'a militias were fuelling instability in Syria and Iraq. All aided and abetted by Iran. Even more alarmingly for Saudi Arabia, Iranian-backed Houthi rebels had overthrown the Yemeni government, leaving the kingdom with a desperately impoverished and lawless neighbour on its southern border. The House of Saud was in a state of constant anxiety about the threat emanating from across the Persian Gulf, with the Crown Prince Mohammed bin Salman going so far as to compare the Iranian regime to Nazi Germany.

The Saudis had been disappointed by Obama's failure to offer them more support in their power struggle with Iran, which they regarded as little short of existential. As far as they were concerned, Iranian proxies could not be allowed to establish a power base on another Saudi border. 'We learned from Europe that appeasement doesn't work. We don't want the new Hitler in Iran to repeat what happened in Europe in the Middle East,' the Crown Prince has said.[8] To the Saudi regime, Yemen seemed to represent a 1939-moment: if they didn't reassert their authority in the region by entering the fray, they risked creeping subjugation by the Iranians.

During the Arab Spring in 2011, Obama had urged a number of old Arab autocracies to make way for democracy, unsettling many Arab leaders. Those that had hoped they could count on the support of the United States in the event of a popular uprising could no longer be so sure. Speaking at the time about the mounting nervousness in Israel, a government official told Reuters: 'The question is, do we think Obama is reliable or not? Right now it doesn't look so. That is a question resonating across the region not just in Israel.[9] The Saudis were equally uneasy, feeling that under Obama, America was not an ally that could be relied upon. They were particularly frustrated by what one senior Saudi royal, Prince Turki al-Faisal, described as Obama's 'lamentable' approach to the civil war in Syria. In October 2013, Saudi intelligence chief Prince Bandar bin Sultan was reported to have told European diplomats that his country was preparing for a 'major shift' in relations with the US.[10]

In reality, there was no significant weakening of this most important diplomatic tie, but the cooling of relations presented an opportunity for Trump. Both the House of Trump and the House of Saud were keen to hit the reset button. During the transition period, Trump's son-in-law, Jared Kushner, who had been handed the Middle East brief, had correctly identified that Saudi Arabia's Crown Prince, Muhammad bin Nayef (MBN), was by no means certain to take over from the ageing king. Though he was the preferred candidate of the CIA and State Department, there were other contenders, most notably a young prince named Mohammed bin Salman.[*] The sixth son of the 25th son of a king, as his biographer points out, 'MBS' seemed destined for obscurity. Fiercely ambitious and ready to schmooze the West, MBS refused to accept that destiny and began setting out a new vision for his country, positioning himself as a radical reformer who would modernise the kingdom. During the transition period before Trump's inauguration, Kushner met the UAE's Crown Prince, Mohammed bin Zayed (MBZ), who had taken MBS under his wing. MBZ put in a good word for the young Saudi prince and, at some point, numbers were exchanged, after which Kushner and MBS reportedly began to communicate via WhatsApp.

---

[*] The line of succession in Saudi Arabia is complex. Normally, the crown is inherited on the basis of seniority between the sons of the king. However, with the emergence of a new generation, the system has begun to shift to the prerogative of the king to choose his successor.

According to Ben Hubbard, whose book *MBS* charts the remarkable rise of the young prince:

The relationship between MBS and Kushner bloomed because both came to believe the other could advance issues they held dear. Kushner saw in MBS someone who could fund American military activities in the Middle East and serve as the skeleton key to unlock peace between Israel and the Arabs. For his part, MBS expected Kushner to push the United States to champion Vision 2030, stand up to Iran and support him in his rivalry with Mohammed bin Nayef to become the kingdom's crown prince.[11]

Two months before Trump's symbolic trip to Riyadh, MBS ventured to Washington to meet the new administration. In a stroke of luck for the young prince, Germany's Chancellor Merkel had been forced to pull out of an engagement with Trump due to a snowstorm. Seizing the opportunity presented by the sudden gap in the President's diary, Kushner slipped MBS into lunch with Trump himself. This was a bold move that breached diplomatic protocol: at the time, MBS was not next in line for the throne. There was a risk that MBN's nose would be put out of joint. It typified the freewheeling diplomatic style the 'First Family' would adopt, which sometimes backfired but, on this occasion, paid off.

Following the lunch between Trump and MBS, one of MBS's advisers told the press:

This meeting is considered a historical turning point in relations between both countries and which had passed through a period of divergence of views on many issues. But the meeting today restored issues to their right path and form a big change in relations between both countries in political, military, security and economic issues.[12]

Trump and Kushner now had a new partner in Riyadh.

In due course, Kushner would welcome a delegation of thirty Saudis to the White House to discuss defence contracts, ahead of the finalisation of the $110 billion deal. When the price for certain pieces of kit became a problem, Kushner took the unorthodox approach of picking up the phone to the CEO of Lockheed Martin to see what could be done. Kushner, who gets little credit for his public service under Trump, had made a series of very good calls. The Trump family's business experience was also coming into play.

As a part of Saudi Arabia's modernisation programme, MBS would travel to the US once again in March 2018, to drum up investment from US corporations. In an interview with *Time* magazine, he argued that Saudi Arabia was only operating at 10 per cent of the country's potential. By 2018, Trump and Kushner's gamble of favouring MBS had paid off: he had achieved Crown Prince status, having elbowed aside his cousin, MBN. It was partly down to hard graft, assiduous networking and sheer force of personality, but his friends in the West would have to turn a blind eye to some rather more dubious manoeuvrings, notably his decision to place hundreds of the country's wealthiest princes, billionaires and senior government officials under house arrest – and subject them to appalling treatment – in the Ritz-Carlton Hotel on charges of corruption.

With his elevated new status, MBS continued his corporate charm offensive in the States, securing meetings with figures including Mark Zuckerberg, Bill Gates and Jeff Bezos. Anyone who could add value to Saudi Arabi was on the list. In 2018, the public investment fund in Saudi Arabia was worth $300 billion; by 2030 MBS hoped it would be worth $2 trillion, with 50 per cent of that figure invested abroad. Between them, Kushner and Trump had dramatically strengthened the relationship between Saudi Arabia and the United States, putting American companies in prime position to benefit from sovereign wealth.

• • •

With an average viewer rating of 3.3/10, *The Emoji Movie* was widely considered to be an absolute turkey. Released in 2017, the animated film was so bad it clinched almost half the awards up for grabs at the 'Razzies,' a kind of 'anti-Oscars' ceremony for the worst films of the year. Universally panned as it was, it seems to have struck a chord with someone in Saudi Arabia, because, in December 2017, it became the first film to be shown at a cinema in the kingdom for thirty-five years, taking its place in history alongside a screening of *Captain Underpants*.

Perhaps the Crown Prince himself supported the screening. After all, he was known to communicate with Kushner via emojis. Indeed, on one occasion, he bombarded Boris Johnson with emojis in WhatsApp messages, leading to speculation that the British Prime Minister's phone had been hacked.

However the choice was made, the re-opening of cinemas was a part of MBS's drive for reform. Saudi Arabia had been in a kind of cultural deep freeze since 1979, when the Grand Mosque of Mecca was seized by armed jihadis demanding the overthrow of the House of Saud. It led to a two-week siege, during which Saudi and French Special Forces attempted to wrest back control of the kingdom's holiest site from the militant religious fundamentalists. Hostages were taken and hundreds of people died. In a bid for self-preservation, the monarchy shifted towards a more conservative form of Islam.

In an interview with Norah O'Donnell on *60 Minutes*, MBS described the profound long-term repercussions of the siege: 'We were living a very normal life like the rest of the Gulf countries. Women were driving cars. There were movie theatres in Saudi Arabia. Women worked everywhere. We were just normal people developing like any other country in the world until the events of 1979.'

After almost four decades, MBS wanted to release a bit of pressure from the tyres. Illustrating the scale of the challenge the young leader faced, Saudi Arabia's highest cleric, Grand Mufti Abdulaziz

Al Sheikh, made no secret of his displeasure at the screening of *The Emoji Movie*. 'We know that singing concerts and cinemas are a depravity,' he proclaimed gloomily. Allowing people to watch silly American movies in cinemas was the thin end of the wedge, he felt. This particular film might be innocent enough fun, but future movie choices might be 'libertine, lewd, immoral and atheist', and cinemas might start allowing men and women to sit together.

MBS pressed on, issuing a historic royal decree allowing women to drive. For Saudi Arabia, this was truly radical: previously it had been an imprisonable offence. Trump was quick to praise, promising to continue supporting the kingdom in its efforts to strengthen Saudi society. Asked in a television interview six months later whether he regarded men and women as equal, MBS replied, 'Absolutely. We are all human beings and there is no difference.'

Shortly after the driving decree, it was revealed that women would also be able to attend live sporting events for the first time, although, to the undoubted relief of the Grand Mufti, they would be confined to family seating areas. In April 2020, the regime announced plans to scrap flogging as a form of punishment, replacing the beatings with prison sentences and fines. Saudi Arabia was still deeply conservative, but these were real liberalisations. In a short space of time, Kushner's man in Riyadh was changing the kingdom in ways many had thought impossible.

The reforms made diplomatic relations between America and the US much easier. Bilateral meetings always involved some awkward exchange, whether it was about war crimes in Yemen, medieval methods of capital punishment or gender inequality. As Deputy Crown Prince, MBS had frequently attended meetings between his father, Salman bin Abdulaziz al Saud, and Obama. Obama would always go through this rigamarole. Perhaps some American voters expected it, but the Saudis found the routine immensely irritating. On Obama's final visit to Riyadh in April 2016, MBS finally snapped. Ben Rhodes, Obama's deputy national security adviser, recalls in

The Atlantic, 'I sat in hundreds of bilateral meetings during eight years in the White House, and I never saw anything quite like what happened next.'[13] The thirty-year-old Deputy Crown Prince rose to his feet to lambast the President, exclaiming that Obama simply did not understand the Saudi justice system. The Saudi royal family was under constant pressure from a deeply conservative population, he argued, and if criminals did not face the type of justice that was routinely meted out, then the stability of the kingdom would be at stake. MBS even offered Obama a briefing on the Saudi justice system. The exchange cannot have done anything to improve relations.

It was, of course, easier not to confront such issues, and Trump was generally happy to avoid the embarrassment of berating his new friends. Human rights activists and others would certainly have preferred to take him to task over atrocities such as the beheading of thirty-seven men in April 2019, the detainment of political activists and the scorched-earth attitude to war in Yemen, where the Saudi Air Force appeared to consider civilians and civilian infrastructure fair game. But, as former CIA director David Petraeus told members of the Royal United Services Institute (RUSI) in October 2020, to operate in the Middle East, Western leaders have to choose their battles, or they will not get anywhere. 'Be very clear about who your friends and also who your enemies are in the Middle East. Recognise and accept that your friends may not be perfect in all respects and there will be some shortcomings about their actions. Try to work through those,' was the way Petraeus put it.[14]

Nonetheless, in October 2018, the House of Saud was associated with an episode so shocking that it could not be ignored by the White House. A journalist named Jamal Khashoggi entered the Saudi consulate in Istanbul to pick up documents allowing him to marry his new fiancée – and never emerged again. Earlier that day, a fifteen-man hit squad had flown to Turkey by private jet from Riyadh, tasked with escorting him back to Saudi Arabia. A struggle ensued, during which Khashoggi was suffocated, dismembered and his body parts loaded into suitcases. The attackers then fled back to Riyadh via Cairo and Dubai.

Khashoggi had once been close to a number of Saudi princes but had gone into self-imposed exile. The Saudi authorities had been particularly unimpressed by his criticism of Trump's contradictory nature at an event at the Washington Institute and had ordered him to stop writing, appearing on television and attending conferences. The worry was that his unhelpful commentary risked destabilising the flourishing bilateral relationship. The journalist subsequently fled Saudi Arabia and turned his pen on the Saudi monarchy, writing columns for the *Washington Post* that undermined MBS's carefully cultivated image as a reformer. His first piece claimed the kingdom was becoming more, not less, repressive, describing it as 'unbearable'.[15] Another article, published in response to the rounding up of the wayward princes, likened MBS to Putin.[16]

According to a leaked intelligence report, a year before Khashoggi's killing, MBS told an aide that if Khashoggi could not be enticed back to Saudi Arabia, where he could be controlled, then he would go after him with a bullet. Following Khashoggi's sudden disappearance from the embassy, Turkish intelligence services launched an investigation, which revealed that an aide to MBS, Maher Abdulaziz Mutreb, was among the hit squad. A telephone call by Mutreb was found to have been made to MBS's office saying, 'Tell your boss deed is done'.[17] In a clumsy attempt to cover their tracks, the assassination team somehow arranged for a body double for the journalist, apparently in the hope that CCTV footage would show that their victim had left the consulate unharmed. The ruse failed when observers spotted that the stunt man was not wearing Khashoggi's shoes.

The murder sparked an international furore. Trump had no choice but to speak out. He publicly condemned the killings, labelling attempts by the hit squad to cover their tracks 'one of the worst in the history of cover-ups'.[18] The question for the President was how far he should go. In the event, he shied away from accusing the monarchy of any involvement, despite a CIA report concluding that MBS had ordered the assassination. Instead, he had to consider the realpolitik. Horrible as the murder was, it did not involve a US citizen, and it seemed insufficient reason to jettison the diplomatic relationship he and Kushner had worked so hard to strengthen. In the end, his strategy was to declare that the US would never know the full story, and to highlight the greater threat posed by Iran. There might be some bad guys in Saudi Arabia, went the message, but they were the lesser evil. Take a look at the country's neighbours, and you'd soon realise they were a whole lot worse.

In a somewhat rambling public statement headlined 'Standing with Saudi Arabia', he emphasised that the world was 'a very dangerous place', calling out Iran for its 'bloody proxy war against Saudi Arabia in Yemen, trying to destabilize Iraq's fragile attempt at democracy, supporting the terror group Hezbollah in Lebanon, propping up dictator Bashar Assad in Syria (who has killed millions of his own citizens), and much more'. Warming to his theme, he railed against Iran killing 'many Americans and other innocent people throughout the Middle East. Iran states openly, and with great force, "Death to America!" and "Death to Israel!" Iran is considered "the world's leading sponsor of terror"'.[19]

Across the Persian Gulf, the ayatollahs were in no doubt who the President considered to be the real enemy.

17

MARTYRS - TRUMP AND IRAN

The Iran 'nuclear deal' was a flagship 'achievement' of the Obama presidency and was supposed to stop Iran from developing nuclear weapons. In exchange for some very warm words about not developing any more bad stuff, the Iranians no longer faced the sanctions that had kept their evil ambitions in check. As a result, their economy boomed. How did they spend the cash? Developing more nuclear weapons and stirring up more trouble in the Middle East, of course.

Trump described the deal as 'one of the worst and most one-sided transactions the United States has ever entered into'.[1] That's a high bar, but he was right.

As befits a man who had just become a martyr, Mohsen Fakhrizadeh was laid to rest with great ceremony. Unusually for these affairs, there were no wailing women falling to their knees as his coffin was paraded through the streets of Tehran – coronavirus restrictions meant members of the public had been told to stay away. But the pandemic did not stop all the big guns turning out for an extravagant display of mourning – and fury – over the violent death of the architect of Iran's nuclear weapons programme. As the formalities got underway, the regime issued a dark warning: Fakhrizadeh's death would be avenged.

Ahead of the main event, his remains were taken to a number of holy Shi'ite shrines in a coffin draped in the red, white and green Iranian flag. Carried by military personnel in splendid black and white regalia, the casket was then brought before Defence Minister General Hatami, who kissed it in the ultimate gesture of respect. The rest of the ceremony took place outside the Ministry of Defence in Tehran, in front of rows of military commanders seated at socially distanced intervals, their cheap, disposable face masks a strange accessory to their immaculate khaki uniforms. A religious singer delivered a plaintive tribute to the deceased, alluding to the martyrdom of a seventh-century holy figure. Above them all, a towering billboard showed a picture of the late nuclear scientist next to Iran's Supreme Leader Ayatollah Ali Khamenei. It fell to Hatami to deliver the most important public message: 'The enemy made a mistake with this assassination.'[2]

Precisely how the head of Iran's rogue nuclear weapons programme met his grisly end is subject to considerable debate. The evidence suggests he was gunned down in a military-style ambush in the town of Absard, to the east of Tehran. Initial accounts told of up to a dozen armed attackers opening fire on his supposedly bullet-proof convoy and a firefight with his bodyguards. Iranian security chiefs subsequently came up with a very different story, however, presumably to spare their blushes at a catastrophic counter-intelligence failure. Their rather fanciful account involved a remote-controlled car and a robotic machine gun. As for who was responsible for the assassination, there was much less doubt. Two years earlier, Israeli Prime Minister Benjamin Netanyahu had openly accused Fakhrizadeh of masterminding Iran's secret nuclear weapons programme: the only real suspects were Mossad agents. Days after the assassination, the Iranian Parliament passed emergency legislation to increase stockpiles of enriched uranium 'for various peaceful purposes'.[3]

Chanting 'Death to America' and 'Death to Israel', lawmakers also called for UN inspectors to be denied access to nuclear sites. The question of how to deal with this rogue state was now even more complicated. Of one thing Trump had never been in any doubt, however – appeasing this hostile state would never work.

• • •

Being a nuclear scientist in Iran is a dangerous business. The Fordow enrichment facility is at least 262ft below ground, reinforced with steel and concrete. Another facility at Natanz lies deep in bunkers under the Iranian desert. Both are safe havens for Iran's nuclear scientists. Nonetheless, between 2010 and 2012, four were assassinated in the streets of Tehran in bombings and drive-by shootings, almost certainly by Mossad.

By 2012, the Israelis were in a state of high alarm about Iran's nuclear activities. A regime that had frequently called for Israel to be 'eliminated' and removed like a 'cancerous tumour' was a matter of months away from acquiring nuclear weapons capability. If Iran developed a nuclear bomb, not only would Israel be in the line of fire, but an arms race would erupt across the Middle East, with Turkey and Saudi Arabia joining the race for nuclear capability. Nuclear non-proliferation would have completely failed. Iran had nearly 20,000 centrifuges and there was enough enriched uranium stockpiled to make eight to ten nuclear bombs. The Iranian nuclear programme was hurtling towards what has been termed a 'zone of immunity': the point at which Iran's nuclear programme would be so developed, it would be immune from any attack. Throughout the year, Israel's Prime Minister, Benjamin Netanyahu, wanted to launch pre-emptive strikes. Briefings suggested that a war could last for thirty days and, in that time, Israel would come under attack from several fronts, including from Hezbollah in Lebanon and from Hamas in the Gaza Strip. Netanyahu would need the support of the United States in the event of any strike on Iran. Obama would not hear of it. Instead, to Netanyahu's fury, his administration began putting it about that Israel's military was incapable of launching an attack that would sufficiently knock out Iran's capabilities. With a US presidential election on the horizon, Netanyahu began courting Republican candidate Mitt Romney instead. By the autumn of 2012, US–Israeli relations were so bad that it was reported by Israel's ambassador to the UN that Obama wouldn't even sit in the same room as Netanyahu.

Alongside the threat of Israeli military action, the international community had ratcheted up sanctions on Iran. In November 2011, the UK had prevented British financial institutions from interacting with their Iranian counterparts. Then, in January 2012, the EU imposed an oil embargo on Iran, decimating the country's main source of income. The thinking was that it would force Iran to divert resources away from the nuclear programme and get its leadership to the negotiating table. The sanctions did their stuff: according to the IMF, in 2012, the Iranian economy contracted 7.7 per cent. That year, the value of Iranian currency hit all-time lows. In 2013, public anger over the state of the economy helped propel the relative moderate Hassan Rouhani to victory in a general election. Iran's new President wanted to rehabilitate his country into the international community.

Since 2006, there had been diplomatic efforts to curb Iran's nuclear programme, involving the five permanent members of the UN plus Germany (the P5+1). All but the US had accepted the need to allow Iran a minimal level of uranium enrichment for energy purposes. In May 2011, the Obama administration had a change of heart. Led by John Kerry, who chaired the Senate Foreign Relations Committee at the time, they began to open up a backchannel with the Iranians via Sultan Qaboos of Oman. The backchannel would build up an understanding between the two sides, eventually leading to US and Iranian delegations meeting in Muscat. Talks dramatically accelerated following the inauguration of Rouhani and the appointment of Mohammad Javad Zarif as Foreign Minister. Zarif had spent many years being educated in the US at San Francisco State University and the University of Denver. In September 2013, just a month after Rouhani took office, Kerry, now Secretary of State, and Zarif became the first foreign ministers of their respective countries to meet since 1979. Eventually, on 14 July 2015, Kerry, Mohammad Javad Zarif and the foreign ministers from the other P5+1 nations signed the Joint Comprehensive Plan of Action (JCPOA), also known as the Iran deal, which would begin to roll back Iran's nuclear programme. Announced amid great fanfare, it was presented as a watershed.

To increase the time it would take for Iran to produce a nuclear weapon, the deal stipulated that for ten years, Iran would reduce its number of centrifuges from approximately 20,000 down to 5,060 at Natanz. For fifteen years, the regime's uranium stockpile would be limited to 300kg at an enrichment level of 3.67 per cent. This was significantly lower than the 12,000kg stockpile Iran had at the time and the 90 per cent enrichment level needed to achieve weapons-grade uranium. For twenty years, there would be cameras on every centrifuge being produced in Iran, and for twenty-five years every ounce of uranium would be accounted for. In exchange, sanctions would be lifted. This included immediate access to more than $100 billion in assets that had been frozen overseas. As a result of these measures, Iran's economy grew 12.5 per cent in 2016. Over time, more sanctions would be removed, including an arms embargo in October 2020. Iran also signed an 'Additional Protocol' which gave international authorities the right to inspect facilities until 2031. If inspections were denied, sanctions would automatically snap back.

There were significant weaknesses in the agreement, however. The main concern was that as the clauses began to expire Iran would quickly be able to scale up its nuclear programme. US allies in the region were also worried about growing Iranian influence in the Middle East. The regime's malign activities through proxies were being oiled by funds released from the relief of sanctions. 'We saw Iran stepping up its aggressive behaviour in the region whether in Syria, whether in Iraq, whether in Yemen, whether in Pakistan, Afghanistan, whether in Africa by using the income it had generated in order to fund its exporting of its revolution,' Saudi Arabia's Foreign Minister, Adel al-Jubeir, told the Chatham House Conference in 2017.[4] Al-Jubeir had his own personal experience of foreign Iranian operations. In 2011, when he was Saudi ambassador to the US, there had been an Iranian plot to assassinate him in Washington DC.

From the outset, the Israelis had bitterly opposed the deal. 'I understand the Iranians are walking around very satisfied in Geneva,' Netanyahu had said after the JCPOA was signed in Switzerland.

As well they should be, because they got everything and paid nothing. Everything they wanted. They wanted relief of sanctions after years of a gruelling sanctions regime. They got that. They are paying nothing because they are not reducing in any way their nuclear enrichment capability. So, Iran got the deal of the century and the international community got a bad deal. This is a very bad deal. Israel utterly rejects it.[5]

As time went by, his government became increasingly alarmed by the regime's activities in the region. '[Iran] is devouring one nation after the other,' the Israeli leader told a Chatham House audience in London in 2017.

It is doing so either by direct conquest, but more usually by using proxies: Hezbollah, they took over Lebanon and Yemen; with the Houthis they're taking over Yemen. They're trying to do the same thing with Shi'ite militias in Iraq. Same thing now in Syria, they want to import tens of thousands of Shi'ites into Syria.[6]

Obama's departure from office was an opportunity for a new start.

• • •

Trump's position on the Iran deal could not have been clearer: it was 'horrible', 'laughable', 'disastrous', 'the worst deal ever', 'one of the worst and most one-sided transactions the United States has ever entered into', and an 'embarrassment to the United States'.[7]

Initially, however, he held off from withdrawing, under pressure from his own defence and intelligence chiefs and international allies. Part of his problem was that, on the face of it, Iran appeared to be honouring its side of the agreement. There were fears that unilaterally coming out of a treaty that had been signed in good faith and was apparently being upheld would set a dangerous precedent in international affairs. Trump simply did not believe that the Iranians were genuinely meeting their obligations – and neither did the Israelis.

Every ninety days, the US administration had to certify that Iran was compliant. When the deadline for Trump's first certification approached in March 2017, his Secretary of State, Rex Tillerson, gave Iran the benefit of the doubt. The President was furious. He allowed Tillerson to certify but ordered him to insert caveats. Iran was put on notice. Tillerson's statement labelled the regime 'a leading state sponsor of terror, through many platforms and methods'.[8] The President would be reviewing America's position on sanctions in due course, the statement indicated.

When the third certification rolled around in October 2017, Trump announced new sanctions on the Iranian Revolutionary Guard Corps and declared that he was preparing to 'address the deal's many serious flaws'.[9] This would become easier in spring 2018, when he replaced his national security adviser H. R. McMaster, who had favoured sticking with the deal, with one of its most vocal critics, George Bush's former UN ambassador, John Bolton.

Bolton was an Iran hawk who, in his own words, believed 'only full-out regime change would ultimately prevent Iran from possessing nuclear weapons'.[10] In an indication of what Trump was up against, it is claimed that the President's own aides consistently worked behind his back to preserve the Iran deal. Recalling an exchange with UK national security adviser Sir Mark Sedwill, Bolton says:

> I ... took a moment to raise the 2015 Iran nuclear deal ... emphasising the likelihood, based on my many conversations with Trump, that America now really would be withdrawing. I emphasised that Trump has made no final decision, but we needed to consider how to constrain Iran after a US withdrawal and how to preserve trans-Atlantic unity. Sedwill was undoubtedly surprised to hear this. Neither he nor other Europeans had heard it before from the administration, since, before my arrival, Trump's advisors had almost uniformly resisted withdrawal.

Other leaders were also adamant that Trump was making a mistake. Around this time, Boris Johnson, then Foreign Secretary in the UK, French President Emmanuel Macron and German Chancellor Angela Merkel all made frantic trips to Washington in an attempt to persuade the White House to stick with the deal. It wasn't perfect, they argued, but it was better than nothing and could be refined.

Trump stood firm. Why would Iran want to renegotiate? The Iranian economy was booming, and they were still allowed to enrich uranium. Previously, the Non-Proliferation Treaty had prevented any enrichment at all. When the JCPOA's sunset clauses come to an end in 2031, the regime would be free to continue where it had left off – having developed considerably more expertise.

On 8 May 2018, Trump confirmed his decision: the US was out:

> The Iran deal is defective at its core. If we do nothing, we know exactly what will happen. In just a short period of time, the world's leading state sponsor of terror will be on the cusp of acquiring the

world's most dangerous weapons. Therefore, I am announcing today that the United States will withdraw from the Iran nuclear deal.[11]

In a swipe at Obama's judgement, he declared that in exchange for lifting crippling economic sanctions on Iran, the deal had only imposed 'very weak limits' on the regime's nuclear activities, 'and no limits at all on its other malign behaviour, including its sinister activities in Syria, Yemen, and other places all around the world.' He went on:

In other words, at the point when the United States had maximum leverage, this disastrous deal gave this regime – and it's a regime of great terror – many billions of dollars, some of it in actual cash – a great embarrassment to me as a citizen and to all citizens of the United States … It didn't bring calm, it didn't bring peace, and it never will.[12]

In what appeared to be a rallying call for regime change, he concluded by appealing directly to the 'long-suffering people of Iran … They are the rightful heirs to a rich culture and an ancient land. And they deserve a nation that does justice to their dreams, honour to their history, and glory to God.'

It would not come any time soon.

•   •   •

The Strait of Hormuz is a narrow entry into the Persian Gulf, through which some 21 million barrels of oil pass every day. That is around a fifth of the world's oil supply – giving anyone who controls this critical maritime passage the power to cut off the flow of fuel to their enemies.

On 12 May 2019, four tankers – two from Saudi Arabia, one from

Norway and one from the UAE – were damaged by limpet mines, explosive devices that can be attached to a ship's hull by a powerful magnet. A month later, limpet mines ripped through the underbelly of two more foreign ships. The ancient right of vessels of any flag to enjoy freedom of navigation in international waters was under unprecedented threat, in one of the most sensitive strategic points in the world. This was the work of the Iranian Revolutionary Guard.

In the days that followed, the US and UK launched a joint maritime operation to patrol shipping lanes. The security of these waters was in everyone's interests, Mike Pompeo declared at the time, and other peaceful nations should play their part.

Tensions escalated when British Royal Marines in Gibraltar seized an Iranian tanker suspected of breaking EU sanctions with Syria by selling 2.1 million barrels of oil to the failed state. The Iranian Revolutionary Guard Corps responded by sending gunboats into the Strait of Hormuz in an attempt to hijack vessels. On 19 July they finally succeeded, swarming the British-flagged *Stena Impero* as it made its way through Omani waters. Iranian Special Forces in balaclavas rappelled from a helicopter and took control of the tanker. The *Stena Impero* was held by the Iranians for over two months.

How had it come to this? The answer is that Trump had launched a policy of 'maximum pressure' on Iran after withdrawing from the JCPOA, and the regime was getting desperate. In what the White House described as 'the toughest sanctions regime ever imposed', in November 2018, restrictions came into force on over 700 entities. The economic impact was immediate and devastating. (According to the IMF, re-imposition of sanctions saw Iran's economy contract 5.4 per cent in 2018, 6.5 per cent in 2019 and 5 per cent in 2020.)

Five months later, Trump tightened the thumbscrews, making it ever harder for Iran to sell oil. Waivers that had allowed China, Greece, India, Italy, Japan, South Korea, Taiwan and Turkey to keep buying were scrapped. If these countries continued to provide custom, they too would be hit by sanctions. The loss of oil revenue hit Iran hard. Production fell from an average of 3.8 million barrels per day pre-sanctions in 2017 to around 1.9 million by August 2020.

Mohammad Ali Jafari, commander of Iran's Revolutionary Guard, had made clear that the regime intended to take this war into the Strait of Hormuz. 'We will make the enemy understand that either all can use the Strait of Hormuz or no one,' he declared.[13]

In September 2019, Iran launched an attack on the Saudi mainland. Waves of drones and missiles began hitting the world's biggest oil-processing plant, owned by Aramco at Abqaiq in eastern Saudi Arabia, and a second plant at Khurais. The smoke from the burning oil could be seen from space. The attack temporarily cut the world's oil supplies by 5 per cent and sent the price of US oil soaring by 14.7 per cent, the biggest jump since 2008. Secretary of State Mike Pompeo accused the regime of orchestrating 'an unprecedented attack on the world's energy supply'.[14] For his part, Jens Stoltenberg, Secretary-General of NATO, accused Iran of 'supporting different terrorist groups and being responsible for destabilising the whole region'.[15]

With typical bombast, Trump warned that the US was 'locked and loaded' for war. As we have seen, however, he had little appetite for discretionary military engagement.[16] 'I'm somebody that would like not to have war,' was how he put it at the time, adding that there was 'no rush'.[17]

Through attacks in the Strait of Hormuz and on Aramco, Iran was trying to disrupt global oil supplies. Few could be in any doubt over its malign influence. In November 2019, there were encouraging signs that Trump's high stakes 'maximum pressure' strategy was fuelling opposition to the regime among its own people. Following a rise in oil prices designed to fill the black hole left in the Iranian budget as a result of sanctions, thousands of young men took to the streets to protest. According to Amnesty, 304 were killed, and a further 7,000 were detained by the authorities. The real number of fatalities may have been as high as 1,500. Thanks to Trump's strong-arm tactics, Iran was beginning to crack.

• • •

Murder, betrayal and a fight for the control of the Seven Kingdoms. The hit television series *Game of Thrones* is a favourite among politicians around the world. Michael Gove, a senior UK government minister, once said his favourite character was Tyrion Lannister, a dwarf who is highly intelligent but heavy-drinking and a social outcast. The show was watched by countless others including former British Prime Minister David Cameron, former Australian Prime Minister Julia Gillard and Obama.

In 2018, Trump took enthusiasm for the series to a whole new level when he posted a photo of himself on Twitter against a wintery background. The caption read: 'Sanctions are Coming: November 5'. A riff on the show's catchphrase 'Winter Is Coming', the tweet was a warning to Iran. Not to be outdone, the Iranians hit back with their own meme. Sticking with the *Game of Thrones* theme, an Iranian commander posted a photo of himself on Instagram with the blueish hue of a White Walker, the zombie-like villains of the show, with the caption, 'I will stand against you.'

The bizarre social media exchange went viral: Trump's message was retweeted nearly 100,000 times and liked by 170,000 accounts. As for the Iranian response, those who assumed it was just harmless banter might have been more concerned had they realised that it was posted by one of the most dangerous men in the Middle East: Qasem Soleimani.

Soleimani was commander of the Iranian Quds Force, an elite branch of Iran's Islamic Revolutionary Guard Corps (IRGC). In April 2019, Trump had formally designated the IRGC a terrorist organisation, the first time the US had ever given an institution of another government this designation. Its soldiers specialised in unconventional warfare and spreading Iranian influence abroad. They were highly valuable instruments of the regime. Soleimani himself controlled a network of Shi'ite militias in Lebanon, Syria and Iraq, whose activities were hugely destabilising. The Quds Force had been instrumental in mounting the insurgency against American troops in Iraq, supplying Iraqi Shi'a militias with improvised explosive devices (IEDs) capable of destroying US armoured vehicles. According to the Pentagon, at least 603 US soldiers killed in Iraq could be attributed to the Iranian-backed militia, accounting for 17 per cent of all US personnel deaths in Iraq between 2003 and 2011.

Between Christmas and New Year in 2019, there was an upsurge in violence in Iraq linked to these Shi'a militias. On 27 December, a US civilian contractor was killed in a rocket attack at an airbase in Kirkuk in northern Iraq. Suspicions fell on an Iraqi Shi'a militia group called Kataib Hezbollah, known to be backed by Iran. Two days later, the US responded with a series of airstrikes on weapons depots owned by Kataib Hezbollah, killing twenty-five militiamen.

The American airstrikes sparked uproar in Baghdad and within the Shi'a community. On New Year's Eve, following the funeral of a number of the dead, a mob waving yellow Kataib Hezbollah flags and chanting 'Death to America' poured through Iraq's highly defended Green Zone – the hub of Iraqi government offices and foreign embassies – and surrounded the US Embassy. Over a thousand insurgents pitched tents and camped outside the embassy. Among US officials, there were fears of an all-out assault on the embassy, similar to events in 1979 in Iran and 2012 in Libya. Trump had hammered Hillary Clinton for the storming of the US embassy in Benghazi. He could not afford anything similar to happen on his watch.

US intelligence officials were in no doubt over who was to blame: the man pulling the strings was Qasem Soleimani. A decision was finally made to take him out. Though he was not as well known, the operation would be considerably riskier than the mission to neutralise either Osama bin Laden or ISIS leader Abu Bakr al-Baghdadi. Soleimani was, after all, a military commander of a sovereign state. It was the equivalent of Iran assassinating Jim Mattis or Joseph Dunford. Tehran was bound to retaliate. On balance, it was nonetheless considered worth the risk.

Just after midnight on 3 January 2020, Soleimani's plane taxied into Baghdad International Airport from Damascus. Just fifteen minutes later, his convoy was obliterated by a US Reaper drone, killing all passengers. Rumours were quickly circulating on social media that something big had happened outside of Baghdad. Soon, a gruesome image of a hand with Soleimani's distinguishable ruby ring still attached was circulating on the internet. Iran's 'shadow commander' was dead.

This was Trump's scalp. 'Soleimani made the death of innocent people his sick passion, contributing to terrorist plots as far away as New Delhi and London,' he declared.

> Today we remember and honour the victims of Soleimani's many atrocities and we take comfort in knowing that his reign of terror is over. Soleimani has been perpetrating acts of terror to destabilise the Middle East for the last twenty years. What the United States did yesterday should have been done long ago. A lot of lives would have been saved.[18]

It was the starkest of warnings to the regime to stop its machinations in the Strait of Hormuz and rein in its militias. It would emerge that Soleimani was actively developing plans to attack American diplomats and service members in Iraq and throughout the region. Trump had acted not to start a war, but to stop one.

Naturally, Iran vowed to avenge Soleimani's death. To date, however, there has been no serious reprisal. Those familiar with the regime's modus operandi believe they will wait until the US least expects it.

Just as foreign policy experts had warned that withdrawing from the JCPOA would be a catastrophe, critics now claimed Trump had gone too far. As the primaries for the Democratic presidential nomination gathered pace, some began warning of World War Three. Bernie Sanders claimed Trump's 'dangerous escalation' had brought the US closer to another disastrous conflict in the Middle East that 'could cost countless lives and trillions more dollars'.[19] The eventual victor, Joe Biden, accused the President of 'tossing a stick of dynamite into a tinderbox'.[20]

It fell to Sir John Sawers, former head of MI6, to give a more balanced view. In a speech to RUSI in October 2020, he said,

> In some ways, one of the things which slightly surprised me was the impact of the killing of Qasem Soleimani on Iran. I think some liberals in the West thought this would only make matters worse. Actually, it has been a salutatory reminder to the Iranians that they can go too far.[21]

The withdrawal from the JCPOA remains one of the most controversial moves of Trump's presidency. While there was broad consensus that the treaty needed to be improved, only Trump recognised that meaningful change would not be possible within the JCPOA's one-sided framework. The rogue state was filling its boots and expanding its influence in the region on the back of the relaxation of sanctions. Its nuclear programme was at best on hold; more likely, it was surreptitiously continuing apace. When the regime overreached itself with militias in Iraq and flouted rules on international freedom of navigation, Trump was not afraid to push back hard, deploying the US Navy to the Persian Gulf and assassinating Soleimani. These were carefully calculated steps, the potential consequences meticulously mapped before the go-ahead. They did not result in disaster.

Not since Reagan had America's adversaries faced such an unpredictable occupant of the White House. And unpredictability can be a great foreign policy advantage.

18

PEACE THROUGH STRENGTH - TRUMP AND ISRAEL

It would be difficult to imagine a more bitter and seemingly intractable problem than 'the Middle East'. For years, countless Presidents, diplomats, politicians and peace brokers had tried and failed to break the deadlock between the Palestinians and the Israelis and their various regional supporters. If ever a different approach was needed, surely it was here. Nothing that had been tried to date had worked – if anything, it seemed to have made matters worse. With such a delicate situation, few would have predicted that a brash, blunt-talking property developer from New York would make any headway. After all, countless 'professionals' had failed miserably. During Trump's presidency, he managed to secure several peace deals in the Middle East. They barely got a mention in the press.

In 2016, John Kerry claimed there would never be peace between Israel and the Arab world. By 2020, Trump had brokered peace deals between Israel and the UAE, Bahrain, Sudan and Morocco. John Kerry has been in politics since 1972 and served as Secretary of State in 2013–17. Donald Trump is a brash New York real-estate developer. Maybe time to let the businesspeople have a go?

On a chill winter night in a dreary commercial district of Tehran, a group of shadowy figures made their way stealthily towards a nondescript warehouse. Just as their year-long surveillance operation had indicated, there were no guards present that night. This was fortunate, because, unlike the ice fog conditions of the previous evening, it was a clear night, and the waxing moon illuminated their every move.

Every step had been planned and choreographed in minute detail. First, they had to disable the alarm system and break through two doors; then, they had to cut through thirty-two enormous safes; finally, they had to leave undetected with thousands of top-secret documents. The precious stash would weigh no less than half a ton.

For all their meticulous preparation, they knew they would have to be ready to think on their feet. But the schedule was strict: whatever happened, they would have to vacate the premises at least two hours before the guards returned at 7 a.m.

Equipped with blowtorches that blasted out flames at 2,000 degrees Celsius, the secret agents burned their way into the selected safes to retrieve what they had come for. After six hours and twenty-nine minutes, they emerged with their treasure: documents that included over 50,000 pages, and 163 CDs containing memos, videos and other plans. They quickly loaded the evidence into trucks and left the country by several different routes. Despite the anticipated nationwide manhunt that followed, no trace of the men nor their haul was ever found.

Three months later, this movie-worthy Israeli spy mission was revealed to the world. It had been a triumph. After privately briefing American President Donald Trump on the details, Israeli Prime Minister Benjamin Netanyahu announced that a group of Tehran-based Mossad agents had successfully retrieved evidence that irrefutably proved what the Israelis had long suspected: Iran's nuclear programme posed an existential threat to the Middle East. This was what Trump needed to strengthen his resolve to abandon the JCPOA and bear down hard on the Iranian regime. The cache of documents showed that the Iran deal was not worth the paper it was printed on, and that the Iranian regime was continuing its clandestine uranium enrichment programme with the intention of using it to build an atomic bomb. The top-secret files also showed that Israel was the key target. Within days of his watershed meeting with Netanyahu, Trump made good on his previous warnings of withdrawing from the Iran deal.

Those who backed Trump's decision knew from experience what many in the West did not want to admit: Iran could not be given an inch. In a televised address, Netanyahu confirmed Israel's full support of the withdrawal. Trump was proving a good friend to Israel – and he would go much further.

• • •

Five days after the US pulled out of the JCPOA, Jared Kushner and Ivanka Trump swept into Israel's Ben Gurion International Airport ahead of one of the most controversial ceremonies of Trump's presidency. The timing of their visit could not have been more sensitive. That very day, 13 May 2018, the Israelis would be celebrating the 70th anniversary of the creation of their state; the following day, the Palestinians would be commemorating what they refer to as the Nabka, or 'Catastrophe', when thousands of their people were displaced from their land as a direct result of the foundation of Israel in 1948. The rolling protests that accompany this anniversary are known as the Great March of Return. Tensions were already rising ahead of the annual demonstrations, with the Israeli military poised to use lethal force.

Trump's daughter and son-in-law had flown into this maelstrom to mark the official opening of the American embassy in Jerusalem. Jerusalem is no ordinary city. With a history that dates back over 3,500 years, it is revered as a holy place to Jews, Christians and Muslims. Often referred to as the City of Peace, it has been besieged, captured and recaptured dozens of times – and destroyed and rebuilt at least twice. Though its strongest ties are arguably Jewish, no piece of real estate is more highly contested.

Today, the status of the city remains at the heart of the Israel–Palestine conflict. Israel regards Jerusalem as its 'eternal and undivided' capital and has built around a dozen settlements on the east of the city, housing some 200,000 Jews, since 1967. Some say the settlements breach international law; others insist on Israel's historic right to the land. For their part, the Palestinians regard East Jerusalem as the capital of a future state. Against this backdrop, Trump's decision to recognise Jerusalem as Israel's capital – a move decried by Palestinian leaders as the 'kiss of death' to the two-state peace solution – was highly symbolic and broke decades of US neutrality on the issue. Put simply, it acknowledged Israel's historic right to the land at the expense of the Palestinian claim.

In diplomatic circles, such a move had long been considered unthinkable. Foreign policy experts generally believed that anyone foolish or fundamentalist enough to recognise Jerusalem as the capital of Israel would also be responsible for widespread riots, if not open war against the State of Israel and her allies. This debate continued up until 'opening day' of the new embassy, which – to widespread relief – came and went without a hitch. Outside the new building, a giant billboard proclaimed that Trump was making Israel 'Great Again'.

In fact, Trump was not the first American President to say that he would move the US Embassy to Jerusalem: previous administrations had also promised to do so but failed to follow through. On 23 October 1995, both Congress and the Senate passed the Jerusalem Embassy Act of 1995. The legislation assigned resources to transferring the American Embassy to Jerusalem, setting 31 May 1999 as the deadline. Despite overwhelming bipartisan support for the move, President Clinton rejected it, arguing that it would derail the Middle East peace process. President George W. Bush promised to relocate the embassy to Jerusalem, but both he and President Obama continually signed security waivers to delay the process.

Whether the experts were wrong all along or whether circumstances have changed is open for debate. What mattered to the

Israelis was that Trump had had the fortitude to make the decision at the right time – without any of the disastrous consequences his predecessors allowed themselves to be persuaded were inevitable.

Moving the embassy seemed dangerous to some and inconsequential to others, when, in reality, it was neither. Acknowledging Jerusalem as the capital of Israel was one facet of a much larger issue: the recognition of Israel's sovereignty over territory it claims as its own – which (naturally) it considers fundamental to its survival and to regional security. For decades, Israel has been facing an existential crisis. Surrounded by neighbours bent on its destruction, it has had to develop creative defensive strategies to avoid being annihilated. However, world-class military technology only goes so far if it is not possible to establish a military presence on the land itself. Trump was much more ready than his predecessors to risk the ire of the Palestinians and their sympathisers in the region, by openly supporting Israel's territorial claims.

In another highly controversial move, as well as acknowledging Jerusalem as the capital city, he recognised the Golan Heights as belonging to Israel. Captured from Syria by the Israeli Defense Forces during the 1967 Six-Day War, the rocky plateau is considered vital to Israel's security. The international community continues to regard the Golan Heights as Syrian territory and rejects the Israeli military occupation. Only the US recognises the area as sovereign Israeli territory.

Paradoxically, Trump's affirmation of Israel's border integrity appears to have been instrumental to regional stability, reinforcing the ability of the Israeli military to monitor (and react to) threats in the wider region.

Danny Ayalon, former Israeli ambassador to the United States, says:

World-renowned jurists support the fact that Israel has a right to this land. This territory is a vital part of maintaining Israel's security. If Israel withdrew then it would not be able to effectively defend itself against attack. Israel also plays a critical role in restraining external threats, including those posed by Iranian-funded terror groups. A strong Israel that includes secure borders impacts other parts of the Middle East because it prevents regional bullies from doing even more damage.[1]

In January 2020, Trump sought to capitalise on these achievements with an agreement he labelled the 'Deal of the Century'. Naturally, it was instantly derided, not least because of this extravagant claim. Nonetheless, it was not without its achievements.

Billed as a 'vision to improve the lives of the Palestinian and Israeli people', it was unveiled at a White House press conference by Trump alongside Netanyahu. Authored by a team led by Kushner, it was rejected by the Palestinians before it was even published.

While it was hopelessly one-sided, it did succeed in solidifying America's stance on important security-related issues. For one, it did not allow the Palestinian Authority to get away with unreasonable territorial demands in exchange for promises of peace. Crucially, it also gave Israel the green light to annex the Jordan Valley – land the Israeli leadership considers vital to the state's defences. Also called Judea and Samaria, this part of the West Bank is home to numerous Jewish historical sites as well as over 400,000 residents. Many of the settlements are located on sites that were home to Jewish communities in previous generations (though they currently cover a mere 1.7 per cent of the land). Naturally, the Israelis were delighted by Trump's decision to endorse their right to remain.

According to retired American Lieutenant General Thomas Kelly, director of operations for the joint chiefs of staff during the Gulf War:

It is impossible to defend Jerusalem unless you hold the high ground ... An aircraft that takes off from an airport in Amman is going to be over Jerusalem in two and a half minutes, so it's utterly impossible for me to defend the whole country unless I hold that land.[2]

The reality is that any missiles launched from the Judean Hills pose an imminent threat to Jerusalem, as well as to Israel's only international airport in Tel Aviv, where even primitive rockets fired from the Hills could cause serious damage. Advanced weaponry from that location could hit any point in Israel. A withdrawal to the 1949 armistice lines (also called the Green Line) would reduce the country's width to 9 miles in one area, rendering it indefensible to oncoming enemy attack.

Trump's 'Deal of the Century' marked a major shift in US policy, abandoning the long-held status quo and setting the US on a different diplomatic path to that still being pursued in the United Kingdom and other European nations. As far as the Israelis were concerned, it was necessary to assert the bare minimum of what they needed to survive in a tough neighbourhood. Indirectly, it also facilitated one of the President's greatest successes: the Abraham Accords.

• • •

On the last day of August 2020, an El Al flight touched down at Abu Dhabi International Airport in the United Arab Emirates. Casual observers who may not have immediately recognised the historic significance of an aircraft operated by the Israeli state landing in an Arab state, might nonetheless have noticed something unusual about the plane, which had been emblazoned with the word 'Peace' in Arabic, English and Hebrew.

Inside the aircraft was Trump's son-in-law, Jared Kushner, and Israel's national security adviser, Meir Ben-Shabbat, along with various officials from both countries. During the three-hour flight, Kushner had made an unusual request of the pilot: was it possible to go any faster? They were on an urgent mission, he told the crew, and wanted to begin work as soon as possible.

Flight LY971 was making the first official flight from Israel to the United Arab Emirates, after the UAE became only the third Middle Eastern country to recognise the state of Israel since 1948. In an indication of the importance of this journey, the aircraft had been allowed to pass through Saudi airspace, which is normally closed to Israeli air traffic. The two countries, long at bitter logger-heads, were taking the first steps towards normalising diplomatic relations.

This was a 'historic breakthrough', Kushner told the media in Abu Dhabi, and it had been a 'tremendous honour' to have joined the flight. 'What happened here was three great leaders came together and they started writing a new script for the Middle East. They said the future doesn't have to be predetermined by the past.'[3]

Raised in a Modern Orthodox Jewish family, Kushner had seemed a natural choice to broker diplomatic relations between Israel and the Arab States. Officially signed on the White House lawn on 15 September 2020, the so-called Abraham Accords represented a new kind of peace that did not require giving up land or paying off debts. This 'peace through strength', as Israeli Prime Minister Netanyahu put it, was ultimately achieved by capitalising on mutual goals like prosperity and defending against the threat of Iran. Though some mixed feelings remained, the achievement was unprecedented.

According to Ryan Mauro, a national security analyst at the Clarion Project think tank, the deal signalled nothing less than 'a new era in the Middle East and the Islamic world'. He went on:

It's not just about an agreement between Arab countries and Israel that is mutually beneficial, though they will have to defend it to their populations after years of promoting slogans like 'death to Israel'. As a result, other Muslim countries will become more comfortable with doing so and extremists will be sidelined. For the first time we can actually envision peace in the Middle East happening in our lifetime.

The agreement normalised diplomatic relations between Israel and these Arab nations on the basis of a mutual desire for peace. It put a firm focus on joint prosperity, with improved economic and military co-operation. It also emphasised a joint approach to the threat posed by Iran. While many European nations reject Israeli goods manufactured in the West Bank, on the grounds that Israeli settlements in the occupied Palestinian territories undermine efforts to create a Palestinian state, these nations would now welcome them, labelling them as from Judea and Samaria.

A few years earlier, a concordat between Israel and Arab States like the UAE and Bahrain had seemed inconceivable. Now, the relationship was being transformed. How had Trump made it happen? Certainly not by accepting the 'tried and tested' but ultimately failed approaches to foreign policy. In 2016, John Kerry had declared that there could be 'no advanced and separate peace with the Arab world without the Palestinian process and Palestinian peace. Everybody needs to understand that.'[4] In other words, Kerry and many others believed that the Arab world would not make peace with Israel until a Palestinian state had been established – not the other way around. Trump recognised that pandering to the corrupt Palestinian leadership had resulted in minimal progress, over a very long period. Instead, ignoring the fury of the powerful pro-Palestinian lobby worldwide, he took a counterintuitive approach to peace. For years, the Palestinian leadership dictated the policies of other Arab nations towards Israel. Today, the opposite is happening. These agreements may even serve as a catalyst for a viable Israeli–Palestinian peace deal in the future.

As we have seen, Trump chose Saudi Arabia for his first international visit as President. During this trip, he validated the strengths and empathised with the fears of the heart of the Muslim world, while emphasising that the US remained a force to be reckoned with and relied upon. This careful positioning would soon be rewarded: his subsequent peace agreements could not have succeeded without Saudi backing.

History had not been on Trump's side. The region bore deep scars from conflicts over the decades. Countless individuals had tried to come to a solution in order to integrate Israel into the Middle East; few had succeeded. During his time as President, Trump was able to facilitate not one but four normalisation agreements between Israel and the Arab world. While those that had once been in the thick of it commentated from the sidelines that it couldn't be done, Trump yet again defied the odds and was able to prove otherwise to Washington's political establishment.

• • •

Perhaps surprisingly for a President that had no foreign policy expertise, Trump appears to have instinctively understood the Middle Eastern mindset better than his predecessors. Peace through strength is a concept widely understood in that part of the world. Past Presidents prided themselves on their Ivy League degrees, pursuing what they considered to be an 'enlightened' approach to foreign policy. Trump had grown up in the rough-and-tumble New York borough of Queens, notorious for its no-bones-about-it, tough, can-do environment. He made his money prior to entering politics – with considerable family help – rather than as a result of his political career. Unlike other Presidents, whose loyalties could be bought, he was free to be as single-mindedly committed to causes as he pleased. He was not a cookie-cutter career politician with talking points that regurgitated the mantras of elitist puppet masters or pandered to the judgement of the media. Trump answered only to his voters and to his own conscience. Just as in his business and personal life, he entered politics as a bulldog that could be petted – but he was also ready to fight. He understood dangerous neighbourhoods and their regional bullies – bullies like Iran and the Palestinian leadership. He also understood the importance of sticking up for your friends – in this case, Israel. This was the level of it, and while lofty elites could (and did) scoff, the results speak for themselves.

The looming threat posed by Iran injected a new urgency and a new opportunity for peace. Princess Hend, former wife of the Emir of Qatar and mother of the crown prince, currently residing in Dubai, believes Trump has made a dramatic contribution to the stability of the region. She said:

> Israel is surrounded by countries who want to destroy them. Before if you were Jewish you would be quiet about it, but now people are excited for Israelis to come. Everyone wants peace and to be surrounded by good people – people who have a future. Trump's bedside manner is lacking, but I look at key performance indicators. I like what the Democrats say, but not what they do. I don't like what the Republicans say, but I like what they do.[5]

By 2020, even Trump's detractors were beginning to acknowledge the significance of his contribution to the Middle East peace process. Chris Coons, a Democrat Senator, said, 'The normalization of relations of any country in the region and Israel is a positive step forward.' And Elizabeth Warren, a Democrat Senator who vied to be the Democrat presidential candidate, said, 'I'm always glad to see steps toward peace.'

Whether or not any liberal Western institution will openly recognise – and honour – these remarkable achievements remains to be seen.

19

GRAVEYARD OF EMPIRES
- AFGHANISTAN

In the aftermath of 9/11, most people in the West supported the decision to send allied troops into Afghanistan. At the time, there was a clear objective: to disrupt the use of Afghanistan as a base for international terror operations and cripple the military capability of the Taliban. Sure, President Bush warned that the job might take a while, but I don't think anybody thought he meant decades. What had started as a limited and highly targeted campaign to root out terror turned into a multi-front war that has now dragged on for longer than the US war with Vietnam.

Long before entering politics, Trump was calling for America to get out. The way he looked at it was simple: how much is this costing us, both in human lives and cold hard cash, and what is it actually achieving? After a while, it just didn't stack up. It is not quite true that the Afghans have always beaten foreign armies, but most have eventually left exhausted and humiliated. The way Trump saw it – and I'm with him on this – if the Afghans want to fight each other once the invaders have left, that's their problem.

On a momentous Sunday afternoon, four weeks after the deadliest terror attack in American history, President George W. Bush announced that the United States was at war. It was 7 October 2001, and the country was still reeling from the horror of

11 September. Almost 3,000 citizens had been killed and more than 25,000 injured in a series of co-ordinated attacks by Islamic extremists on the twin towers of the World Trade Center and at the Pentagon. Now, the most powerful military in the world was preparing to retaliate.

Dressed in a suit and tie in colours that perfectly matched the stars and stripes of the American flag behind him, the President sat behind his desk in the Treaty Room of the White House – the birthplace of many historic peace deals – and announced that he had given the order for military strikes in Afghanistan. Somewhere in the labyrinthine caves and mountains of the country known as the 'Graveyard of Empires', the mastermind of the 9/11 attacks, Osama bin Laden, was hiding. America would smoke him out.

In the days that followed, the terrorist training camps and installations of al-Qaeda and the Taliban regime faced a ferocious onslaught from land-based bombers, carrier-based F-14 Tomcat and F-A/18 Hornet fighters, and Tomahawk cruise missiles launched from both US and British ships and submarines. Called 'Operation Enduring Freedom', the initial invasion was designed to disrupt the use of Afghanistan as a terrorist base and clear the way for what Bush called a 'sustained, comprehensive and relentless operation' to destroy al-Qaeda's terror network and dismember the extremist fundamentalist Taliban government that had dominated Afghanistan since 1996.[1] In his initial address to the nation, Bush repeatedly signalled that the mission would take time. The terrorists were likely to 'burrow deeper into caves and other entrenched hiding places', he warned. Given the nature and reach of the enemy, it would require 'the patient accumulation of successes'. Patience would be 'one of the nation's great strengths'.[2]

Watching at home on their television sets, few Americans gave much thought to the likely length of the overseas mission. When Bush warned that it would 'take time to achieve our goals', most of those listening probably assumed that he meant months, not years.

Had they known that the conflict would drag on for the best part of two decades, spanning the administrations of three Presidents, public support for the operation, which was overwhelming at the start, would surely have evaporated.

Fast-forward a decade after that speech, and America remained mired in a NATO-led operation that achieved some spectacular successes at the start but which slowly unravelled. It took coalition forces little over a month to seize control of the capital Kabul, a very tangible early result. By December, Kandahar, Afghanistan's second largest city and the last Taliban stronghold, had also fallen and Taliban chief Mullah Mohammed Omar had fled. By Christmas, al-Qaeda had initiated a truce, and their bunker and cave complex in the Tora Bora mountains had been taken. Soon, Afghanistan would have a new President, Hamid Karzai, a figure who had supported the coalition effort against the Taliban and with whom the allies felt they could work. To the relief of political leaders in the NATO member states involved in the operation, the war appeared to be going to plan.

As Afghanistan took the first tentative steps towards democracy, however, Taliban fighters were quietly regrouping in the mountainous border area with Pakistan. They could not match the conventional firepower of the International Security Assistance Force (ISAF) – but on hostile terrain they knew how to navigate far better than their enemies; they could position snipers to pick off American soldiers one by one and plant improvised explosive devices to blow up their convoys. Through relentless guerrilla warfare, far more expensive for the ISAF than it was for the Taliban, they would gradually wear down the Western invaders.

By 2011, some 2,700 NATO troops and 10,000 Afghan civilians had been killed, and NATO allies had spent £258 billion on a war that was, in the words of a top US general, 'little better than halfway' towards achieving its aims.[3]

Among the many public figures who despaired at the loss of blood and treasure was Donald Trump. On 7 October 2011, ten years to the day since Operation Enduring Freedom began, the property tycoon and showbiz star voiced his anger over the seemingly endless war. 'When will we stop wasting our money on rebuilding Afghanistan? We must rebuild our country first,' he tweeted.[4]

Earlier that year, Trump had made his first speaking appearance at the Conservative Political Action Conference and given a number of speeches in early primary states, prompting speculation that he was considering a tilt at the White House. The rumours were quashed when, in May 2011, he announced he would not run. His political ambitions were on hold, but Afghanistan continued to rile him. Every time he saw pictures of grief-stricken widows of fallen US servicemen and coffins draped in the American flag, his view hardened. For the next few years, he periodically fired off tweets labelling the war a 'disaster'. 'It is time to get out,' he complained in 2012.[5]

While he was just a celebrity businessman and TV personality, there was no need to trouble himself with the complexities of the conflict. In due course, however, he would no longer be just another angry observer. The misery of Operation Enduring Freedom would become very much his problem.

•　•　•

Unlike Steve Bannon, a former naval officer, Trump had zero experience in military matters. His position was that you did not need to be any kind of defence expert to see that his two predecessors had screwed up over Afghanistan.

When Obama took over from Bush, the security situation was rapidly deteriorating. The new President did what new political leaders usually do when they inherit a long-running problem and commissioned a strategic review, in the hope it would offer some answers. According to a well-placed former State Department official, however, even this got off to the wrong start, as the President 'dithered' and procrastinated and asked the wrong questions.

In a damning account of Obama's record in Afghanistan, Vali Nasr, now a professor of Middle East Studies and International Affairs at Johns Hopkins University, says the President was 'busybodying the national security apparatus by asking for more answers to the same set of questions, each time posed differently'. He appointed an outstanding diplomat, Richard Holbrooke, as a special representative in Afghanistan and Pakistan, but Nasr claims Holbrooke was given neither the support nor the authority he required to make a difference. 'Obama has earned plaudits for his foreign policy performance ... [but] my time in the Obama administration turned out to be a deeply disillusioning experience. The truth is that his administration made it extremely difficult for its own foreign policy experts to be heard,' Nasr has said, adding that the President had a 'truly disturbing habit of funnelling major foreign policy decisions through a small cabal of relatively inexperienced White House advisors whose turf was strictly politics'.[6]

The upshot of Obama's review was a surge in troop numbers. To counter the growing insurgency, in December 2009 (a week before he jetted to Oslo to pick up a Nobel Peace Prize), he announced that 30,000 additional servicemen and women would be going to Afghanistan. By mid-2010, there would be 100,000 young American soldiers in the country. Knowing just how badly this would go down with a US electorate already sickened by the mounting death toll, at the same time as announcing the additional troops, Obama set out a timetable for withdrawal. 'After eighteen months, our troops will begin to come home,' he promised.[7]

Defence chiefs were furious. Such mixed messages risked undermining everything they were trying to achieve. If the Taliban knew the Americans and their friends would be leaving in eighteen months, the troop surge would not frighten them. All they had to do was dig in and wait.

Trump's former national security adviser, Lieutenant General H. R. McMaster, would subsequently label the conflict a 'one-year war fought twenty times over'. He later said, 'As in the Vietnam War, our nation's soldiers were taking risks and making sacrifices without understanding how those risks and sacrifices contributed to a worthy outcome. If the objective was withdrawal, why were soldiers still in harm's way?'[8]

Ronald Neumann, the former US ambassador to Afghanistan, is also scathing about the way coalition forces approached the conflict during this period. In a blunt exchange with ISAF Commander-General Stanley McChrystal in May 2010, he said nobody seemed to know why they were there. 'While everyone spoke of needing significant progress by 2011, there was no definition of what this meant or what would happen if it were achieved – or not achieved. If we did not know how to define progress for ourselves, how could we expect the Afghans to understand?'[9]

When the withdrawal began in June 2011, Obama used language that could have come from Trump's America First policy. 'America, it is time to focus on nation building here at home,' he declared.

The first drawdown saw 10,000 troops return, followed by 33,000 more by summer 2012. However, Afghanistan was little, if any, more stable than before, and US politicians and military chiefs remained deeply divided over strategy.

Describing the confusion during this period, Obama's deputy national security adviser, Ben Rhodes, has recalled the contradictory strategies pursued by Obama's Defense Secretary, commander of the ISAF, chairman of the joint chiefs of staff and Secretary of State:

> When the shortcomings of the Afghan government were pointed out, [Robert] Gates said that we should not give 'one dollar or soldier' for a corrupt government – even though that's exactly what we were doing. [David] Petraeus said our goal was not to defeat the Taliban but to deny them population centres. [Michael]

Mullen talked about the psychological piece – the need to create the impression that the Taliban will lose. For the same reason, [Hillary] Clinton said that putting in troops wouldn't work but you still need to put in troops.[10]

Trapped in a place that seemed as dangerous and unstable as it had been when they arrived, the allies were getting desperate. Raising the stakes, amid great secrecy, the Obama administration began seeking to establish a backchannel to Taliban leaders. Unable to crush these fanatical guerrilla fighters with any permanent effect, perhaps there was nothing for it but to invite the enemy to the table? And so it was that in 2010, unofficial peace talks began, orchestrated by Holbrooke and Obama's Secretary of State, Hillary Clinton.

Recalling the decision in her memoirs, Clinton writes, 'History tells us that insurgencies rarely end with a surrender ceremony on the deck of a battleship. Instead they tend to run out of steam thanks to persistent diplomacy, steady improvements in quality of life for people on the ground, and unyielding perseverance by those who want peace.'[11]

Unfortunately, the Obama administration couldn't even win over America's supposed allies in Afghanistan, never mind the Taliban. Part of the problem was Karzai, who was very difficult to deal with. Vice-President Joe Biden apparently 'detested' him.[12] As a Senator, Biden had visited Karzai to discuss his concerns over corruption in Afghanistan. When the American didn't like what he was hearing, he threw his napkin on the table in front of the Afghan Cabinet and declared, 'This dinner is over.'[13] In her memoir, Clinton describes Karzai as 'proud, stubborn, and quick to bristle at any perceived slight'. She writes, 'Talking to Hamid Karzai, the President of Afghanistan, was often a frustrating exercise' – but, unfortunately, there was no way round him. 'Like it or not, Karzai was a linchpin of our mission in Afghanistan.'[14]

Obama's relationship with the Afghan leader was also difficult.

He had significantly less personal contact with Karzai than Bush had managed, which did not help. And the debacle over a surprise visit to US troops at Bagram airfield in December 2010 had further strained relations. Poor weather meant Obama could not fly to Kabul to see Karzai as planned; rather than wait for conditions to clear, the President left without seeing the Afghan leader. Karzai was put out.

In any case, he always kept the Americans at arm's length, once telling sixty Afghan parliamentarians: 'If you and the international community pressure me more, I swear that I am going to join the Taliban.'[15] For a man whose father was gunned down by the Taliban, that was quite a statement. They got nowhere.

Obama had made Afghanistan his top overseas priority when he entered office, but in eight years and two terms, he neither ended the war nor the violence. He did eventually manage to reduce the number of troops from 100,000 to 8,400, but the killing and maiming of Afghan citizens continued apace. The number of civilian injuries increased every single year during his time in office, from 3,557 in 2009 to 7,925 in 2016 when he left the White House. Civilian fatalities also increased from 2,412 to 3,527. The security situation in Afghanistan deteriorated rather than improved. In total 24,850 Afghan civilians were killed and 45,347 injured during his tenure as President. If the objective was to bring stability to Afghanistan, then the Obama administration had achieved the opposite.

In his excoriating piece, written in 2013, Vali Nasr writes of Obama:

It was to court public opinion that Obama first embraced the war in Afghanistan. And when public opinion changed, he was quick to declare victory and call the troops back home. His actions from start to finish were guided by politics, and they played well at home. Abroad, however, the stories the United States tells to justify its on-again, off-again approach do not ring true to friend or foe. They know the truth: America is leaving Afghanistan to its own fate. America is leaving even as the demons of regional chaos that first beckoned it there are once again rising to threaten its security.[16]

As Obama left the White House in 2016, the question was whether Trump could do better.

• • •

Of all the fake, sun-baked beachfront developments in Dubai, the Palm Jumeirah is the most jaw-dropping. Sometimes dubbed the 'eighth wonder of the world' in recognition of the extraordinary feat of engineering and construction required to create the man-made archipelagos in the shape of a palm tree, the artificial islands are the jewel in the crown of the United Arab Emirates. Among the many high-profile figures who invested in swanky apartments there were David and Victoria Beckham; Brad Pitt and Angelina Jolie; Michael Schumacher – and a political family whose multi-million-pound property portfolio on the islands raised more than a few eyebrows. Their surname was Karzai – and they were close relatives and associates of the Afghan President. Hamid Karzai's own brother, Mahmoud, lavished millions of pounds on glitzy waterside properties there, using Kabul Bank, then Afghanistan's biggest and most controversial private bank, to bankroll his purchases. Much of the money flowing through the troubled bank came from international aid, donated to support public-sector salaries. The purchase of swanky properties in Dubai by members of the Karzai family raised fears that it was being syphoned off in a corrupt fashion.

Since Operation Enduring Freedom began in 2001, the World Bank has consistently ranked Afghanistan in the top ten most corrupt nations. Billions of US taxpayers' dollars were purloined by Afghan officials and warlords. A report by the Special Inspector

General for Afghanistan Reconstruction argues that corruption became so prevalent in Afghanistan due to 'continuing insecurity, weak systems of accountability, the drug trade, a large influx of money, and poor oversight of contracting and procurement related to the international presence'.[17] The influx of money into the economy was a particular concern. In 2010, US reconstruction assistance provided more cash than the size of the entire Afghan economy, totalling around $15 billion just that year. Trump picked up on this at the time. In February 2012, he tweeted, 'We are building roads and schools for people that hate us. It's not in our national interests.' A month later he exclaimed that the Afghans were 'robbing us blind!'[18] By the time Trump entered office the war had cost American taxpayers at least $662 billion. His inaugural address left little doubt about his intention to draw the line. The US had, he declared, 'subsidized the armies of other countries while allowing for the very sad depletion of our military'. It had 'spent trillions of dollars overseas while America's infrastructure has fallen into disrepair'.[19] With his arrival in the White House, he made clear, that era was coming to an end.

As we have seen, before Afghanistan became his problem, Trump had been all for withdrawing US forces immediately. That was his instinct, and, as he told one crowd, he'd always made a habit of following his gut. To the same audience, however, he also acknowledged that this approach to decision-making might not work quite so well in the Oval Office. And so it was that once he became President, he had to listen – at least somewhat – to his generals.

Dubbed the 'axis of adults' by a liberal media neurotic about where Trump's instincts might lead and desperately seeking reassurance that his actions would be tempered by advisers with a more analytical approach to international affairs, these 'grown-ups' were led by General Jim 'Mad Dog' Mattis. Mad Dog was a nickname he'd been given by the media. It had been seized on by Trump, although he was also known as the Warrior Monk due to his vast collection of books. An outspoken critic of Obama's Middle Eastern policy, he had famously advised Marines in Iraq to 'be polite, be professional, but have a plan to kill everybody you meet'.[20]

Mirroring Obama's first move, in the first few weeks of his presidency, Trump ordered Mattis to launch a comprehensive review of US strategy in Afghanistan. Unlike Obama, Trump did not meddle with the process – he had never been interested in the detail. The result of Mattis's review was a five-point plan, based on ending the Obama era's arbitrary timetables for troop withdrawals. Decisions would now be based entirely on conditions on the ground. The second pillar was the integration of diplomatic, economic and military instruments of American power. The third sent a stark warning to neighbouring Pakistan. Trump said:

We can no longer be silent about Pakistan's safe havens for terrorist organizations, the Taliban, and other groups that pose a threat to the region and beyond. Pakistan has much to gain from partnering with our effort in Afghanistan. It has much to lose by continuing to harbour criminals and terrorists.[21]

Fourthly, with Pakistan seen as a hindrance, America would increasingly turn to that country's old foe, India, for assistance in the South Asia region. Finally, Trump would ensure America was properly equipped for the fight. That meant giving the military more freedom to face down the enemy.

The number of strikes on Afghanistan showed Trump meant business. In 2015, there were only 947 airstrikes in Afghanistan as part of Operation Freedom's Sentinel, the mission that followed Operation Enduring Freedom which had officially ended in 2014. In 2016 the figure increased slightly to 1,337. Under Trump, the number of airstrikes in 2017, 2018 and 2019 soared to 4,361, 7,362 and 7,423, respectively.

Trump remained impatient for results. He simply was not willing to tolerate an approach that looked like 'more of the same'. By September 2018, he was becoming increasingly agitated. He couldn't understand why the US was still there. Even America's top general, Joseph Dunford, was beginning to sound pessimistic. In late 2018, Dunford told a security forum, 'They [the Taliban] are not losing right now, I think that is fair to say. We used the term stalemate a year ago and, relatively speaking, it has not changed much.'[22] America was no closer to getting out. A new approach was required.

Firstly, Trump began to build pressure on Pakistan to stop providing the safe haven for terrorists he had previously warned about. Pakistan's Inter-Services Intelligence Directorate had a long history of aiding and abetting the Taliban. As a result, the US would cut foreign aid by $300 million. A more significant development was the creation of a new position in the Trump administration: the US Representative for Afghanistan Reconciliation. Appointed to the role was Afghan-born diplomat Zalmay Khalilzad. Khalilzad had a wealth of diplomatic experience and got on well with members of the Afghan government. Under President Bush, he had been the US ambassador in Iraq, Afghanistan and finally the UN. Members of the Taliban had already begun to reach out to him, expressing an interest in coming to the table. The appointment signalled a new direction. Bill Clinton's former Assistant Secretary of State for South and Central Asian Affairs, Robin Raphel, told National Public Radio, 'I think everybody realises – and I include in this the Taliban – that things in Afghanistan are getting too fractured, that there are too many players and Afghanistan could become the next Syria if attention is not paid to the political as well as the military dimensions.'[23] Obama had never been convinced by the case for pursuing a diplomatic solution with the Taliban. By contrast, Trump believed that however distasteful the notion of talking to tyrants who had yet to lay down their arms, negotiations were almost always worth a try.

• • •

In the wooded hills of the eastern Appalachians, unmarked on park maps, lies the country retreat of US Presidents. The long list of foreign dignitaries who have stayed at Camp David in Catoctin Mountain Park, Maryland, includes Margaret Thatcher, Tony Blair and Russian President Vladimir Putin. In September 2019, the most trusted senior officials at the residence began preparing for a very different type of foreign delegation. The 'VIP' visitors in question were Taliban leaders. By affording them the same status as overseas heads of state, their host, President Trump, was taking a huge political risk. It was imperative that the plan remain top secret.

The impetus to seek peace with the Taliban came from Secretary of State Mike Pompeo – though, as we have seen, it was not an entirely new policy. Moreover, there were divisions within the administration over whether it was a good idea, particularly between Pompeo's State Department and the national security team led by John Bolton. Many senior figures baulked at the thought of doing deals with the Taliban, who were hardly the most trustworthy negotiating partners. Other defence and foreign policy experts continued to believe that the US should stay in Afghanistan almost indefinitely, in order to prevent another 9/11. 'This was about keeping America safe from another 9/11, or even worse, a 9/11 where the terrorists had nuclear, chemical, or biological weapons. As long as the threat existed, no place was too far away to worry about,' John Bolton has written in his memoirs.[24] Republican Senator Lindsey Graham warned Trump in private: 'Do you want on your résumé that you allowed Afghanistan to go back into the darkness and the second 9/11 came from the very place the first 9/11 did?'[25]

There was a significant flaw to this argument, namely bin Laden's original 'justification' for 9/11, which was born of a grievance over the presence of US troops in Saudi Arabia. Maintaining a US presence in Afghanistan risked painting a permanent target on the back of the US. As for staying to train Afghan security forces, there had already been more than enough time to do that. America had poured tens of billions of dollars into the Afghanistan Security Forces Fund. US taxpayers were entitled to assume they were now equipped to sort themselves out.

And so, Trump encouraged the diplomatic effort. Under Khalilzad, secret negotiations with the Taliban made good progress. On 16 August 2019, a number of administration officials and advisers met with Trump at his golf club in Bedminster to update him. 'Just completed a very good meeting on Afghanistan. Many on the opposite side of this nineteen-year war, and us, are looking to make a deal – if possible!' Trump tweeted enthusiastically, after the meeting.[26]

All this was about to be thrown into jeopardy. In the 1980s, it had been the Americans aiding the Mujahideen to take out and bog down the Soviet troops. Now, the tables had turned: disturbing evidence was emerging that the Russians were placing bounties on the heads of US soldiers for the Taliban to claim. Just as the US had tried to keep the Soviet Union in Afghanistan, Putin was now trying to weaken the US by keeping the debilitating conflict going. Khalilzad spent the first week of September 2019 in Kabul, briefing Afghan President Ashraf Ghani, who had replaced Karzai in 2014, and other Afghan leaders on a deal to end eighteen years of fighting. All it needed was Trump's sign-off, he said. If they were ready to back it, it could be signed, sealed and delivered at a historic summit at Camp David.

A wave of violence in the capital that week fuelled Ghani's reservations. When a spate of suicide bombs killed a US serviceman, Trump too pulled back. Whether figures linked to Putin's regime had a hand in the attacks is unclear – though there were certainly those who did well out of the status quo. The war was a lucrative business for the vested interests of opium dealers, senior ideological Taliban leaders and those creaming off US reconstruction appropriation funds. Either way, Trump was furious: the Camp David visit, which had always been opposed by John Bolton, was off.

Trump tweeted:

Unbeknownst to almost everyone, the major Taliban leaders and, separately, the President of Afghanistan, were going to secretly meet with me at Camp David on Sunday … They were coming to the United States tonight. Unfortunately, in order to build false leverage, they admitted to an attack in Kabul that killed one of our great, great soldiers, and eleven other people. I immediately cancelled the meeting and called off peace negotiations. What kind of people would kill so many in order to seemingly strengthen their bargaining position? They didn't, they only made it worse! If they cannot agree to a ceasefire during these very important peace talks, and would even kill twelve innocent people, then they probably don't have the power to negotiate a meaningful agreement anyway. How many more decades are they willing to fight?[27]

To take a quote from *The Godfather* trilogy, 'Just when I thought I was out, they pull me back in!' After this characteristic outburst, Trump calmed down. Two months later, he made a surprise visit to see US troops in Afghanistan over Thanksgiving. During the trip, he revealed that diplomatic channels with the Taliban had been reopened. Sitting alongside Ghani, he told the press:

Well, as you know, for a period of time, we've been wanting to make a deal and so have the Taliban. Then we pulled back. We were getting close and we pulled back. We didn't want to do it because of what they did. It was not a good – it was not a good thing they did with the killing a soldier. They knew he was a soldier, but he was a soldier, an American soldier from Puerto Rico. And they killed him. They killed a United Nations soldier. And they also killed – they killed a total of twelve people. They thought that was good negotiating power. I said, 'No, that's bad negotiating power.'

That was not good what they did. And since then, we've hit them so hard, they've never been hit this hard. In the history of the war, they have not – never been hit hard. And they want to make a deal. So we'll see what happens. If they make it, fine. If they don't make it, that's fine.[28]

Talks had moved from a red light to amber.

In February 2020, he gave the green light. Taliban elders and senior US officials, including Secretary of State Mike Pompeo, arrived in the Qatari capital of Doha, where the Taliban had established their political office. After nearly nineteen long years of war, a war where US soldiers were now being deployed despite not even being born when 9/11 occurred, peace between the US and the Taliban was on the horizon. Khalilzad and the Taliban's deputy leader, Mullah Abdul Ghani Baradar, would sign an agreement bringing an end to hostilities between the United States and the Taliban. The historic deal saw the US commit to withdrawing their entire presence within fourteen months. In the first 135 days, it would reduce troop numbers from around 14,000 to 8,600. In order to create trust between the two sides, confidence-building measures, such as prisoner exchanges, would occur. Some 5,000 Taliban prisoners would be freed in exchange for the release of 1,000 government soldiers. The US would also begin to review sanctions on members of the Taliban. In return, the Taliban would not co-operate with any groups or individuals who sought to threaten US national security and would prevent its members from using Afghan soil to co-ordinate attacks against the US and its allies. This would alleviate the concerns of US Congressmen and generals who tried to justify the US remaining in Afghanistan in order to prevent another 9/11.

Not everyone was thrilled. Trump's former national security adviser, H. R. McMaster, described the peace deal as 'ill conceived', claiming the negotiations 'set up the Afghan government for more difficulty'. He continued:

If it was our objective to leave, just leave! But don't cut a deal first with the Taliban that then puts the Afghan government in a massively difficult position. Don't coerce them to release 5,000 of the most heinous people on earth who are now going to be free to establish a terrorist infrastructure much like the release of al-Qaeda in Iraq prisoners did to establish ISIS in Syria and Iraq after December 2011.[29]

In a damning riposte, he labelled the deal 'a classic case of strategic narcissism, wishful thinking and ultimately self-delusion'.

Bolton, who might reasonably be described as a disgruntled former employee, having been ousted by the President soon after the Camp David debacle, was equally scathing: 'Signing this agreement with Taliban is an unacceptable risk to America's civilian population. This is an Obama-style deal. Legitimizing Taliban sends the wrong signal to ISIS and al-Qaeda terrorists, and to America's enemies generally.'[30] Bolton instead wanted to leave enough troops in the country to at least assist with counterterrorism efforts.

However, Afghanistan's former President was ecstatic. Ahead of the signing, Hamid Karzai said, 'I was right like hell, yes. Very much I told the Afghan people the Taliban were our brothers. They are from this country and that this war is not ours. This is a foreign-imposed war for foreign objectives and neither us nor the Taliban should fall victim to it.'[31]

Fortunately, Trump stopped short of describing the Taliban as his 'brothers' – which would have been an insult to the families of US servicemen and women killed in action in Afghanistan and too much for most Americans to stomach – but he had shown there could be merit in talking to tyrants. After years of stalemate, it was tangible progress.

• • •

Of course, Trump benefited from the sheer passage of time in Afghanistan: by the time he became President, the war effort was already petering out. He also benefited from the hindsight of mistakes made by his predecessors.

Yet, he deserves credit for the clarity of his strategy from the start, and his genuine readiness to seek and embrace diplomatic solutions. Inviting Taliban leaders to Camp David was nothing if not bold; rescinding the invitation when they failed to curb violent attacks in Kabul showed he was neither desperate nor a soft touch.

At the time of writing, the deal he backed is holding up. Between April and October 2020 there was not a single US fatality in Afghanistan – the longest period without a death for the US military since the start of the war in October 2001 (though, of course, there were many fewer US targets by then.) However, Afghanistan remains deeply troubled. Attacks on local security forces have continued, and in the space of two years, from 2018 to 2020, some 4,400 civilians have been killed. In a depressing new low, an attack on a maternity ward in May killed twenty-four mothers and babies. June 2020 witnessed the most violent week in the nineteen-year conflict, with 422 bloody incidents across thirty-two provinces. Western forces had all but left, but there could be no peace while warring factions within Afghanistan continued to slug it out.*

In mid-2020, the next step was for the Afghan government to engage in face-to-face talks with the Taliban. This had never before been achieved. Talks were originally scheduled to begin on 10 March 2020, but were delayed by a series of roadblocks, including disagreements over prisoner releases; a contested election; and escalating violence including the attempted murder of one of the women on the Afghan government's negotiating team. After countless false starts, the two sides eventually came together in Doha on

---

* Some will say that the continuing unrest is a product of the withdrawal. Most American voters probably care less about the internal state of Afghanistan than whether it still constitutes a national security threat to the US – the impetus for being there in the first place. The British failed to control the Afghans, the Russians failed to control the Afghans and the US has failed to do the same. Bitter experience has demonstrated that it is a highly tribalised nation that will never be brought to heel via a foreign military presence.

12 September 2020, one day after the nineteenth anniversary of the 11 September attacks, where it all began. Twenty-one negotiators from each side faced off across the Qatari ballroom, in a scene like an awkward school disco. The Taliban negotiating team was not a typical diplomatic delegation: among the group were five men who had been released from Guantanamo Bay in 2014 and Anas Haqqani, the son of the founder of the Haqqani Network, an insurgent group with strong links to Pakistan. Meanwhile, across the floor, representing the Afghan government was Ashraf Ghani's election opponent, Abdullah Abdullah. When asked what the peace talks meant for the Afghan people, Abdullah said, 'It means that we are in a different stage in our history. It means that hopefully, God willing, history is about to turn. That is the significance of this moment.' He added, 'There is no winner in the war and there is no loser in an inclusive peaceful settlement.'[32]

At the time of writing, 2,318 US personnel have now given their lives to the fight in Afghanistan and an additional 20,666 have been wounded in action since 2001. The costs have continued to soar to an estimated $826.7 billion as of July 2020. According to other estimates, American taxpayers have shelled out more than one trillion dollars. Trump promised to end the endless wars before entering office. People had not expected the war to last ten years; now, nineteen years in, who is to say it couldn't last thirty? The fact that Trump ultimately managed to bring the Taliban to the negotiating table and then sign a deal is a significant achievement. Obama couldn't even bring them to the table. There is now a timetable of withdrawal to escape from the Graveyard of Empires, honouring promises from the 2016 election. A politician is actually delivering on a pledge and body bags filled with young US soldiers are no longer flying home as regularly. With a deal struck between the US and the Taliban, it remains to be seen whether the Afghans can strike a deal between themselves. As far as Trump is concerned, that is no longer America's problem.

DAY OF THE SUN – TRUMP AND NORTH KOREA

North Korea's nuclear weapons programme has been troubling US Presidents for decades. None of them ever seemed to get anywhere with it. The truth is, usually there were more pressing problems. Whatever one thinks of the despicable regime, they posed no real threat to the might of the US military. As Trump once said of Kim Jong-un: 'I too have a Nuclear Button, but it is a much bigger and more powerful one than his, and my Button works!'

His historic face-to-face meeting with the dictator was a master-stroke. It didn't magically end North Korea's nuclear weapons pro-gramme, but it reset rapidly deteriorating relations. It seems to have contained Little Rocket Man – at least for the time being.

The Day of the Sun is a very special festival in North Korea. It takes place on 15 April, and the 'Sun' in question is the late Kim Il-sung, grandfather of current leader Kim Jong-un and the man who established North Korea as a communist state in 1948. Every year, the nation commemorates his birthday over a three-day holiday. The celebration is often equated to Christmas in the West and is associated with various traditions, including laying flowers at Il-sung's many statues, the exchanging of gifts and a dazzling firework display over the Taedong river.

The year 2012 marked the 100th anniversary celebration, and so extra razzmatazz was in order. Of course, there would be the usual ceremony in Kim Il-sung public square in the capital Pyongyang, involving thousands of goose-stepping soldiers, displays of military hardware and marching bands. On this occasion, however, the regime wanted to put on a show so spectacular it would attract global attention. This was a moment of great national pride, and the dictator wanted to demonstrate just what the country long derided as the 'hermit kingdom' could do.

How could publicity be guaranteed? They could always boost the fireworks budget and choreograph an even more theatrical display of singing schoolchildren and gymnastic routines performed by thousands of young women in identikit red leotards. These colourful events were guaranteed to capture a few seconds of TV airtime around the world, especially if they were accompanied by a dramatic flypast. The fact that Kim Jong-un himself, newly installed as Supreme Leader following the sudden death of his father Kim Jong-il just months earlier, would be making his first ever public address would help drum up interest. But this momentous date called for something more. Since the overriding theme of the public celebrations would be North Korea's military prowess, it made sense to showcase their most impressive technology. Amid much fanfare, the armed forces would launch a satellite.

The word *Kwangmyŏngsŏng* means bright star, and the North Korean regime hoped the object it launched into orbit aboard a carrier rocket at 07.39 on 13 April 2012 would prove a shining example of what it could achieve. Publicly, the DPRK claimed the satellite was for weather-forecast purposes, but nobody outside North Korea took that seriously. While the stunt was a failure – the rocket exploded ninety seconds after launch – Western defence and intelligence officials knew what they had been watching was a ballistic missile test. It would require a response.

On 16 April, the US issued a statement condemning the stunt as 'provocative'. Just a month earlier, the two countries had struck a deal after a meeting in Beijing, in which North Korea had committed to suspend its uranium enrichment operations, allow international monitors and suspend nuclear testing in exchange for food aid from the US. It was now painfully clear that the agreement would not be honoured. The US suspended the food aid.

That August, President Obama dispatched Daniel Russell and Sydney Seiler (special assistant to the President and senior director of Asia respectively) to Pyongyang from Guam, a US territory in Micronesia in the western Pacific Ocean, in an attempt to ease diplomatic tensions. The pair left North Korea feeling that something had been achieved, only for the North Koreans to launch a second rocket on 12 December. This time it was successful.

The Unha-3 was fired in three stages: the first stage fell into the Yellow Sea; the second into the Philippine Sea; but it finally entered orbit in the third stage, a moment of significant pride for the regime and anxiety for the West. The Day of the Sun had been properly commemorated – albeit eight months late.

What happened in 2012 is broadly illustrative of the state of relations between the US and North Korea since the dissolution of the Soviet Union in 1991.The past thirty years have been characterised by an endless cycle of rising tensions interspersed with periodic lulls, during which the regime lies low before embarking on a new round of nuclear missile tests. Trump would approach the challenge very differently to his predecessors, however, with a series of high-stakes gambles that achieved mixed results but were nonetheless remarkable in their originality and audacity. While he was determined to lay down markers with the North Korean regime, he was also ready to be 'friends' with the Supreme Leader in a way that had been unthinkable to other occupants of the White House.

When Bill Clinton became President in 1993, he set the tone for successive US administrations, approaching North Korea as if it were little more than a dangerous irritant, as opposed to a regime worth attempting to understand and cultivate in the interests of world peace. Ahead of a diplomatic visit to Pyongyang in 1994, aimed at convincing Kim il-sung to negotiate with the Clintons over nuclear weapons, Jimmy Carter, former US President from 1977 to 1981, acknowledged that there could be something to be gained by showing the regime some respect. 'You haven't told me what Kim il-sung wants. What he wants is my respect. And I am going to give it to him,' he is said to have told reporters.[1]

The effects of Carter's softer approach were not long-lasting. It seems successive Presidents simply did not consider it worth investing the time and political capital. While US defence chiefs were in no doubt that the regime posed a real military threat, both to its southern neighbour via conventional weapons and to the United States and the rest of the world through nuclear capabilities, the risk seemed neither imminent nor very serious. These assumptions, encouraged by the collapse of the Soviet Union, persistently undermined any negotiating process.

The second Bush administration was more confrontational, making little secret that it sought regime change. Facing what it felt was an existential threat, the DPRK dug in, enhancing its conventional and nuclear arsenal.

Kim Jong-il's sudden demise in December 2011 – the result of a massive heart attack – and Kim Jong-un's new leadership presented an opportunity for change. After all, the new young leader was no stranger to the West. He is thought to have been educated in Switzerland for several years, attending the public school of Liebefeld near Bern under the pseudonym Pak Chol. Ri Tcheul, who acted as North Korea's ambassador to Switzerland for nearly three decades, also acted as a mentor to Kim Jong-il's sons. In diplomatic circles, there were hopes that he might have helped coach Kim Jong-un in Western values and customs. In an encouraging sign, North Korea's new Supreme Leader was rumoured to enjoy Western action movies, particularly those starring Jean-Claude Van Damme and NBA legend Michael Jordan. There was some optimism that his background, shrouded in mystery as it was, might help bridge the yawning cultural divide between this isolated regime and the Western world.

By the time Obama came to power, however, North Korea's status as a hostile state was entrenched. His strategy, criticised in some quarters as overly cautious, revolved around increased espionage and the use of sanctions. Supporters of this approach characterised it as 'strategic patience'. To others, it looked more like a 'policy of bemused inaction'.[2] North Korea gleefully continued to grow its ballistic missile capabilities and insult Obama in outrageously racist terms. 'It would be better for him to live with other monkeys at a wild animal park in Africa ... and licking breadcrumbs thrown by onlookers,' one citizen wrote in a series of essays published by a state-run media organisation, Pyongyang's Korean Central News Agency.[3] The even-tempered Obama brushed off the offence, doubtless hoping that the playground bully would eventually tire of being provocative. Little changed for the better.

The relationship Trump inherited was ugly, openly hostile and aggressive – at least on North Korea's side. It needed a careful hand, the precise opposite of what Trump would demonstrate in his early days in the White House. His initial approach was extraordinarily inflammatory – and risky.

Just four months into his presidency, the Commander-in-Chief ordered a navy strike group to move towards the Korean peninsula. It was a dramatic shift away from Obama's 'strategic patience'. Trump made a show of his willingness to tackle North Korea's threats with or without international support. China's role would be pivotal, but Trump made clear that he was not going to hang around waiting to get President Xi on side. 'China will either decide to help us with North Korea or they won't,' he told the *Financial Times*. 'If they do, that will be very good for China, and if they don't, it won't be good for anyone.'[4]

As the USS *Carl Vinson* supercarrier sallied forth from Singapore to the Korean Peninsula, complete with fighter jets, two guided-missile destroyers and a guided-missile cruiser, the North Korean regime held its nerve. A foreign ministry spokesperson said that the US would be held 'wholly accountable for the catastrophic consequences to be entailed by its outrageous actions. [North Korea] is ready to react to any mode of war desired by the US.'5

In South Korea and Japan, there was mounting alarm. Trump's presidency was so new that his wife Melania and son Baron had yet to move into the White House. As the aircraft carrier set off, he was also firing missiles at an air base in Syria, in what the White House said was a signal to the rest of the world. Nobody could be sure how far he would go. Pang Zhongying, a professor at Renmin University in China, told the *Financial Times*, 'North Korea is not Syria ... Syria has fallen apart and is not capable of fighting back. North Korea is totally different and even a surgical strike could bring disastrous consequences. The US is bluffing.'6

However, Bong Youngshik, a North Korea expert from Yonsei University in Seoul, supported the move, arguing that symbolic military action served as an 'indirect warning to Pyongyang that once North Korea crosses a red line, Trump will not hesitate to turn US power into action', which is 'far more effective in terms of etching a strong image of the Trump administration in the mind of Kim Jong-un'.7

In the days and months that followed, Trump continued to ramp up the rhetoric, hinting that if the North Korean regime continued its programme of nuclear missile testing, it would be annihilated. In a series of provocative tweets in summer 2017, he questioned whether Kim Jong-un had 'anything better to do with his life?', famously warning a month later that if North Korea continued to threaten the US, it would be 'met with fire and fury like the world has never seen.'8

So far from backing down, the North Koreans responded that they were considering a strike around Guam, home to two strategic

US military bases. The US Air Force had been flying bombers from Guam over the Korean Peninsula on a regular basis to ensure the regime did not forget that America was there. Kim Jong-un threatened to create 'an enveloping fire' around the island. Fortunately, he soon thought better of it. Trump called it 'a very wise and well-reasoned decision'. They had avoided what the President had warned would be 'catastrophic' consequences.[9]

While Trump's supporters defended his military manoeuvrings and aggressive rhetoric as carefully calculated brinkmanship, critics feared he'd tub-thump his way into a world war. Senator John McCain, chairman of the Armed Services Committee (and no admirer of the President), warned that Trump's positioning was only bringing the US 'closer to some kind of serious confrontation'.[10] Yet, the traditional approach of successive White House administrations had self-evidently not worked.

Mark Dubowitz, chief executive of the Foundation for Defense of Democracies (a non-profit think tank), has argued that, in some ways, the President was out of options: 'This is a more dangerous moment than faced by Trump's predecessors,' he told the *New York Times*. 'The normal nuanced diplomatic rhetoric coming out of Washington hasn't worked in persuading the Kim regime of American resolve. This language underscores that the most powerful country in the world has its own escalatory and retaliatory options.'[11]

• • •

Cindy and Fred Warmbier were on tenterhooks as they waited to collect their son Otto from Lunken Airport in Cincinnati in April 2017. The 22-year-old, a curious and adventurous soul, had travelled to North Korea with a pioneer group in 2015, to celebrate New Year's Eve before beginning a year abroad in China. After one festive drink too many, he thought it would be a lark to make off with some memorabilia from his hotel, evidently imagining that what he was doing was no more serious than pinching a traffic cone after a night out in his hometown of Cincinnati.

Unfortunately, the item in question was a propaganda poster, and its unauthorised removal from a restricted part of the premises, in a country run by an unstable dictator, was never going to be without consequence.

In North Korea, this was considered a serious and dangerous crime. On 2 January 2016, as Otto prepared to leave North Korea to embark on his studies in China, he was arrested at Pyongyang International Airport, on charges of subversion. According to his roommate, he didn't resist as he was led away; he 'sort of half-smiled', almost as if he were resigned to his fate.[12] In due course, he would be sentenced to fifteen years of hard labour in North Korea, an extraordinarily draconian punishment for a foolish drunken act.

The young man's incarceration prompted months of diplomatic wrangling. Unbeknown to the outside world, behind bars he was in a terrible state. It would later emerge that soon after his imprisonment, he had suffered a devastating neurological injury, which had left him unconscious. The North Korean authorities did not tell anyone about his condition for over a year, when they casually announced that he had fallen into a coma as a result of contracting botulism and taking a sleeping pill. A month later, they agreed to allow him home.

This move was unexpected, and, at the time, many of those involved were puzzled by the sudden change of heart. His parents are both on record criticising the Obama administration for failing to do more to push for his release. Given just how sick he turned out to be, however, Otto's release was no great surprise. Keeping him alive was becoming difficult and expensive.

Waiting for their son, the Warmbiers were nervous. Diplomatic officials had led them to believe that his condition would be quite treatable once he was back in the States and could be taken to Cincinnati Medical Center. In reality, as they were about to discover, he had spent fourteen months in a coma and was in a vegetative state.

Fred heard Otto before he saw him – guttural, brutal sounds that did not sound like they could possibly come from his son. Out of the plane came Otto, strapped onto a stretcher and howling. His wavy hair had been shorn, his limbs seemed 'totally deformed' and his bottom teeth had been knocked out.[13] There was a feeding tube attached to him. He would die in hospital six days later. While a post-mortem did not reveal any fractures to his skull, the coroner's report stated that he died from an unknown injury causing lack of oxygen to the brain. A year later, a US federal court found North Korea liable for his torture and death. The regime did not attempt to present any case for the defence.

The appalling demise of this young man had a profound impact on public opinion in America. He was a powerfully tragic symbol – an aspiring investment banker at the top of his class, killed by a regime he yearned to explore and understand via an educational trip. His death shone a spotlight on the Obama administration's inaction on North Korea. Senator John McCain released a statement: 'Let us state the facts plainly. Otto Warmbier, an American citizen, was murdered by the Kim Jong-un regime.'[14] Michael Kirby, former chairman at the United Nations Commission of Inquiry on Human Rights in North Korea, wrote, 'In 1945, the world promised that never again would it turn away from crimes against humanity. That promise has not yet been delivered. We owe it to Otto Warmbier, but also to the people of North Korea who still live in the shadows, to deliver on the promise.'[15] Trump was under pressure to do something about it.

On 30 June, in a joint news conference with South Korean President Moon Jae-in, Trump expressed his frustrations at decades of inaction over North Korea's 'brutal' and 'reckless' regime, adding, 'The years of strategic patience with the North Korean regime has failed … Frankly, that patience is over.'[16]

That summer, North Korea continued to fire and test ballistic missiles, and the US continued flying sorties from Guam. At the 2017

UN General Assembly in September, Trump threatened to 'totally destroy' North Korea. Two days later, he continued the offensive, slapping additional sanctions on the state. Kim Jong-un responded with a strongly worded statement in which he referred to Trump as a 'dotard' and a 'frightened dog'.[17]

Then something extraordinary happened: word reached the White House that the North Korean dictator might be willing to meet. The message came via South Korean diplomat and Seoul's national security office chief, Chung Eui-yong. It was an unexpected gesture from the regime. This was exactly how Trump liked to do business: face to face; principal to principal; eyeballing the enemy. Any encounter with Kim Jong-un was guaranteed to be a big show. Moreover, surely even his left-wing critics would have to appreciate his attempt at jaw-jaw? By 9 March 2018, Trump's mind was made up: he would do it.

The landmark decision was announced by Chung Eui-yong outside the White House: 'The Republic of Korea, the United States and our partners stand together in insisting that we not repeat the mistakes of the past,' he said, 'and that the pressure will continue until North Korea matches its words with concrete actions.'[18]

Secretary of State Rex Tillerson admitted that the choice to accept the bombshell invite was made by Trump alone, and it has been speculated that Tillerson wasn't made aware of it until Eui-yong's announcement.

The President's team found themselves on the back foot; only a day earlier, Tillerson had told press in a morning news conference that the US was 'a long ways from negotiations' with North Korea. The State Department, seemingly as thrown by the news, suddenly had to put together a team for Trump's meeting, apparently to be held in May. If it went well, it could draw a line under decades of hostility and pave the way towards a radically different relationship. If it went badly – well, it probably wouldn't make anything worse.

While Trump received plaudits for getting the Supreme Leader to the table, foreign policy experts urged caution. The question was whether the contretemps between two of the most unpredictable figures on the world stage would amount to anything more than great television.

• • •

Sentosa Island, off the southern coast of Singapore, is, according to a translation of the Malay name, a place of 'peace and tranquillity'. Until 1830, it was simply known as Pulau Panjang, which means 'long island', but later it would become Pulau Blakang Mati, Malay for 'The Island of Death Behind'. Quite how it acquired this dark moniker is a matter of some debate among historians. Some say it derived from the island's history of piracy; others point to the outbreak of a dreadful disease; while a third group has put it down to the infertile soil, which means much of the land is unproductive.

During the Second World War, the island was used as a British military base and a Japanese prisoner-of-war camp before being renamed Sentosa, in a move to develop it into a tourist destination in the 1970s. Today, it is one of the most popular resorts in Singapore. This hopeful history, and, more importantly, the privacy and security the island afforded, made it the ideal place for the first ever meeting between a US and a North Korean leader.

The run-up to the summit was accompanied by feverish anticipation. How would the swaggering Trump, an imposing 6ft 2in.-tall figure, match up to little 5ft 7in. Kim, and could two such enormous egos in one room manage to keep their discussions amicable for long? What would the personal chemistry be like? Would they even shake hands? Amid all the excitement, the White House even released a commemorative coin to mark the meeting.

Such was the excitement that over 2,500 journalists were camped out at the mainland's dedicated media centre. Seven carefully selected American journalists and seven North Korean representatives were allowed to go to Sentosa itself to witness the meeting.

Trump was first to arrive at the hotel for the one-on-one and was forced to wait for Kim, who was seventeen minutes late. After pleasantries, they sat down to a working lunch, followed by a joint ceremony. The one-on-one meeting, with interpreters only, kicked off with a twelve-second handshake, which was forensically examined by press. It led on to what Trump would later describe as a 'very heartfelt conversation'.[19]

In a mark of transatlantic unity, the menu featured food from both East and West, such as beef short-rib confit and sweet-and-sour crispy pork. For dessert, the delegations could choose between a dark chocolate ganache tartlet and Häagen-Dazs vanilla ice cream with cherry coulis and *tropézienne*. A Singaporean government camera and photographers were present, but no American members of the press were given access.

Later, Trump and Kim took a stroll. In what has been described as a 'classic alpha male move', the US President showed off the Secret Service's bullet-proof limousine (nicknamed 'The Beast') to the North Korean leader before the signing ceremony.[20]

The elaborately named 'Joint Statement of President Donald J. Trump of the United States of America and Chairman Kim Jong-un of the State Affairs Commission of the Democratic People's Republic of Korea at the Singapore Summit', committed both countries to work towards 'prosperity' as well as 'a lasting and stable peace regime on the Korean Peninsula'.[21]

Naturally, Trump hailed the summit a tremendous success, describing his meeting with the Supreme Leader as 'very, very good'.[22] Both sides could be relieved that discussions had remained cordial, and that the viciousness of the personal insults they had once traded had been set aside.

The trouble was that the United States had made precious few concessions relative to the North Koreans. As David Chan-oong Kang, director of the USC Korean Studies Institute, observed in the *New York Times*, North Korea had made promises to dismantle its most prized assets, shut down ICBM facilities and stop missile and nuclear tests among other things, while the US had pledged to do very little.

In reality, US defence and intelligence chiefs were never naïve enough to imagine that North Korea suddenly posed a much-diminished threat. The regime had learned that stockpiling nuclear weapons was a reliable way for a tiny nation to attract international attention. It gave a country whose entire GDP was about the same as the annual budget of a mid-sized UK government department a completely disproportionate status on the world stage. Only a year before the summit, North Korea had fired its first intercontinental ballistic missile and declared itself a 'proud nuclear state'.[23] If the regime abandoned this quest, it would slip into the same obscurity as other countries of similar size and economic power. The way North Korean leaders saw it, being an international pariah was very much more appealing than irrelevance.

In summer 2018, the news came that seasoned North Korea observers had always predicted: the regime was up to its old tricks again. For all the presentational success of the summit, there had been no metamorphosis. Intelligence chiefs were reported to have uncovered disturbing evidence of an increase in production of fuel for nuclear weapons at 'multiple secret sites'.[24] That November, the New York Times reported that satellite images showed the regime had continued to secretly build up missile bases.

Had it all been for nothing? At the very least, Trump's efforts had maintained the status quo and demonstrated that however gravely he was insulted, however inflammatory his own rhetoric, he would not rush into a potentially catastrophic military confrontation. Following his election in 2016, emotional left-wingers had fretted that he was so bombastic and thin-skinned that he could not be relied upon not to press the nuclear button. This was to misunderstand his fundamental and profound aversion to dragging the United States into any unnecessary foreign conflict. In his approach to

North Korea, he showed that he was not too proud to engage with foreign leaders who had personally insulted him, nor too arrogant or vainglorious to consider them unworthy of his time. His attitude to North Korea was neither fatalistic nor defeatist. In short, he was willing to give peace a try. It is easy to imagine the rapturous praise Obama would have received for a similar effort, and the long-term credit he would have gained, while most of those who briefly praised the President for getting Kim to the negotiating table quickly forgot the achievement.

The Hanoi summit, in February 2019, which was cut short, high-lighted the scale of the challenge that remains. The conference took place at the Metropole Hotel (Hanoi's first international hotel), Vietnam having been chosen to host the talks because of its strong diplomatic relationship with both the US and North Korea. The event was abandoned after two days, when it became obvious that negotiations were not getting anywhere. Trump accused the North Koreans of making unreasonable demands: an end to all sanctions in exchange for what did not amount to much more than the closure of one weapons facility. With typical optimism, he nonetheless declared that the talks had been productive, adding, 'I think we'll end up being very good friends.'[25]

Frustrated North Korean officials called a press conference hours later, claiming Kim had demanded only the ending of partial sanctions in return for shutting down the north's main nuclear complex. The event had been a disappointment, but it had not broken up in acrimony: all the main players, including South Korea and Japan, made clear their readiness to continue talking.

On 30 June, Trump became the first US President to set foot in the so-called Demilitarised Zone, the border that divides the Korean peninsula, to shake hands with the Supreme Leader once again. The meeting, spurred by an impulsive presidential tweet saying he'd meet with Kim 'at the Border/DMZ', even if it was 'just to shake his hand and say Hello', also involved South Korea's President Moon Jae-in.[26]

It seemed largely symbolic, with Trump insisting that a good deal takes time. Soon after, satellite imagery indicated that North Korea had little intention of denuclearisation: the Sohae satellite launch site (where engines and technologies for the country's ICBM programme are also tested), which it seemed to be dismantling after the 2018 summit, was in fact being rebuilt.

In summer 2020, North Korea's Foreign Minister, Ri Son Gwon, would release a statement on North Korean state media, saying it was pulling away from the US relationship. 'Never again will we provide the US chief executive with another package to be used for achievements without receiving any returns,' he said. 'Nothing is more hypocritical than an empty promise.'[27]

North Korea then ceased communication hotlines with South Korea, effectively erasing any hope of continuing diplomatic efforts between the two leaders. This halted all attempts at a productive relationship with the US.

In bringing Kim Jong-un to the negotiating table, Trump had achieved more in relation to North Korea than his three predecessors combined. While the medium-term outcome was disappointing, the very fact of it was a spectacular diplomatic coup. No other US President has contemplated anything like it, still less made it happen.

Some will argue that having started a good thing, Trump gave up too easily. Had he secured a second term, perhaps he would have tried again. In any case, sometimes the best that can be hoped from diplomacy is to maintain the status quo, however bad that may be, because preventing deterioration is a huge challenge in itself. The US–North Korea dynamic that Joe Biden inherits is certainly no worse than what Trump inherited from Obama.

It remains to be seen whether Joe Biden will do any better. The signs are not encouraging. In 2019, he criticised Trump's policy on North Korea, labelling Kim Jong-un a 'murderous dictator'.[28] In reply, North Korea compared him to a 'rabid dog' that should be 'beaten to death with a stick'. In a jumbled statement, the regime declared:

> Anyone who dare slanders the dignity of the supreme leadership of the DPRK, can never spare the DPRK's merciless punishment whoever and wherever. And he will be made to see even in a grave what horrible consequences will be brought about by his thoughtless utterances.[29]

Biden argues that in treating North Korea as a serious negotiating partner, Trump did more harm than good, 'legitimizing a dictator'.[30] This is like the argument Western governments use in relation to hostage taking: publicly, they say they will not negotiate with terrorists to secure the release of innocent citizens; behind the scenes, some discussions are almost always taking place. Showman that he is, Trump simply did it in full public gaze. His calculation was that there was very little to lose. He made it very much easier for a successor to repeat the attempt. Perhaps next time the two nations will be able to keep talks going for more than forty-eight hours.

CONCLUSION

When I first started writing this book, I was absolutely convinced that Trump would win a second term – by a landslide. His first victory had been a complete shock, but before coronavirus took its toll, there was a widespread view that he would secure another four years. Biden was, after all, a candidate who had been routinely derided by members of his own party, including by his future running mate Kamala Harris, who said she believed allegations that he was guilty of sexual abuse.[1] Then there was his advanced age and disturbing propensity to muddle his words. My thinking was that Biden was a kind of throwaway candidate. I guessed that the Democrats knew they couldn't win in 2020 and didn't want to sacrifice their best talent to a doomed campaign. I assumed their strategy was to let Trump have his second term, wait for the pandemic to trash the economy and then steam in with a truly impressive candidate in 2024.

Until the very early hours of 4 November, the morning after election day, it still looked as if he would win. Then something strange started to happen. Some key swing states stopped counting. Observers were told to go home. Counting then resumed, in some cases without observers present. There were hundreds of thousands of additional votes to process, approximately 78 per cent of which favoured Biden. Pennsylvania, which had Trump ahead by nearly 700,000 votes at one stage, started to turn for Biden. Sure, a big

Democrat push on postal voting was paying off – but 78 per cent? That didn't seem right, and Trump and his supporters were suspicious. Various lawsuits and investigations followed, which failed to shed much light on the matter. They generally concluded that nothing untoward had taken place.

It is beyond the remit of this book to examine what jiggery-pokery may or may not have occurred, but it is worth reviewing the facts. Trump got more votes than any previous incumbent: 11 million more than in 2016. (By contrast, in 2012, Obama was re-elected with 3.5 million *fewer* votes than he received in 2008.) Trump increased his support among black voters by 50 per cent, perhaps aided by Biden's misguided assumption that he was automatically entitled to the support of this demographic. 'If you have a problem figuring out whether you're for me or Trump, then you ain't black,' were his actual words.[2] (Just imagine the outcry had Trump said something similar about white voters!)

Trump's share of the Hispanic vote also increased to 35 per cent. He won Florida, Ohio and Iowa by huge margins. Since 1852, anyone who has won these three states has become President (with the notable exception of Nixon in 1960 – that election itself the subject of debate as to fraud). Biden won more votes than any President in history – some 11.7 million more than Obama in 2008. This despite the fact that he won a record low of 17 per cent of counties – 477 compared to the 873 Obama won in 2008.

The number of ballot papers that were rejected was a record low, particularly in swing states. In Pennsylvania, for example, just under 1 per cent of papers were thrown out in 2016. In 2020, the figure was 0.28 per cent, despite a surge in postal votes.

In an essay labelling the result 'deeply puzzling', US pollster Patrick Basham highlights a long list of curiosities, including the fact that every 'non-polling metric' predicted that Trump would win.[3] These measures, which look at factors such as party registration trends, how candidates fare in their respective presidential primaries, how many donations they receive and their popularity ratings, have consistently proven accurate in the past.

All of this could be completely above board. Perhaps Joe Biden really is the most popular President in US history. Certainly, Trump exhausted all legal avenues to contest the result, and those who supported him had no choice but to accept the outcome. For my own part, I remain deeply suspicious. I simply do not believe that a mumbling career politician – a man who has been doing the political rounds for fifty years, hitherto without attracting star status; a man who has been casually divisive; a man so disliked by his Vice-President that she declared she believed allegations of sexual abuse against him; a man whose campaign rallies attracted only a few hundred people (partly because they were deliberately socially distanced, for sure, but the masses were hardly clamouring to get in); and perhaps most decisively, a man whose approval rating on day one of his presidency was lower than Trump's approval rating on his final day[4] – could have so dramatically stormed to victory without some funny business. Was there a fraud? In my view, yes. The only question in my mind is how much.

In this book, I have not so much played devil's advocate as attempted to give Trump the fair hearing he was consistently denied. Having examined his record, my conclusion is this: for all the awful events in the dying days of his administration, Trump's halo is only invisible if people are determined not to see it. Amid his fury at losing to Joe Biden, and with his conviction that he had been robbed of victory clouding his judgement, the halo slipped, with horrible consequences. But that does not mean that it was never there.

For me, one of the most sickening aspects of the events of 7 January 2021, when his supporters breached the US Capitol in a violent protest in which five people lost their lives, was the knowledge that it would be used as incontrovertible evidence of all the worst things his critics had always said about him. The fact that it was entirely his own fault did not make the ferocity of the backlash any less painful for his admirers.

No one would defend what happened in the Capitol Building that day, and, indeed, no one tried. What did Trump think would happen when he called for a march on the seat of American democracy to 'stop the steal' (as his supporters described the outcome of the 2020 election)?

By 'rallying the troops' in an extraordinary thirty-minute tirade against all those he felt had let him down, including many members of his own party, he made a catastrophic mistake. All that was required from everyone who opposed him or had an interest in letting events spiral out of control was to sit back and watch. Democrats knew that once the Capitol was breached, it was game over for Trump. It was always unlikely that the Electoral College votes would have been sent back to state legislature, as he had wanted; the minute the doors of the Capitol were breached and the first protestor walked in, there was no hope. Add some professional protestors into the mix and the Trump presidency came to an undignified and tragic end.

Afterwards, his detractors went even further than I had anticipated, whipping themselves into a frenzy of righteous indignation. Around the world, there was a Mexican wave of virtue-signalling and clamour to remove him from office. Social media chiefs raced to cancel him, suspending or permanently removing him from the platforms he had always used to communicate directly with voters: Twitter, Facebook and Instagram. Shopify banned Trump stores. Among media organisations that had always loathed him, there was a feeding frenzy around the entrails of his administration.

Hysteria reached new heights when Speaker of the US House of Representatives Nancy Pelosi suggested he could not be trusted not to blow up the world. 'This morning, I spoke to the chairman of the joint chiefs of staff, Mark Milley, to discuss available precautions for preventing an unstable president from initiating military hostilities or accessing the launch codes and ordering a nuclear strike,' she declared pompously.[5]

The observation that if he was insufficiently responsible to have a Twitter account then he should not be allowed near any instruments of war became commonplace.

It is not necessary to have any sympathy for Trump personally to feel disturbed by the glee with which a President of the United States was cancelled by so-called tech giants. Where does that leave free speech? With my businessman hat on, I would say, well, these are their platforms, they can do what they like. And, of course, they can. Yet these media giants have special protections under US law, exempting them from various restrictions faced by traditional publishers. How much power should they have? Is it OK for figures like Mark Zuckerberg to decide which politicians are and are not allowed to communicate with the public who elected them? How much influence do other governments have over these companies? Complex questions for another day...

Either way, following these seismic events it seems inevitable that the 45th President will be portrayed with even more venom than he attracted while in office. Already Joe 'time for peace and unity' Biden has labelled his predecessor 'the most incompetent President in the history of the United States of America.'[6] As I have set out in this book, however, the facts tell a different story. Among the troops he brought home, those who benefited from the blue-collar jobs he created, the poor he lifted out of poverty, the swathes of unwanted and ignored voters to whom he gave a voice, I suspect he will remain a hero.

On the economy, on defence, in the war on terror, on China, Israel, Iran and the wider Middle East, his administration made remarkable achievements. Where he did not ultimately succeed – on North Korea, on his handling of coronavirus, indeed on re-election to a second term – it was never for want of trying; never for fear of a fight in which he might be politically bloodied or wounded; never for the fatalism that considers difficult and bad things too difficult to change. To the end, he went down fighting, with an indomitable spirit and energy that further infuriated all those who just wanted him to exit the stage.

I have given a lot of thought as to why Establishment types always hated him, and I cannot escape the conclusion that it started with snobbery. He just wasn't anything like the experts, the commentators, the so-called opinion leaders and all the others with honorary doctorates and Ivy League degrees. He had next to nothing in common with these liberal elites, with their comfortable, careful, conventional lives in which 'giving something back' means attending the occasional charity benefit. He was brash, he was crass and, in Melania, he probably had the wrong kind of wife. For her part, the First Lady looked a bit too perfect, didn't smile enough, had an accent. He didn't play the game, and neither did she – and who can blame her? She never wanted to be in the White House.

Under relentless attack from the moment he secured the Republican nomination in 2016, Trump cannot possibly have found it a *pleasure* being President. It was a constant battle, as of course it is for any occupant of the White House, but all the more for those who deliberately set out to shake up the system.

As a political novice when he entered the White House, he knew how neither Washington nor the government administrative system worked. The more irregular, controversial and ambitious his ideas, the more resistance he met and the more frustrated he became – hence the 'fire and fury' he so often displayed.

Those who have worked at the heart of governments in powerful democracies know just how hard it is to get things done. Overcoming bureaucracy and institutional inertia can require a kind of demented focus. Often, it is just no use being 'nice': ensuring that manifesto pledges and policy targets are met demands a kind of ruthlessness and drive that is sometimes incompatible with unfailing politesse. It is clear from numerous accounts that working for

Trump could be rough and tough, and he had an unfortunate habit of turning on those who did not stick it out. His detractors have generally assumed that this must be because he has a nasty streak; the more generous interpretation is simply that he was not interested in anyone who was not fully signed up to delivering on the commitments he made to the American people. He felt compelled to honour those pledges and, as I have sought to demonstrate, by and large, he did.

The hour-to-hour, day-to-day responsibility of his position was overwhelming, as it is for all Presidents. Already in his seventies, Trump must have found it exhausting – and not particularly good for his health. Under these circumstances, why on earth did he want a second term? Because he's a power-hungry egomaniac? Naturally, that is what his critics think. As we have seen, however, the President of the United States has considerably less power than people believe. Trump was often exasperated by the impotence of the position.

So, I do not believe he sought a second term – and kept fighting for it till he had exhausted all legal avenues – simply so he could 'rule the world'. I think he truly believed he could continue to make life better for ordinary Americans. To that end, he was ready to carry on putting up with all those who continued to ridicule him, to scoff at his ideas and the way he expressed himself, and, worst of all, to question his fundamental decency and integrity. To me, that in itself deserves a halo.

St Donald? Not quite. Frustratingly for those who could see the light, his flaws had a habit of obscuring the shimmering circle above his head. When the liberal elite finally overcome the trauma of his presidency, however, perhaps they will realise that he was not the monster they made him out to be. While I am not holding my breath, a good dose of mumbling, bumbling, tax-raising Joe Biden might just produce some nostalgia for his predecessor.

One thing is for sure: Trump supporters will not just go away.

I dare say the 45th President of the United States will spend the next few years using his remarkable fan base to continue what he started: being a thorn in the side of the Establishment and standing up for the United States of America. That he loves his country, no one could doubt.

NOTES

INTRODUCTION

1   Elise Viebeck, 'A visual history of Trump's battle with the *N.Y. Daily News*', *Washington Post*, 10 February 2016.
2   August Brown, '"I feel good for speaking up": YG on his 2016 protest anthem that goes after Donald Trump', *Los Angeles Times*, 17 November 2016.
3   'Trump in Ocala: "I never knew the Washington swamp was this deep"', Bloomberg Quicktake [video], YouTube, uploaded 16 October 2020.
4   Heather Saul, 'Barack Obama on Stephan Colbert: "To be honest, I still don't know what my Nobel Peace Prize was for"', *The Independent*, 19 October 2016.
5   Mythili Sampathkumar, 'Donald Trump puts "America First" stating he is not "president of the world"', *The Independent*, 5 April 2017.

1: ALIENS – TRUMP AND IMMIGRATION

1   William Jefferson Clinton, 'State of the Union 1995 (delivered version) – 24 January 1995', available at: http://www.let.rug.nl/usa/presidents/william-jefferson-clinton/state-of-the-union-1995-(delivered-version).php
2   'Full text of President Obama's speech on immigration plan', Reuters, 21 November 2014.
3   Annie Linskey, 'In 2006, Democrats were saying "build that fence!"', *Boston Globe*, 2017.
4   Joshua Green, *Devil's Bargain: Steve Bannon, Donald Trump and the Nationalist Uprising* (New York: Penguin Books, 2017), p. 111.
5   Jill Colvin, 'AP Fact check: Trump exaggerates cost of illegal immigration', AP News, 5 December 2018.
6   'Yale study finds twice as many undocumented immigrants as previous estimates', Yale Insights, 21 September 2018.
7   Philip Bump, 'The toxic power of Trump's politics', *Washington Post*, 15 July 2019.
8   Glenn Kessler, 'A history of Trump's promises that Mexico would pay for the wall, which it refuses to do', *Washington Post*, 8 January 2019.
9   Jonathan Capehart, 'Donald Trump's "Mexican rapist" rhetoric will keep the Republican Party out of the White House', *Washington Post*, 17 June 2015.
10 Martin Pengelly, '"Offensive and inaccurate": Marco Rubio rejects Donald Trump's Mexico remarks', *The Guardian*, 4 July 2015.
11 Philip Sherwell, 'Republicans cast into turmoil as Donald Trump rides the populist surge', *Daily Telegraph*, 5 July 2015.
12 Ibid.
13 Milco Baute, *Democrats vs Republicans: For Whom Should We Vote?* (Tampa: Baute Production Publisher, 2018), p. 92.

14 Walter Williams, 'Why Dems changed course on illegal immigration', *Boston Herald*, 17 January 2019.
15 Pippa Norris and Ronald Inglehart, *Cultural Backlash and the Rise of Populism: Trump, Brexit, and Authoritarian Populism* (Cambridge: Cambridge University Press, 2019), p. 186.
16 'Attorney General Sessions delivers remarks to the Association of State Criminal Investigative Agencies 2018 spring conference', The United States Department of Justice, 7 May 2018.
17 'Trump sends 5,200 troops to Mexico border as caravan advances', Reuters, 29 October 2018.

2: HEADS YOU WIN, TAILS I LOSE – RACE AND RIOTING
1 'Democrats lose control of presidential event', CNN, 19 July 2015.
2 Martin Pengelly, 'O'Malley and Sanders interrupted by Black Lives Matter protestors in Phoenix', *The Guardian*, 19 July 2015.
3 Rebecca Leber, 'Martin O'Malley apologized for saying "All Lives Matter." Should Hillary Clinton?', *New Republic*, 20 July 2015.
4 Nick Gass, 'Trump calls O'Malley a "disgusting, little, weak, pathetic baby"', Politico, 21 August 2015.
5 Sabrina Siddiqui, 'Donald Trump strikes muddled note on "divisive" Black Lives Matter', *The Guardian*, 13 July 2016.
6 'George Floyd death: Trump threatens to send in army to end unrest', BBC News, 2 June 2020.
7 'Public-health experts are not hypocrites', *The Atlantic*, 11 June 2020.
8 'Biden: Trump "despicable" for invoking George Floyd', BBC, 6 June 2020.
9 Guy Adams, 'Revealed: The British arm of Black Lives Matter's full agenda – abolish the police, smash capitalism … and close all prisons', *Daily Mail*, 19 June 2020.
10 'Remarks by President Trump in press briefing', The White House, 11 August 2020.
11 Harriet Alexander, 'Trump tells Mayor de Blasio to rehire all the cops who lost their jobs when he cut $1bn from NYPD budget in response to BLM protests as crime and homelessness escalates in NYC', *Daily Mail*, 12 August 2020.
12 'Full transcript of Michelle Obama's D.N.C. speech', *New York Times*, 17 August 2020.
13 Haven Orecchio-Egresitz, 'The white St. Louis couple who pointed guns at Black Lives Matter protestors outside their mansion say they support the movement', Insider, 29 June 2020.

3: BARBARIAN AT THE GATE – FREE SPEECH AND POLITICAL CORRECTNESS
1 'How might Trump "drain the swamp"?', BBC News, 18 October 2016.
2 Interview with research team.
3 Hannah Fingerhut, 'In "political correctness" debate, most Americans think too many people are easily offended', Pew Research Center, 20 July 2016.
4 Steve Kolowich, 'Trump said he would "end" political correctness on campuses. Could a President do that?', *Chronicle of Higher Education*, 20 October 2016.
5 Glenn Kessler, 'Trump's outrageous claim that "thousands" of New Jersey Muslims celebrated the 9/11 attacks', *Washington Post*, 22 November 2015; '"Drug dealers, criminals, rapists": what Trump thinks of Mexicans', BBC News, 31 August 2016; Holly Yan, 'Donald Trump's "blood" comment about Megyn Kelly draws outrage', CNN Politics, 8 August 2015.
6 'It's Intersex Awareness Day – here are five myths we need to shatter', Amnesty International, 26 October 2018.
7 'Gender Pronouns', LGBTQ+ Resource Center, available at: https://uwm.edu/lgbtrc/support/gender-pronouns/
8 'Impact of transgender personnel on readiness and health care costs in the US military likely to be small', Rand Corp., 30 June 2016.
9 'The Pentagon spends a lot of money on Viagra', CBS News, 20 February 2015.
10 Kathy Frankovic, 'American views of transgender people: the impact of politics, personal contact, and religion', YouGov, 11 October 2019.

NOTES

11 Negassi Tesfamichael, 'Trump: "I'm doing the military a great favor" by banning transgender troops', Politico, 8 October 2017.
12 'Remarks by President Trump at South Dakota's 2020 Mount Rushmore fireworks celebration', The White House, 4 July 2020.
13 Nick Givas, 'CNN slights Mount Rushmore as "monument of two slaveowners" after extolling its "majesty" in 2016', Fox News, 3 July 2020.
14 Susan Svrluga, 'Trump lashes back at Berkeley after violent protests block speech by Breitbart writer Milo Yiannopoulos', Washington Post, 2 February 2017.
15 'President Donald J. Trump is improving transparency and promoting free speech in higher education', The White House, 21 March 2019.

4: WITH FRIENDS LIKE THESE – TRUMP AND THE UK
1 Oliver Wainwright, 'Trump's $3m White House redesign? It's as drab as a downmarket hotel', The Guardian, 24 August 2017.
2 'Global Security: UK–US Relations, Examination of Witnesses', Foreign Affairs Committee, 2 December 2009.
3 Ibid.
4 'Question time (13/10/16): Hard Brexit, unfit Trump, IndyRef 2 and Labour opposition', Incorrigible Forever [video], YouTube, uploaded 14 October 2016.
5 'Donald Trump protests attract millions across US and world', BBC News, 21 January 2017.
6 'Trump claims media "dishonest" over crowd photos', BBC News, 22 January 2017.
7 J. Frank Bullitt, 'Trump's "The Squad" tweet: the right message said the wrong way', Issues and Insights, 16 July 2019.
8 Charlotte Tobitt, 'BBC correspondent showed bias against Trump in article, complaints unit rules', PressGazette, 7 August 2020.
9 'Block Donald J Trump from UK entry', Petitions UK Government and Parliament, available at: https://petition.parliament.uk/archived/petitions/114003
10 Douglas Murray, 'It's time to consider the real Trump', The Spectator, 12 November 2016, p. 10.
11 'Marcus Fysh – should Donald Trump be banned from Britain?', 21 January 2016, available at: https://www.marcusfysh.org.uk/news/marcus-fysh-should-donald-trump-be-banned-britain
12 Commons debates, 18 January 2016, available at: https://publications.parliament.uk/pa/cm201516/cmhansrd/cm160118/halltext/160118h0002.htm
13 'Donald Trump debate: ban risks making tycoon a "martyr"', BBC News, 18 January 2016.
14 'Donald Trump: I love the people of the UK', ITV News [video], YouTube, uploaded 29 February 2016.
15 'May under fire for dismissing Farage's alliance with Trump', Daily Telegraph, 14 November 2016.
16 Aletha Adu, 'Michael Gove says he would have voted for Hillary Clinton after interview with Trump', Daily Express, 17 January 2017.
17 'Lord Jones calls Trump baby balloon "disgusting"', CNBC, 11 July 2018.
18 Matthew Weaver, 'Timeline: Donald Trump's feud with Sadiq Khan', The Guardian, 16 June 2019.
19 'Donald Trump calls Mayor of London Sadiq Khan a "stone cold loser"', BBC News, 3 June 2019.
20 Will Worley, 'John Bercow on Donald Trump's parliamentary address: speech in full', The Independent, 6 February 2017.
21 Isabel Oakeshott, 'Britain's man in the US says Trump is "inept": leaked secret cables from ambassador say the President is "uniquely dysfunctional and his career could end in disgrace"', Mail on Sunday, 6 July 2019.
22 Rebecca Davison, '"How vile and evil to get joy from the suffering of others": GMB viewers slam Dominic West for telling Kate Garraway he "jumped for joy" over Trump's Covid diagnosis despite her husband Derek battling the disease', Daily Mail, 2 October 2020.

23 Ryan Parker, 'John Cleese revels in Donald Trump Covid-19 diagnosis', *Hollywood Reporter*, 2 October 2020.

24 'Glasgow City to wear Ruth Bader Ginsburg name on kit', BBC Sport, 23 September 2020.

5: MUCH ADO ABOUT A NOTHINGBURGER? - TRUMP AND RUSSIA

1   Jane Mayer, 'The inside story of Christophe Steele's Trump dossier', *New Yorker*, 26 November 2019.

2   Ibid.

3   'Dossier author Christopher Steele's libel trial ends in London', *Washington Times*, 1 September 2020.

4   Tom McCarthy, '"Russia is fake news": Trump decries reports of pre-election communication', *The Guardian*, 16 February 2017.

5   Kate Sullivan, 'Mueller explains why his family left Trump's golf club', CNN, 18 April 2019.

6   Joe Concha, 'CNN's Van Jones: O'Keefe Russia "nothingburger" video "a hoax"', The Hill, 29 June 2017.

7   Andrew Weissmann, *Where Law Ends: Inside the Mueller Investigation* (New York: Penguin Random House, 2020).

8   Bess Levin, 'Jared Kushner: my ignorance could be the key to world peace', *Vanity Fair*, 13 May 2019.

9   Natasha Turak, 'Trump handing northern Syria to Turkey is a "gift" to Russia, Iran, and ISIS, former US envoy says', CNBC, 7 October 2019.

10 'Putin: Voters' choices of Trump and Brexit "disrespected"', BBC News, 20 December 2018.

11 Matt Mathers, '"Brazen abuse of power": Pelosi slams Trump's decision to pardon Michael Flynn', *The Independent*, 26 November 2020.

12 Edith M. Lederer, 'Russia envoy: Tensions with US are probably worst since 1973', AP, 16 October 2016.

13 Joby Warrick and Karen DeYoung, 'From "reset" to "pause": The real story behind Hillary Clinton's feud with Vladimir Putin', *Washington Post*, 3 November 2016.

14 Ben Smith, 'Hillary: Putin "doesn't have a soul"', Politico, 6 January 2008.

15 'Donald Trump's tweet about "best friend" Putin is most retweeted from final debate', *Hollywood Reporter*, 19 October 2016; 'This extensive mashup confirms Trump's love for Putin', *Rolling Stone*, 31 July 2020.

16 'Read the full transcript of Trump's first solo press conference', CNBC, 16 February 2017.

6: TEN MEN - TRUMP'S ATTITUDE TO WOMEN

1   Hillary Clinton, tweet, 9.55 p.m., 7 October 2016, https://twitter.com/HillaryClinton/status/784497331647422464

2   'Kaine: Lewd Trump tape "makes me sick to my stomach"', Reuters, 8 October 2016.

3   Ilana Nathans, 'Clinton's 1975 rape case', FactCheck, 17 June 2016.

4   Anita Kumar, 'Meet the four women who say they have been wronged by the Clintons', *Fresno Bee*, 9 October 2016.

5   'Inside Team Trump', *Newsday*, 18 September 1989.

6   Stuart Greer, 'Female engineer behind Trump Tower reveals what it's like working with the President of the United States', *Manchester Evening News*, 1 October 2018.

7   'New book by former Trump aide alleges early racist comments', *Los Angeles Times*, 16 October 2020.

8   'Ivana Trump: Hard work, discipline and self-reliance', *Tampa Bay Times*, 26 September 1988.

9   'Inside Team Trump', op. cit.

10 Nicole Horning, *The Women's Movement and the Rise of Feminism* (New York: Greenhaven Publishing, 2019), p. 12.

11 'Madonna at Women's March: "I have thought an awful lot about blowing up the White House"', CBS News, 21 January 2017.

12 Roslyn Layton, 'Hundreds of women have lead roles in the Trump administration. 45 more await senate confirmation', *Forbes*, 29 June 2019.

13 'Donald Trump defends Bill O'Reilly amid sexual harassment claims', *The Guardian*, 5 April 2017; Cher, tweet, 7.52 p.m., 19 April 2017, https://twitter.com/cher/status/854769725498302464; Rosie O'Donnell, tweet, 9.31 p.m., 19 April 2017, https://twitter.com/Rosie/status/854794680827072513; Stephen King, tweet, 10.25 p.m., 19 April 2017, https://twitter.com/stephenking/status/854808092684320769?lang=en

7: DRILL, BABY, DRILL – TRUMP AND THE ENVIRONMENT

1 Timothy Cama, 'Trump "really didn't care about" ANWR initially', *The Hill*, 1 February 2018.

2 Ben Adler and Rebecca Leber, 'Donald Trump once backed urgent climate action. Wait, what?', Grist, 8 June 2016.

3 Edward Wong, 'Trump has called climate change a Chinese hoax. Beijing says it is anything but', *Washington Post*, 19 November 2016.

4 'Statement by President Trump on the Paris Climate Accord', The White House, 1 June 2017.

5 Ibid.

6 Ibid.

7 Ibid.

8 'Trump dumps Paris climate deal: reaction', *Science*, 1 June 2017.

9 '"Height of egotism": North Korea blasts US withdrawal from Paris climate accord', RT, 7 June 2017.

10 'Biden vows to ban new drilling on public lands. It won't be easy', *Washington Post*, 19 November 2020.

11 'President Donald J. Trump is supporting hydraulic fracturing and other technologies to protect our jobs, economic opportunity, and national security', The White House, 31 October 2020.

12 Nina Lakhani, 'Trump has made fracking an election issue. Has he misjudged Pennsylvania?', *The Guardian*, 10 October 2020.

13 Julian Borger, '"Secure the oil": Trump's Syria strategy leaves Pentagon perplexed', *The Guardian*, 8 November 2019.

14 Matthew Robinson, 'Save Alaska fisheries from mining, Trump Jr urges father', *The Times*, 5 August 2020.

15 'Remarks by President Trump at signing of H.R. 1957, The Great American Outdoors Act', The White House, 4 August 2020.

8: MOON TO MARS – TRUMP'S RECORD ON JOBS

1 W. J. Hennigan, 'Exclusive: Strange Russian spacecraft shadowing US spy satellite, general says', *TIME*, 10 February 2020.

2 Joey Roulette, 'US builds alliances in "wild, wild west" of space: general', Reuters, 18 September 2019.

3 'Remarks by President Trump at a meeting with the National Space Council and signing of space policy directive-3', The White House, 18 June 2018.

4 Ben Allen, 'Space Force is a colossal waste of time, money and talent', *GQ*, 28 May 2020.

5 Interview with research team.

6 'Donald Trump vows to create 25 million jobs over next decade', *New York Times*, 16 September 2016; 'Trump's promise to create 25 million jobs in a decade seems wildly unrealistic', Vox, 25 January 2017.

7 'Happy (deregulated) New Year! Trump still the all-time record rule-cutter', Investor's Business Daily, 31 December 2018.

8 Interview with research team.

9 'Remarks by President Trump at a meeting with the National Space Council', op. cit.

10 'Four astronauts on way to International Space Station – as it happened', *The Guardian*, 16 November 2020.

11 Jeff Cox, 'Trump has set economic growth on fire. Here is how he did it', CNBC, 7 September 2018.

12 'Fact check: How Trump's economy compares to Obama's', CNN, 19 February 2020.

13 Barack Obama, tweet, 3.46 p.m., 17 February 2020, https://twitter.com/BarackObama/status/1229432034650722304

14 Andrew Buncombe, 'Obama trolls Trump on President's Day with comment about economy', *The Independent*, 18 February 2020.

15 Interview with research team.

16 Nina McCollum, 'Here's what most people don't know about "being on food stamps"', HuffPost, 19 December 2019.

17 David Brett, 'How big was the global Trump rally – and where does it leave valuations', Schroders, 19 January 2017.

9: STEEL RESOLVE – TRADE DEALS, TARIFFS AND MANUFACTURING JOBS

1 'A guide to decide: twelve tests to choose between Clinton and Trump', *Pittsburgh Post-Gazette*, 6 November 2016.

2 Interview with research team.

3 Ibid.

4 'Steel certain: Trump vows to make Pittsburgh great again', Politico, 13 April 2016.

5 'Donald Trump vows to create 25 million jobs over next decade', op. cit.

6 Rebecca Savransky, 'Obama to Trump: "What magic wand do you have?"', *The Hill*, 1 June 2016.

7 'US to become world's greatest magnet for job creation: Donald Trump', NDTV, 4 January 2017.

8 'Remarks by President Trump at Made in America product showcase', The White House, 17 July 2017.

9 Jacob Pramuk, 'Trump blasts General Motors: Make Chevy Cruze model in US or "pay big border tax"', CNBC, 3 January 2017.

10 Louis Nelson, 'Trump targets Toyota: Build plant in US or pay "big border tax"', Politico, 5 January 2017.

11 'Trump gives remarks on US–Mexico–Canada deal', CNN, 1 October 2018.

12 'Trump imposes steel tariffs on imported solar panels and washing machines', *The Guardian*, 23 January 2018.

13 'Trump dealt blow as US trade deficit jumps', BBC News, 6 March 2019.

14 'Trump threatens Mexico with tariffs over immigration', Politico, 31 May 2019.

15 Ian Kullgren, 'Yes, Clinton did call TPP the "gold standard"', Politico, 9 October 2016.

16 'A timeline of Trump's complicated relationship with the TPP', *Washington Post*, 13 April 2018.

17 'The Woodward book comes for James Mattis', *The Atlantic*, 6 September 2018.

18 'Bob Woodward: Trump's aides stole his papers "to protect the country"', CNN, 5 September 2018.

10: WINNING – TRUMP AND CHINA, PART ONE

1 Quint Forgey, 'Trump on "Chinese virus" label: "It's not racist at all"', Politico, 18 March 2020.

2 'Steve Bannon full address and Q&A', Oxford Union [video], YouTube, uploaded 16 November 2018.

3 Interview with research team.

4 'Wince Philip: Prince's most famous comments and clangers', *The Guardian*, 4 May 2017.

5 'Transcript of the second debate', *New York Times*, 10 October 2016.

6 Xi Jinping, *The Governance of China* (Beijing: Foreign Language Press, 2014).

7 Rob Crilly, 'Donald Trump finding out that winning as president does not come easy, as dealmaker-in-chief comes up short on healthcare', *Daily Telegraph*, 24 March 2017.

8 'Steve Bannon, first interview with the former Trump adviser', PBS Frontline, 13 January 2020.

9 Stephen Moore and Arthur Laffer, *Trumponomics: Inside the America First Plan to Get Our Economy Back on Track* (New York: St Martin's Publishing Group, 2018), p. 13.

10 Tom Miller, *China's Asian Dream: Empire Building Along the New Silk Road* (London: Zed Books, 2017), p. 25.

11 'Trump, reforming the US–China trade relationship to make America great again', available at: https://assets.donaldjtrump.com/US-China-Trade-Reform.pdf

12 Interview with research team.

13 'Trump, reforming the US–China trade relationship to make America great again', op. cit.

14 Jeremy Diamond, 'Trump: "We can't continue to allow China to rape our country"', CNN, 2 May 2016.

15 'Full transcript: first 2016 presidential debate', Politico, 27 September 2016.

16 'A President Trump could destroy the world economy', *Washington Post*, 5 October 2016.

17 Lawrence Summers, 'The economic consequences of a Donald Trump win would be severe', *Financial Times*, 5 June 2016.

18 Ali Vitali, 'Trump dines with China leader: "We have developed a friendship"', NBC News, 7 April 2017.

19 'Trump announces tariffs on steel and aluminium', BBC News, 1 March 2018.

20 'President Trump signs steel and aluminium tariffs proclamations', C-Span, 8 March 2018.

21 Ibid.

22 Ibid.

23 Interview with research team.

24 'Remarks by President Trump at the World Economic Forum, Davos, Switzerland', The White House, 21 January 2020.

25 Richard Milne, 'Norway sees Liu Xiaobo's Nobel Prize hurt salmon exports to China', *Financial Times*, 15 August 2013.

26 Demetri Sevastopulo, 'Democrats harden their stance on China', *Financial Times*, 15 May 2019.

27 'Conservatives should support Joe Biden's "Buy American" initiative', *Washington Post*, 18 November 2020.

11: BLITZKRIEG – TRUMP AND CHINA, PART TWO

1 '"Huawei is something that is very dangerous," says Trump', France 24 English [video], YouTube, uploaded 24 May 2019.

2 Arjun Kharpal, 'Huawei says it would never hand data to China's government. Experts say it wouldn't have a choice', CNBC, 4 March 2019.

3 Ibid.

4 'Defence Sub-Committee, oral evidence: the security of 5G', House of Commons, 2 June 2020, available at: https://committees.parliament.uk/oralevidence/448/html/

5 Julie Wernau, 'Forced tech transfers are on the rise in China, European firms say', *Wall Street Journal*, 20 May 2019.

6 Bob Woodward, *Fear: Trump in the White House* (New York: Simon & Schuster, 2018), p. 273.

7 Christopher Wray, 'The threat posed by the Chinese government and the Chinese Communist Party to the economic and national security of the United States', Federal Bureau of Investigation, 7 July 2020.

8 'Chinese consulate in Houston ordered to close by US', BBC News, 23 July 2020.

9 'Trump says additional Chinese embassy closures possible', Arab News [video], YouTube, uploaded 22 July 2020.

10 'Remarks by President Trump on United States 5G deployment', The White House, 12 April 2019.

11 Robert C. O'Brien (ed.), 'Trump on China: putting America first', The White House, p. 77.

12 Ibid.

13 Ibid., p. 97.

14 Oliver Dowden, Hansard, 14 July 2020.

15 Tom Cheshire, 'Trump and China respond to UK's ban on Huawei', Sky News, 15 July 2020.

16 'National security strategy of the United States of America', The White House, December 2017, p. 25.

17 'Remarks by President Obama and President Xi of the People's Republic of China in joint press conference', The White House, 25 September 2015.

18 Michael R. Pompeo, 'US position on maritime claims in the South China Sea', US Department of State, 13 July 2020.

19 Barney Henderson and Chris Graham, 'China lodges formal complaint with US over Donald Trump's call with president of Taiwan', *Daily Telegraph*, 3 December 2016.

20 Ibid.

21 'Steve Bannon, first interview', op. cit.

12: LEAVE NO MAN BEHIND – TRUMP'S ATTITUDE TO NATO AND THE MILITARY

1 'Greece, out of ideas, requests global aid', *New York Times*, 24 April 2010.

2 Ali Vitali, 'Trump calls for increased defense spending, more military might', NBC News, 7 September 2016.

3 'Trump worries Nato with "obsolete" comment', BBC News, 16 January 2017.

4 'Full transcript of interview with Donald Trump', *The Times*, 16 January 2017.

5 'Trump says Nato "no longer obsolete"', BBC News, 12 April 2017.

6 Samantha Schmidt, 'Breaking down Trump's shove', *Washington Post*, 26 May 2017.

7 'Trump pushes past Montenegro's PM', BBC News [video], YouTube, 26 May 2017.

8 'Emmanuel Macron warns Europe: NATO is becoming brain-dead', *The Economist*, 7 November 2019.

9 David Reid, 'Trump slams Macron for "insulting" and "disrespectful" NATO comments', CNBC, 3 December 2019.

10 'Nato alliance experiencing brain death, says Macron', BBC News, 7 November 2019; 'Are you "brain dead"? Turkey's Erdogan raps Macron before NATO summit', Reuters, 29 November 2019.

11 'Remarks by President Trump and NATO Secretary General Stoltenberg after 1:1 meeting', The White House, 3 December 2019.

12 Robert D. Blackwill, 'Trump's foreign policies are better than they seem', Council on Foreign Relations, Council Special Report, No. 84, April 2019.

13 'Trump claims credit for Nato spending boost', *Financial Times*, 2 December 2019.

14 Tim Marshall, *Prisoners of Geography: Ten Maps that Tell You Everything You Need to Know About Global Politics* (London: Elliott & Thompson, 2015).

15 'US election 2020: Has Trump delivered on his promises?', BBC News, 15 October 2020.

16 'US delivering "peace through strength": President Trump tells UN', UN News, 22 September 2020.

17 Ali Vitali, 'Trump calls for increased defense spending, more military might', NBC News, 7 September 2016.

18 'Remarks by President Trump in joint address to Congress', The White House, 28 February 2017.

19 'Trump touted his colossal spending Bill as a blessing for the military. Here's what the Pentagon is getting', CNBC, 23 March 2018.

20 Ibid.

21 'Guided by National Defense Strategy, defense department increases force lethality', US Department of Defense, 5 August 2020.

22 Loren Thompson, 'Top five steps Trump has taken to prepare the US military for whatever comes next', *Forbes*, 6 January 2020.

23 Valerie Insinna, 'Trump makes the "out of control" F-35 his latest target', Defense News, 12 December 2016.

24 Loren Thompson, 'Trump drives down price of F-35 fighter 25 per cent from Obama level', *Forbes*, 17 June 2019.

25 'Somalia force posture announcement', US Department of Defense, 4 December 2020.
26 'Remarks by President Trump before Marine One departure', The White House, 29 July 2020.

13: PEACE, MAN – NO NEW WARS

1   Daniella Diaz, 'Corker: Trump setting US "on the path to World War III"', CNN, 9 October 2017.
2   'Steve Bannon, first interview', op. cit.
3   'US foreign policy after Trump', Chatham House, 28 October 2019.
4   James M. Lindsay, 'Rally "round the flag"', Brookings, 25 March 2003.
5   Patricia Zengerle, 'With eye on Afghanistan talks, Trumps vows to stop "endless wars"', Reuters, 6 February 2019.
6   'US foreign policy after Trump', op. cit.
7   'Remarks by President Trump in joint address to congress', The White House, 28 February 2017.
8   'State of the reunion! Tears of joy as Trump reunites army family', Tribune India, 5 February 2020.
9   Tim Stanley, 'Don't write off Trump – he is the candidate of unfashionable America', Daily Telegraph, 24 August 2020.
10 'Steve Bannon and Lanny Davis debate (English version)', CTK [video], YouTube, uploaded 22 May 2018.

14: RED LINES – TRUMP'S RECORD IN SYRIA

1   'US President Barack Obama in "red line" warning to Syria over chemical weapons', The Telegraph [video], YouTube, uploaded 21 August 2012.
2   David Cameron, For the Record (London: William Collins, 2019), p. 460.
3   'Legislators push for vote before strikes', New York Times, 29 August 2013.
4   Jake Sherman, 'Boehner to Obama: Make Syria case', Politico, 28 August 2013.
5   'Statement by the President on Syria', The White House, 31 August 2013.
6   Cameron, For the Record, p. 466.
7   Ben Rhodes, The World As It Is: Inside the Obama White House (London: Bodley Head, 2018).
8   'Remarks by the President in address to the nation on Syria', The White House, 10 September 2013.
9   'Statement by the President on US–Russian agreement on framework for elimination of Syrian chemical weapons', The White House, 14 September 2013.
10 Scott Shane, 'Weren't Syria's chemical weapons destroyed? It's complicated', New York Times, 7 April 2017.
11 Jim Garamone, 'Trump orders missile attack in retaliation for Syrian chemical strikes', US Department of Defense, 6 April 2017.
12 Woodward, Fear, p. 146.
13 Katie Forster, 'Donald Trump said US should "stay the hell out of Syria" as "many very bad things will happen" in previous tweets', The Independent, 7 April 2017.
14 Rex W. Tillerson, 'Secretary Tillerson's remarks at a press availability in Italy', US Embassy & Consulates in Russia, 11 April 2017.
15 Max Greenwood, 'Schumer says Trump strikes "appropriate," warns against greater involvement in Syria', The Hill, 13 April 2018.
16 'Pelosi statement on US airstrikes in Syria', Speaker of the House, 7 April 2017.
17 'Rubio statement on US airstrikes in Syria', US Senator for Florida, 6 April 2017.
18 Alice Woodhouse, 'US politicians react to Syria missile attack', Financial Times, 7 April 2017.
19 Mark Hensch, 'CNN host: "Donald Trump became president" last night', The Hill, 7 April 2017.
20 Woodward, Fear, p. 151.
21 'Bashar al-Assad goes old school in response to Trump's "animal" insult', Sky News, 31 May 2018.

22 'Trump fires Rex Tillerson as secretary of state', BBC News, 13 March 2018.
23 John Bolton, *The Room Where It Happened* (New York: Simon & Schuster, 2020), p. 146.
24 Ibid.
25 'Syria air strikes: Trump hails "perfect" mission', BBC News, 14 April 2018.
26 'Full transcript: third 2016 presidential debate', Politico, 20 October 2016.
27 'A conversation with James Clapper', Council on Foreign Relations, 25 October 2016.
28 'Trump: Clinton's foreign policy plan would start WW3', BBC News, 26 October 2016.
29 Ibid.
30 Zaid Jilani, 'In secret Goldman Sachs speech, Hillary Clinton admitted no-fly zone would "kill a lot of Syrians"', The Intercept, 10 October 2016.
31 Matt Chorley, 'Something must be done but we're waiting for instructions', *The Times*, 13 April 2018.
32 Julian Borger and Martin Chulov, 'Trump shocks allies and advisers with plan to pull US troops out of Syria', *The Guardian*, 20 December 2018.
33 'James Mattis' resignation letter in full', BBC News, 21 December 2018.
34 Lindsey Graham, tweet, 3.09 p.m., 19 December 2018, https://twitter.com/LindseyGrahamSC/status/1075407801327984641
35 Lindsey Graham, tweet, 4.56 p.m., 19 December 2018, https://twitter.com/LindseyGrahamSC/status/1075434823949402112
36 'Trump says others must fight in Syria', *Newcastle Star*, 20 December 2018.
37 'Maximum pressure on the Assad regime for its chemical weapons use and other atrocities', Hudson Institute, 12 May 2020, p. 11.
38 'Statement from President Donald J. Trump', The White House, 4 April 2017.

15: SHADOWS IN THE DARKNESS – TRUMP'S RECORD IN THE WAR ON TERROR

1 Thomas Johnson, 'Listen: soldier's widow shares her call with Trump', *Washington Post*, 19 October 2017.
2 Robert Burns, 'Officials: no need for Trump's approval to use massive bomb', AP News, 14 April 2017.
3 'Donald Trump: "Knock the hell out of Isis and make America great again"', Politics Wire [video], YouTube, uploaded 13 August 2016.
4 'Full transcript: second 2016 presidential debate', Politico, 10 October 2016.
5 Catherine Philp, 'President Trump makes good on his promise to pound Islamic State', *The Times*, 20 January 2018.
6 'Trump: "I want surveillance of certain mosques"', AP Archive [video], YouTube, uploaded 16 November 2016.
7 Peter Holley, '"Radical Islamic terrorism": three words that separate Trump from most of Washington', *Washington Post*, 28 February 2017.
8 Amy Sherman, 'Trump: Clinton won't use the term "radical Islamic terrorists"', PolitiFact, 9 October 2016.
9 'October 9, 2016 debate transcript', The Commission on Presidential Debates, 9 October 2016.
10 'The inaugural address: remarks of President Donald J. Trump', The White House, 20 January 2017.
11 'Gorka: American leadership can defeat radical Islam', Fox News, 1 March 2017.
12 'Timeline: the rise, spread, and fall of the Islamic State', Wilson Center, 28 October 2019.
13 David Remnick, 'Going the distance: on and off the road with Barack Obama', New Yorker, 20 January 2014.
14 'Foley beheading video shocks the world, Obama says', BBC News, 20 August 2014.
15 'Timeline: the rise, spread, and fall of the Islamic State', op. cit.
16 'Trump urges "shutdown" on Muslims entering US', AP [video], YouTube, uploaded 16 November 2016.
17 Marco Rubio, tweet, 12.14 a.m., 8 December 2015, https://twitter.com/marcorubio/status/674019172800704512?s=20]

18 Bernie Sanders, tweet, 10.16 p.m., 7 December 2015, https://twitter.com/BernieSanders/status/673989470912299008

19 'Susanna Reid debates Steve Bannon over Trump's Brexit criticism', *Good Morning Britain* [video], YouTube, uploaded 13 July 2018.

20 Iman Amrani, 'Thousands protest Trump Muslim ban in London', *The Guardian*, 30 January 2017.

21 'May tells ministers to raise travel ban with their US counterparts', *The Guardian*, 29 January 2017.

22 Katie Forster and Lizzie Dearden, 'Donald Trump calls judge's suspension of immigration ban "ridiculous" and says it will be overturned', *The Independent*, 4 February 2017.

23 'Attorney General Xavier Becerra joins sixteen attorneys general condemning un-American executive order to protect individual freedoms from the federal government', State of California Department of Justice, 29 January 2017.

24 John Murray Brown, 'Donald Trump's travel ban suffers fresh court setback', *Financial Times*, 30 March 2017.

25 'Trump travel ban: "unprecedented judicial overreach"', BBC News, 16 March 2017.

26 Jennifer Sinco Kelleher, 'Judge halts newest Trump travel ban, saying it has some woes', *Seattle Times*, 17 October 2017.

27 'Statement regarding court action affecting the President's proclamation regarding travel to the United States by nationals of certain countries', The White House, 17 October 2017.

28 'Remarks of undersecretary for terrorism and financial intelligence David S. Cohen at the Carnegie Endowment for International Peace, "attacking ISIL's financial foundation"', US Department of the Treasury, 23 October 2014.

29 Bob Woodward, *Rage* (New York: Simon & Schuster, 2020), pp. 4, 37.

30 Philip Bump, 'Trump says the Islamic State's defeat is imminent – as he has for months', *Washington Post*, 20 March 2019.

31 'Speech: Donald Trump in Birmingham, AL – November 21, 2015', Factbase Videos [video], YouTube, uploaded 30 August 2019.

32 'Hillary Clinton: I would go after Baghdadi', CNBC [video], YouTube, uploaded 9 October 2016.

33 Nancy A. Youssef, 'US says it destroyed Baghdadi compound to prevent shrine to terror leader', *Wall Street Journal*, 30 October 2019.

34 Mike Calia, 'Trump will address the nation Sunday morning with a "major statement" after cryptic tweet', CNBC, 26 October 2019.

35 'Remarks by President Trump on the death of ISIS leader Abu Bakr al-Baghdadi', The White House, 27 October 2019.

36 'Fragile States Index 2016', The Fund for Peace, 2016, p. 7.

37 'UAE says Trump travel ban an internal affair, most Muslims unaffected', Reuters, 1 February 2017.

16: THE LESSER EVIL – TRUMP AND SAUDI ARABIA

1 'President Trump's speech to the Arab Islamic American summit', The White House, 21 May 2017.

2 'Steve Bannon, full address and Q&A', op. cit.

3 'Saudi FM: Trump visit is coup for peace', BBC News, 19 May 2017.

4 'Donald Trump says isolation of Qatar may be "beginning of the end of the horror of terrorism"', *Daily Telegraph*, 6 June 2017.

5 Tom Finn, 'US, Qatar sign agreement on combating terrorism financing', Reuters, 10 July 2017.

6 'Remarks by President Trump and Amir Tamim bin Hamad Al Thani of the state of Qatar before bilateral meeting', The White House, 10 April 2018.

7 William D. Hartung, 'Trump is an aggressive arms dealer. So were his predecessors', *The Nation*, 19 November 2019.

8 'Iran's supreme leader "the new Hitler", says Saudi crown prince', BBC News, 24 November 2017.

9 Douglas Hamilton, 'Israel shocked by Obama's "betrayal" of Mubarak', Reuters, 31 January 2011.

10 'How serious is the "rift" in US–Saudi relations', BBC News, 23 October 2013.

11 Ben Hubbard, *MBS: The Rise to Power of Mohammad Bin Salman* (London: William Collins, 2020).

12 'Saudi deputy crown prince, Trump meeting a "turning point": Saudi adviser', Reuters, 14 March 2017.

13 Ben Rhodes, 'A fatal abandonment of American leadership', *The Atlantic*, 12 October 2018.

14 'An online conversation with two former spymasters', RUSI, 22 October 2020.

15 Jamal Khashoggi, 'Saudi Arabia wasn't always this repressive. Now it's unbearable', *Washington Post*, 18 September 2017.

16 Jamal Khashoggi, 'Saudi Arabia's crown prince is acting like Putin', *Washington Post*, 6 November 2017.

17 'Khashoggi killing: "Tell your boss deed is done"', Aljazeera, 13 November 2018.

18 'Trump calls Khashoggi killing "one of the worst in the history of cover-ups"', *Washington Post*, 23 October 2018.

19 'Trump Saudi statement: what the President's words reveal', BBC News, 20 November 2018.

17: MARTYRS - TRUMP AND IRAN

1 'Remarks by President Trump on Iran strategy', The White House, 13 October 2017.

2 'Was assassination carried out by remote-controlled machine gun?', Jewish Voice, 3 December 2020.

3 'At nuke chief's funeral, defense minister vows vengeance, nuclear progress', *Times of Israel*, 30 November 2020.

4 'In conversation with HE Adel al-Jubeir, Minister of Foreign Affairs, Saudi Arabia (full session)', Chatham House [video], YouTube, uploaded 25 October 2017.

5 'Israeli PM Netanyahu says deal with Iran is a bad idea after meeting Kerry', AP Archive [video], YouTube, uploaded 31 July 2015.

6 'In conversation with Benjamin Netanyahu', Chatham House [video], YouTube, uploaded 3 November 2017.

7 'Trump on the Iran deal: "Worst, horrible, laughable"', BBC News, 26 April 2018.

8 'Trump orders Iran nuclear deal review despite compliance', BBC News, 19 April 2017.

9 'Trump threatens to rip up Iran nuclear deal unless US and allies fix "serious flaws"', *The Guardian*, 13 October 2017.

10 Bolton, *The Room Where It Happened*.

11 'President Trump says the Iran deal is defective at its core. A new one will require real commitments', The White House, 11 May 2018.

12 'Remarks by President Trump on the joint comprehensive plan of action', The White House, 8 May 2018.

13 'Iran's Guards say Strait of Hormuz is for all or "no one"', Reuters, 5 July 2018.

14 'Washington blames Iran for "unprecedented attack" on world's energy supply', Radio Farda, 15 September 2019.

15 'NATO chief "extremely concerned" after attacks on Saudi', France 24, 16 September 2019.

16 Bianca Quilantan, 'Trump says US "locked and loaded" after attack on Saudi oil', Politico, 15 September 2019.

17 Steve Holland and Rania El Gamal, 'Trump says he does not want war after attack on Saudi oil facilities', Reuters, 16 September 2019.

18 'President Trump statement on Soleimani', C-Span [video], YouTube, uploaded 3 January 2020.

19 Bernie Sanders, tweet, 4.50 a.m., 3 January 2020, https://twitter.com/BernieSanders/status/1212959357425651713

20 Edward Helmore, 'Democratic presidential candidates condemn killing of Iran general', *The Guardian*, 3 January 2020.

21 'An online conversation with two former spymasters', RUSI, 22 October 2020.

18: PEACE THROUGH STRENGTH – TRUMP AND ISRAEL

1 Interview with research team.

2 'Fact sheets: the 1967 border – the "green line"', Jewish Virtual Library, 24 May 2011.

3 'Israel and UAE in historic flight following peace deal', BBC News, 31 August 2020.

4 Seth J. Frantzman, 'Why John Kerry and others were wrong about peace and Israel – analysis', *Jerusalem Post*, 17 September 2020.

5 Interview with research team.

19: GRAVEYARD OF EMPIRES – AFGHANISTAN

1 Michael Smith, 'Operation endures without the freedom', *Daily Telegraph*, 5 November 2001.

2 'Text: Bush announces strikes against Taliban', *Washington Post*, 7 October 2001.

3 Ian Drury, '2,753 soldiers killed, £258bn spent… but top general says we're only "halfway there" on tenth anniversary of invasion of Afghanistan', *Daily Mail*, 7 October 2011.

4 'Trump announces new strategy for Afghanistan that calls for a troop increase', *Washington Post*, 21 August 2017.

5 'Tracking Donald Trump's evolving positions on Afghanistan', PolitiFact, 22 August 2017.

6 Vali Nasr, 'The inside story of how the White House let diplomacy fail in Afghanistan', *Foreign Policy*, 4 March 2013.

7 'Remarks by the President in address to the nation on the way forward in Afghanistan and Pakistan', The White House, 1 December 2009.

8 H. R. McMaster, *Battlegrounds: The Fight to Defend the Free World* (New York: Harper, 2020).

9 Ronald E. Neumann, 'Failed relations between Hamid Karzai and the United States: How can we learn?', United States Institute of Peace, May 2015, p. 6.

10 Rhodes, *The World As It Is*.

11 Hillary Rodham Clinton, *Hard Choices: A Memoir* (New York: Simon & Schuster, 2014), p. 141.

12 Rhodes, *The World As It Is*.

13 Dexter Filkins, 'Leader of Afghanistan finds himself hero no more', *New York Times*, 7 February 2009.

14 Clinton, *Hard Choices*, p. 132.

15 'Karzai's words leave few choices for the West', *New York Times*, 4 April 2010.

16 Nasr, 'The inside story of how the White House let diplomacy fail in Afghanistan'.

17 'Corruption in conflict: lessons from the US experience in Afghanistan', Special Inspector General for Afghanistan Reconstruction, September 2016, p. 6.

18 Zack Beauchamp, 'The case against Trump's decision to keep fighting in Afghanistan, explained by Trump', Vox, 21 August 2017.

19 'The inaugural address', op. cit.

20 'Trump's transition: Who is General "Mad Dog" Mattis?', BBC News, 2 December 2016.

21 Nahal Toosi, 'Pakistan terrorism crackdown "necessary" to Trump's Afghanistan strategy', Politico, 22 August 2017.

22 Jamie Crawford, 'Top US military officer says Taliban "are not losing"', CNN, 17 November 2018.

23 'Zalmay Khalilzad appointed as US special adviser to Afghanistan', NPR, 5 September 2018.

24 Bolton, *The Room Where It Happened*.

25 Woodward, *Fear*, p. 121.

26 'Trump gets update from aides on Afghan plan with troop pullout possible', Reuters, 16 August 2019.

27 Meridith McGraw, 'Trump cancels secret meeting with the Taliban at Camp David after deadly bombings', ABC News, 8 September 2019.

28 'Remarks following a meeting with President Ashraf Ghani Ahmadzai of Afghanistan and an exchange with reporters from Bagram Airfield, Afghanistan', The White House, 28 November 2019.

29 'Former US national security advisor H. R. McMaster on his new book (full stream 9/29), Washington Post [video], YouTube, uploaded 29 September 2020.

30 Steve Holland, 'Trump hails Afghanistan deal, plans to meet Taliban leaders soon', Reuters, 1 March 2020.

31 Ben Farmer, '"I was right like hell": former Afghan president Hamid Karzai says peace deal vindicates talking to the Taliban', Daily Telegraph, 23 February 2020.

32 'Afghanistan's Abdullah: There's no loser in a peaceful settlement', Aljazeera, 17 September 2020.

20: DAY OF THE SUN – TRUMP AND NORTH KOREA

1 Damien McElroy, 'Donald Trump's summit with Kim Jong-un could be a game-changing encounter', National News, 9 March 2018.

2 'Obama's "strategic patience" strategy toward North Korea is over – but Trump could make the region safer', The Independent, 9 April 2017.

3 Hyung-jin Kim, 'North Korea unleashes racist slurs against Obama', ABC News, 9 May 2014.

4 'Donald Trump in his own words', Financial Times, 2 April 2017.

5 Justin McCurry and Tom Phillips, 'North Korea "ready for war" after US redeploys navy strike team', The Guardian, 11 April 2017.

6 Demetri Sevastopulo and Tom Mitchell, 'US carrier's Korea mission: a message to the world', Financial Times, 10 April 2017.

7 Ibid.

8 '"Nothing better to do?" Trump mocks Kim Jong-un's latest missile launch', The Guardian, 4 July 2017; 'Trump says North Korea will be met with "fire and fury like the world has never seen" if it escalates nuclear threat', The Independent, 8 August 2017.

9 'US airbase in Guam threatened by North Korea as Trump promises "fire and fury"', The Guardian, 9 August 2017; 'Trump praises North Korean leader for "wise" decision', Reuters, 16 August 2017.

10 'Trump threatens "fire and fury" against North Korea if it endangers US', New York Times, 8 August 2017.

11 Ibid.

12 'Opinion: Otto Warmbier's North Korea roommate speaks out', Washington Post, 15 June 2017.

13 'Otto Warmbier "systematically tortured" by N Korea say parents', BBC News, 27 September 2017.

14 'John McCain: Otto Warmbier was "murdered by the Kim Jong-Un regime"', Business Insider, 19 June 2017.

15 Michael Kirby, 'Beyond the Tragedy of Otto Warmbier', Sydney Institute, 21 June 2017.

16 Meghan Keneally, 'From "fire and fury" to "rocket man", the various barbs traded between Trump and Kim Jong-un', ABC News, 12 June 2018.

17 'Kim Jong-un calls President Trump "dotard" and "frightened dog"', NBC News, 21 September 2017.

18 'South Korea and White House on talks with North: full transcript', The Guardian, 9 March 2018.

19 'Read the full transcript of Trump's North Korea summit press conference', Vox, 12 June 2018.

20 'Donald Trump shows who's boss by giving Kim Jong-un sneak peak inside £1.5m limo The Beast', The Sun, 12 June 2018.

21 'Trump Kim summit: Full text of the signed statement', BBC News, 12 June 2018.

22 '"Very, very good", Trump says of his meeting with Kim Jong-un', ABC News [video], YouTube, uploaded 12 June 2018.

23 'North Korea crisis: How events have unfolded under Trump', NBC News, 3 May 2017.

24 Tom Embury-Dennis, 'North Korea has increased nuclear fuel production at secret sites, US officials say', *The Independent*, 20 June 2018.

25 Jesse Johnson, 'Remarks by President Trump in press conference, Hanoi, Vietnam', The White House, 28 February 2019.

26 'Trump says he wants to "shake hands" with North Korea's Kim at DMZ', BBC News, 29 June 2019.

27 'North Korea says little reason to maintain Kim–Trump ties – KCNA', Reuters, 11 June 2020.

28 Jesse Johnson, 'Biden says no way to unconditional meeting with North Korea's Kim', *Japan Times*, 15 January 2020.

29 'North Korea calls Joe Biden a "rabid dog" who deserves to be beaten to death', *Washington Post*, 14 November 2019.

30 'President-Elect Biden on Foreign Policy', Council on Foreign Relations, 7 November 2020.

CONCLUSION

1 Danielle Zoellner, '"I believe them": From supporting Biden's assault accusers to policing, where Kamala Harris has clashed with running mate', *The Independent*, 12 August 2020.

2 'Biden tells voters "you ain't black" if you're still deciding between him and Trump – video', *The Guardian*, 22 May 2020.

3 Patrick Basham, 'Reasons why the 2020 presidential election is deeply puzzling', *The Spectator*, 30 November 2020.

4 'Daily presidential tracking poll', Rasmussen Reports, 8 February 2021.

5 'Pelosi asks Joint Chiefs about preventing Trump from launching nukes', Politico, 8 January 2021.

6 Tom Gillespie, 'Donald Trump is "most incompetent president" in US history, says Joe Biden', Sky News, 8 January 2021.

INDEX